Attitudes to Careers in Tourism

Attitudes to Careers in Tourism

Manoj Sharma

RANDOM PUBLICATIONS
NEW DELHI (INDIA)

Attitudes to Careers in Tourism

ISBN 978-93-5111-327-0

Published in 2014 in India by

RANDOM PUBLICATIONS

4376-A/4B, Gali Murari Lal, Ansari Road
New Delhi-110 002
Phone : +91-11-43580356, +91-11-23289044
e-mail: randomexports@gmail.com, sales@randompublications.com, info@randompublications.com

Reprinted 2026

Type Setting by : Keystoneprintads, Delhi-110051
Digitally Printed at: Replika Press Pvt. Ltd.

Preface

Tourism as a global industry is essentially a post Second-World War phenomenon. Though a number of research papers and articles have been written on different aspects of tourism, there has been a need for an authentic. The characteristics of tourism employment and careers have been widely documented. Although the development of the tourism industry can create new employment opportunities, it is often criticized for providing primarily low-skilled and low-paying jobs. If today's students are to become the effective practitioners of tomorrow, it is fundamental to understand their perceptions of tourism employment.

It is a vital for the professionals in the tourism industry to identify trends early and design proactive strategies to gain competitive advantage as the global tourism industry continues to expand and become more complex. Tourism marketing is one of the important fields of tourism industry and this book gives an in depth and comprehensive coverage of key marketing principles applied to tourism. This book focuses on a sample of India students studying tourism at university level in order to analyze their perceptions towards tourism careers. The results showed that, overall, the respondents' perceptions are neither favorable nor unfavorable. The findings also indicated that: willingness to study tourism; willingness to work in tourism after graduation; and work experience; are important factors in shaping their image of tourism careers.

I thank all members of my team who have helped in the preparation of the book. My special thanks go to "Random Publications" who have published the book.

—Manoj Sharma

Contents

1

Tourism: An Introduction

AN OVERVIEW

BACKGROUND TO RESEARCH

Tourism is the world's largest industry and predicted to double in size in the next 20 years. It has the potential to bring major benefits to destinations, but can also be damaging to the people living there and to their environment. Other industries have already understood this ambivalent nature of trade and have adopted the triple bottom line of social, environmental and economic responsibility. It is now time for the tourism industry to rise to this challenge–the challenge of ethical tourism.

The big question, though, is how to put these ethics into practice. As a development charity, Tearfund is concerned to increase the positive impact of tourism to developing countries, particularly on the lives of the poor, and to mitigate any negative effects. In January 2000, Tearfund carried out some market research, which showed that the majority of tourists want a more ethical tourism industry, and would be willing to pay more for it. This current report, one year on, asks how the industry is responding.

It looks at 65 UK-based tour operators, highlights examples of their good practice in ethical tourism and suggests ways in which this can be replicated and built upon. Ethical tourism is in the best interests of all involved. It offers tour operators a competitive advantage and safeguards the future of the industry by ensuring the long-term sustainability of a destination. It offers the tourists a richer experience, as holidays will draw on the distinctive features of a destination. It is also in the interests of those living there and those working for development, as it can help to combat poverty and contribute to sustainable development.

TRENDS IN THE TOURISM INDUSTRY

The tourism industry is highly competitive and tour operators are under increasing pressure to differentiate their products. Research suggests that once the main criteria for a holiday are satisfied (location/facilities, cost and availability), clients will make choices based on ethical considerations such as working conditions, the environment and charitable giving. Clients are also looking for increased quality and experience in their holiday. In this climate, companies would do well to differentiate their products according to consumer demand i.e. based on ethical criteria.

The industry is already responding. Some operators are moving from a cut-price to an experience-focused approach, and there is a rise in small-scale and specialist operators. Since the Earth Summit in 1992, many operators have started to address their environmental responsibility. AITO (Association of Independent Tour Operators) have been working over the past year to produce a responsible tourism code for their members.

In November 2000 ABTA (Association of British Travel Agents) published their own detailed research into clients' ethical preferences. Any tour operator who fails to respond risks being left behind. They also fail to fulfil their role as a responsible company in the 21st century. Furthermore, they risk damaging the very resources upon which the industry depends–people and their environment. This report offers some ways forward for those who wish to rise to this challenge.

BRINGING BENEFITS TO THE LOCAL COMMUNITY

This stage highlights the benefits tour operators bring to local communities, the factors that enable this to happen and some of the barriers that operators face. It considers whether these benefits can be replicated elsewhere, and places these findings in the context of increased consolidation in the industry and consumer pressure for change. It then suggests some initial steps that companies can take to increase benefits they bring.

FINDINGS

Do you have any Examples of where your Company has had a Positive Impact on Local Communities

Many companies had positive stories to tell about supporting the local economy. This focused on using locally-run hotels and service providers, sourcing goods locally, and training and employing local people. It enabled the money from tourism to go directly to people in the destination and support their development.

For some operators it included a year-round commitment to the destination, which helped to provide secure employment and ensure that tourism was a viable way of earning a living. In rural communities, tourism helped reverse the flow to the cities to look for work and enabled people to remain in their families and communities. There were also examples where the income from tourist visits had directly contributed to better standards of health and education. Some of the larger operators provided a significant proportion of employment in some destinations.

What Factors are Necessary for Local People to Benefit

When asked what key factors are necessary in order for people in the destination to benefit from tourism, there were some very clear views expressed across the industry.

Support for the Local Economy

This was considered most important. The emphasis was on using locally-owned and locally-run accommodation and transport, employing and training local people, and giving tourists the confidence and information to use local restaurants and buy local crafts. It confirms 'conventional' wisdom that strengthening local linkages will have the greatest positive impact in the tourism industry.

Good Relationships and Long-term Investment

This included the benefits of a long-term partnership, working with hotels or ground handlers over many years, and the need to build trust between tour operator and supplier. It also focused on the desire for good and regular communication.

Quality and Commercial Viability

This was central as operators stressed the necessity of an attractive product which will sell. There is no use having a product that could potentially bring enormous benefit to the local area, if no-one is interested in going and no-one uses it!

Many also stressed the need for an interesting product, different from what others may be offering. This difference and added quality is based on a good knowledge of the area and time spent doing the necessary research. Smaller operators felt that the time invested up-front paid off later on in terms of clients' enjoyment and repeat visits.

Positive Attitudes of Clients

This was included by over half the respondents, emphasising the need for clients to be educated about the destination, the culture and the people, and to know how to behave in a way that respects the environment.

Other Areas

These included tour operators understanding and responding to local need, and the government providing support to local businesses.

Would it be Possible to do Something Similar Elsewhere

When asked if their good examples could be repeated in other settings, the overwhelming response was yes, given the right conditions. Out of the 54 companies with good examples, nearly 90% (47) said that this could be done in other places, showing a strong optimism that change is possible and that as suggested, be able to see many more of these good examples in the future.

What are the Barriers to Bringing Benefits

However, despite all of these potential benefits that tourism can bring, many of the tour operators expressed frustration at the difficulties in implementation.

Profit-driven

This is clearly important as tour operators need to make money to stay in business. Many of those interviewed simply said, 'We are a commercial company, we need to make money and therefore cannot do as much as we would like to.' Often the biggest operators are working on such small margins (typically around 2%) that they use economies of scale to reduce costs wherever they can.

This means that smaller, local service providers in the destinations miss out. Also, the larger operators often do not allow the time to do the research to find viable alternative service providers. Resort reps may have a few days to find all of the necessary information in a destination and therefore go to the places that others are already using.

Client Expectations

The high demands by clients for Western standards was cited by nearly half of the operators as a barrier to bringing greater benefits to the destination, as was the fact that few clients are talking directly to the companies themselves to demand holidays that bring more benefits to the local economy. A significant minority of operators mentioned the tourists' lack of awareness of the economic reality in a destination i.e. tourists may spend two weeks in a hotel in the Caribbean without realising the extent of the poverty a few hundred metres away.

Some also mentioned that tourists may fear the poverty that exists because it is new to them and they are unsure how to cope with it. Significantly, ten operators spoke of a lack of respect by tourists for local people, and relationships having broken down as a result.

Provision on the Ground

The supply side was cited by the majority of operators with a third of operators complaining that they could not find good quality ground agents, and almost the same number saying that the local government could be doing more to encourage local business through training and affordable loans. Others spoke of the poor communications to remote towns and villages, the lack of marketing of local features, and the lack of understanding of client expectations.

Bureaucracy

The fact that under the EU Package Travel Directive a tour operator may be liable for anything that happens to their clients when they are on holiday, has made many operators much more cautious about what they do, and the local services they recommend to clients. Many of the bigger operators who arrange package tours said they were keen to promote local restaurants and services, but were afraid that if something went wrong, they would be sued when the client came back to the UK. The high standards of health and safety required by the legislation means that Western-owned hotels are often favoured as they are already known to meet these standards. 20% of operators mentioned difficulties working with local or national governments, particularly when offering to clean up a particular beach or river, or helping with the rebuilding of a local site of interest.

How much Money Remains in the Local Economy

When asked what percentage of the holiday, excluding the flight, remains in the local economy, most operators found this difficult to answer. Many of the answers were very rough estimates. None of the bigger, mass tourism operators were able to give us an estimate of what remains locally. This was partly due to the many different holidays they offer, and partly due to the fact that hotels and local services are often owned by people who live outside the local area. Medium-sized companies (taking more than 5,000 people per year, but fewer than 100,000) gave an average estimate of 35% of the cost of their trips remaining locally. The smaller, more specialist operators gave an average estimate of around 70%.

COMMENTARY

Industry Trends

The tourism industry is undergoing an unprecedented period of consolidation. This can work against quality, as costs are cut through economies of scale and standardisation. Only the biggest operators will be able to win in terms of price, and others will need alternative strategies in order to ensure their future survival and success. Recent research into the industry has shown that clients choose their holidays on the basis of destination, price and availability.

Tearfund research in January 2000 found that clients choose their holidays in terms of cost, weather and facilities/location. Although slightly different, both of these pieces of research showed that once the main criteria are satisfied, clients start to base their choices on other more ethical issues. For many larger companies, cost does not vary much, and many will offer similar holidays in similar destinations so clients' main criteria can be satisfied reasonably easily. How they choose their holidays will then come down to issues such as how the company treats the environment, the working conditions and wages of the staff, local cultural experiences or the information and advice made available. Although clients may not be choosing their holidays at the moment on these criteria, this is probably because such holidays are not available or, if they are, they are not well advertised. However, if the recent market research has accurately predicted future trends, companies who take the lead on ethical issues are likely to be rewarded with increased sales. The research findings show that most tour operators have some good examples of where their operations are making a positive difference to the lives of local people. They believe that this can be replicated in other places, and that this is best achieved by supporting the local economy wherever possible, educating tourists and long-term investment in the destination.

The mention of a long-term commitment to a destination is encouraging, because this is vital to enable tour operators to bring more investment, help local businesses to develop and meet clients' needs, and will ensure that tourism is viewed favourably by local people. However, this professed long-term commitment is in stark contrast to the current activities of some operators, who may move on very quickly to new destinations. Problems encountered include time and financial pressure on the industry, the quality of local services, the increased liability due to the EU Package Travel Directive and tourist attitudes (whether ignorance or very high expectations). The frequency with which operators mentioned the lack of good-quality services is surprising, given that few operators are doing much to help with training and building the capacity of local service providers.

In terms of customer expectations and understanding, companies need to respond to two main challenges. In a market that is demanding a high-quality experience, companies that make stronger connections with local people and their culture will become increasingly appealing, as they will draw on the distinctive features of a destination, and offer a richer holiday experience. Tour operators are also in a unique situation to provide information and advice to ensure that tourists travel in an informed way, and operators have a responsibility to ensure that this happens. Finally, many operators complained that they could not afford to change, as it cost too much money and took too much time. However, as the industry moves in this direction and clients increase their pressure for change, the question is increasingly likely to be 'can we afford not to change?' Ethical issues may not be mainstream at the moment, but the move is certainly in that direction. Companies that fail to respond to this change are likely to be left behind in five or ten years' time.

RECOMMENDATIONS

Action

Companies cannot do everything at once. Change comes gradually and sustainable change needs to be integrated into normal business practice.

Possible initial action includes:

- *Share best practice*: Tour operators can start by writing down more examples of where their operations have had a noticeable and positive impact on the local community. This will help to see which factors are important to bring benefits, and what can be done elsewhere.
- *Speak to local groups*: For new destinations especially, companies can make an effort not just to speak to the big hotel owners, but to speak to local community representatives, tourism associations and environmental groups as well as the hotels.

  They can find out about some of the local issues, details of local businesses and possible ways that they can be more integrated into the tourism industry. Development and environment charities in the UK working in these destinations may be able to help with contact details. This process is likely to add an extra day or two onto a trip, but the initial extra cost will be more than recouped later. Companies will be able to provide better-quality holidays, which draw on more of the local character, and ensure that local people benefit from tourism.
- *Consider how to overcome barriers*: Rather than accepting barriers to bringing greater benefits, tour operators can seek to overcome them e.g. by supporting local training initiatives, providing more detailed information for clients, and taking a longer-term approach to a destination.
- *Experiment with a few examples*: Companies can start in one or two destinations to experiment with using smaller operators and providing a more unique service that reflects the character of the destination. They can then get feedback to check whether this is the kind of holiday that is appealing to their clients.
- *Integrate into normal business processes*: No movement towards more responsible tourism will be sustainable unless change becomes integrated into normal business processes. Companies therefore need to take a long-term view of their future, and of how they will operate in a changing industry.

CHARITY BEGINS OVERSEAS

This stage looks at which companies give money to charity, how much they give and whether they favour charities based overseas or in the UK. It shows how tourism companies encourage tourists to give to charities, and what sort of advice they offer to them.

It places this charitable giving in the context of trends across many industries (not just tourism) and draws out some recommendations on how to give effectively, and advice to give to tourists

FINDINGS

Does your Company Donate Money to Charity

Information on charitable giving was relatively hard to come by. Few companies could provide the exact details for the previous year. Some were involved in charitable activities in the host destinations but had no records of this in the head office. Other companies gave donations in kind but did not seem to know if a record was kept or, if one was kept, where this might be. However, out of the 61 companies whom we interviewed (excluding the four who are actually charities), over three quarters (46) said they donated money to charity.

In what ways does your Company Give to Charity

There were almost as many ways of distributing charitable money as there were companies engaged in the activities. There were also strong ideas about what was good to do and what was not, with some of these ideas in direct contradiction to each other. Examples were: setting up a charitable trust which the tour operator administered e.g. MasterSun, Specialist Trekking Co-operative; giving to global environmental or development charities based in the UK but working overseas such as Friends of Conservation, WWF-UK and Survival International; giving £1 or £2 from every booking to a specified charity; giving to a well-known UK charity working in the UK; using money to buy things that are needed by projects that the tour operator visits; matching 'pound for pound' the donations that tourists give; and donations in kind in the form of training or advice.

To which Type of Charities did you Donate Money

Out of the 46 companies who gave money, the majority (33) gave directly to projects in the destinations in which they were working, often projects that they visited or used or had a long-term relationship with. Half gave money to UK-based charities working overseas, either in development work in the destination or with a global environmental remit. Six operators (mainly the larger ones) gave to charities working in the UK.

How much Money did you Donate During the Previous Financial Year

A total of £700,000 was given to charity in 1999/2000 (by the 46 companies who could provide information). The bigger the company, the more money they gave away. Big companies gave on average £43,000 in the financial year, whereas medium companies gave £13,000 each and the smaller ones each gave £5,300 away.

However, when this was considered in relation to profit, the smaller and medium-sized companies paid a higher proportion of profits to charity. Some of the larger companies gave as little as £1 for every £1,000 pre-tax profit, which is about 0.1%. The medium-sized operators who did give to charity gave an average of 1% pre-tax profit. The smaller operators gave varying amounts. From the data we were able to use, these companies gave the equivalent of around 5% pre-tax profits away to charity.

Several of the smaller companies did not give to charity as they placed an emphasis on paying fair prices throughout the whole operation and viewed this as a more sustainable and long-lasting contribution of the company to development in the destination. For example, Tribes Travel, who advertise themselves as the UK's only fair-trade tour operator, integrate their ethical principles throughout their operations by favouring locally-owned and locally-run businesses and community initiatives, and paying a fair wage for the expertise and services they use.

Do you Encourage your Clients to Give to Charity

Of the 46 companies who give money (and two that do not), two thirds offer some sort of advice or encouragement to tourists about how to engage in charitable giving.

- *Giving direct to projects*: Some operators encouraged tourists to give money when they visited projects, or to bring out goods that they could give to the people they visited.
- *Giving money away in the street*: Some operators gave advice to tourists not to give money out in the street, especially to children. Some then added that it is better to bring pens to give away while some said that tourists should speak to the rep or to their tour leader about possible local projects to support.
- *Optional donations*: A few operators added an optional extra charge on the invoice, and specified which charity it would go to.
- *Contact with tourists when they returned*: Many of the smaller companies, particularly those who are keen to encourage repeat visits, will send out a newsletter or new brochure to all clients when they are back in the UK. This often has details of projects to support.

COMMENTARY

Industry Trends

The nature of charitable giving has changed significantly in the past few years.

The main changes are:

- *Strategic approach*: Companies have aligned their giving with long-term business objectives by funding projects that directly impact key stakeholders e.g. suppliers, customers, employees. This allows more focused giving, which is integrated into business processes and therefore more likely to last, even when margins are tight.

- *In-kind contributions*: In addition to giving money away, companies are giving time, expertise and equipment which is often more focused on specific business needs and therefore more valuable in bringing about long-term change and building partnerships.
- *Evaluation*: Various tools have been developed to measure the impact of giving, and therefore to be able to continuously increase the impact, and determine the most strategic and relevant inputs.
- *Participation*: More and more companies are including different stakeholders (e.g. non-governmental organisations, employees, local communities) in designing and implementing their giving activities, so that they are more effective in meeting real needs, more integrated into community activities and therefore more sustainable.
- *Terminations*: It is encouraging that so many companies are giving money to charity. It is also encouraging that over half of those giving money are targeting charities in destinations in which they are operating. This means that the tour operators are contributing in a positive way to those whose lives may be adversely affected by any tourism development in their area, or who may be missing out on direct economic benefits. They are also helping to reverse some of the decline of the natural environment. However, the larger companies are more likely to give to charities operating in the UK. While these charities may be doing good work, the tourism industry surely has a responsibility to support people overseas whose lives they are affecting by their presence in their communities? With increasing pressure for profits, charitable giving that is more targeted and aligned with business interests is likely to be more sustainable, both for the industry and for the charities themselves. There is a wide variety of ways of engaging in charitable giving, and a range of advice given to tourists. Advice from one company may contradict advice from another, which shows the potential usefulness of some basic guidelines. These would give operators confidence in their charitable activities, and encourage consistency and adherence to good practice across the industry. However, charity is no substitute for ethical practice. So, while charitable giving is to be encouraged, it can only ever be seen as one part of a company's responsible behaviour.

RECOMMENDATIONS

Actions to Ensure More Effective Charitable Giving by Tour Operators

Below are ten suggested steps that companies could take to ensure that their charitable giving is integrated, effective and sustainable. They draw on the Business for Social Responsibility website and The Cause Related Marketing Guidelines.

- Integrate charitable giving into the overall company mission and objectives. Develop a clear understanding and articulation of how it fits into normal business operations, and ensure support at the highest level. This will help establish a clear set of values by which to decide where and how to give.
- Appoint a staff member who will have specific responsibility to oversee and develop charitable giving activities.
- Initiate effective research into the possibilities of funding, particularly in the destinations in which you work. Take some time to speak to staff and to the development and environment charities there. Find out their views on the real problems and ways they think you can best help. It is better to give less money in the first year and to spend time doing the initial research well, in order to ensure that future money is spent well. Consider working with a local organisation that can help you with the research and distribution of funds. UKbased development and environment groups may be able to help you find suitable partners.
- Commit to a funding level and stick to it. This will enable you and the charities to plan better. Possible methods to decide a suitable level include: fix a set level of pre-tax profits either using a sliding percentage based on profitability, or a fixed percentage; set an amount for each year, regardless of profit; or give a per capita rate for each employee or visitor.
- Combine charitable giving activities with other company activities such as provision of training, in-kind donations, shadowing and placements. Consider how you can help to build the capacity of local entrepreneurs who could be integrated into the tourism industry in the destination. Fund projects that directly impact key stakeholders e.g. suppliers, customers, employees. This will strengthen your supply chain and help bring sustainable change.
- Develop long-term partnerships with the charities you are working with. This will ensure that the giving brings lasting change. Develop a formal agreement so that both sides know what to expect from the relationship. Ensure that regular communication happens.
- Focus on the poor as they will often be left out of any tourism activities, and may bear the brunt of any negative effects. Try to support some charities that are working with the poorest people in the destinations.
- Focus on the destination and try to give to charities that are either UK-based and working in the destination, or are based in the destinations themselves.
- Evaluate your activities regularly to ensure that you are doing the most with your money, and to make changes if necessary. Consider bringing in an independent assessor.

- Brief your staff in the destinations and in the UK about your charitable giving policies and the information you offer to clients.

Actions to Ensure more Effective Charitable giving by Clients

Below are some ways to encourage clients to give to charity, and to help them respond compassionately when they encounter poverty in the destinations.

- *Before they go*: Publicise the charities you support in your brochure and include fuller information in your pre-departure pack. Consider collecting charitable donations before the tourists travel, possibly through a voluntary supplement to the invoice.
- *Bringing goods to give away*: If you think that tourists may bring goods for local people, find out beforehand what is most suitable to bring and let them know. Arrange for any goods that they have brought to be collected by the rep or tour guide and distributed through a local agency once the tourists have gone.
- *Understanding and responding in the destination*: Use the welcome meeting to help tourists understand the extent of poverty or other problems in the destination e.g. environmental destruction. Explain the causes of the problems and what they are likely to encounter e.g. begging, children asking for money. Inform tourists about possible responses they can make, including giving to local charities when they are there, giving when they get back home and giving away goods.
- *Responses to begging*: Begging is often the greatest concern for tourists. Encourage people to seek local advice on how to respond and place begging within its local cultural context. Some may choose to give to local charities, others may choose to buy food, or give money. Whatever they choose to do, encourage a compassionate and respectful attitude. Help them to be sensitive about how giving away money or sweets to children may affect their attitudes towards school i.e. they could see begging as more rewarding than gaining an education.
- *Visiting local projects*: Offer the opportunity for tourists to go to visit any projects you support. However, actively discourage ostentatious shows of charity when they are there, as this can reduce the dignity of the beneficiaries. Collect a fee from each tourist beforehand, which will go directly to the development work in the project.
- *Collecting and distributing money*: Encourage the local rep to collect any money in the destination and to distribute it discreetly through a local agent once the tourists have gone.
- *Back in the UK*: Provide information and advice for tourists for when they return home so they can continue to support the charities that are connected with your business.

DEVELOPING LOCAL PARTNERSHIPS

This stage looks at whether tour operators consider themselves to be in partnership with businesses in the destinations, and what they mean by the word 'partnership.' It also considers what type of training and advice they offer. It puts this in the context of increased community involvement across all industries, and suggests some principles that should underpin this, and some possible actions to take now.

FINDINGS

Would you use the Word 'Partnership' to Describe the Relationship with your Suppliers

When asked whether tour operators would consider their relationships with their suppliers as a partnership, the overwhelming majority (80%) said yes.

What do you Mean by Partnership

When asked to define what this meant for them, a variety of different answers were given, but many strong common themes appeared.

Relationships at the Centre

Over 70% of those questioned who considered themselves to be in a partnership with their ground operators, spoke of this in terms of long-term commitment. The other areas of a good relationship were spending time together, trust, listening and good communication. This emphasises the importance of good relationships in tour operating, an industry still characterised as exploitative of its purchasing power. Breaking this down according to company size, roughly half of all of the small and medium-sized operators placed a significant emphasis on the centrality of good relationships, whereas the larger operators barely mentioned it.

Joint Business Approach

It is common that tour operators will work closely with ground operators or service providers to develop the necessary services in the destination. Many of the smaller specialist operators plan their trips together with those in the communities they visit. This ensures that the communities are happy with the way tourism develops, and can cope with the number of tourists coming. For the larger groups, partnership often focused on sharing the same view of customer service and being able to provide the necessary standard of service, but little more than that. A few of the smaller UK operators also mentioned financial openness, but this was a low priority.

Local Community Involvement

One third of those who answered emphasised the need to properly recognise skills and experience and to pay a fair wage for them. This focuses on paying for quality as opposed to paying the lowest price possible. Other operators, mainly those set up with strong development aims in mind, thought it was vital that a partnership would meet local needs, particularly those of the poor. Finally, a significant minority emphasised the need for local communities to be able to determine the direction of their tourism development. The emphasis on local community involvement came almost exclusively from the smaller operators, with one mention from a medium-sized operator and no mention from any of the larger operators.

What Type of Training do you Provide

Many of those who spoke of being involved in partnerships were involved in some form of training. However, for most it was a relatively small part of their operations, and it was not seen as a high priority. Some of those who did not provide training said that the relationship with their ground handlers overseas was so close that they discussed everything and worked together in all aspects of the business. Others operators did not provide any training as they tried to find service providers who could already provide the services they wanted.

Skills Development

This ranges from working with guides to improve their skills (including bringing some to the UK, or paying for others to shadow those who were already trained), paying for reps to have language training, and working with people in villages to help them prepare food in a way that clients will like.

Understanding Consumers and Customer Service

This involves training staff, particularly those in hotels, to treat tourists in a way that they expect. It enables both tour operator and local business to be confident that their services meet the clients' expectations. Some companies also give more general advice to smaller, community tourism initiatives to help them pitch their product at different operators in the European and North American travel market. (Companies also offer advice to tourists on how to treat those in the destination, but this is covered in the next stage on responsible tourism.)

Health and Safety

Many operators provide advice and training to hotels so that they can meet the health and safety requirements of the EU Package Holiday Directive. This may involve written guidelines or sending experts to those hotels to run training workshops e.g. on food preparation.

Product Development

Operators who are in long-term relationship with groups or service providers may help them to develop their product to increase the quality of experience for the client. In many cases this involves helping communities develop a series of activities, which can be done in a single day or in two days. This enables a visit to rural village or community tourism initiative to become viable as part of a standard package tour, and is not just limited to those wanting to have a completely alternative holiday.

Bureaucracy

This involves helping suppliers to undertake the necessary paperwork in registering themselves and in meeting the legal requirements of being a business.

Environment

This is mainly working with rural groups to support them in maintaining their wilderness and local environment to ensure that tourism does not do any damage.

COMMENTARY

Industry Trends

The role of the company in modern society is changing. It used to be acceptable to see a company's role as providing jobs and making a profit for its shareholders. However, the economic bottom line (profit) has given way to the triple bottom line (economic, social and environmental) and a company's responsibilities are now to its stakeholders, not only its shareholders. There is a growing body of research to suggest that responsible organisations are already more commercially successful. Part of this overall trend is increased involvement with the local community.

This spans a wide range of activities and includes developing local infrastructure, enhancing jobs skills of local residents, introducing technology, sharing business practice and supporting local business development. If done well and in partnership with the local community, it has the potential to bring many benefits. However, if done badly, it can further marginalise local groups. Increased involvement with the local community also brings benefits to the companies involved.

It provides a trained local labour pool that will be able to meet the company's needs, and increases understanding of local cultures and norms, so that local operations are smoother and more integrated. It also improves relationships with the community, supports the local infrastructure to improve logistics and service provision and increases employee skills and training. Finally, it enhances brand image which will, in turn, increase competitive advantage as clients include ethical principles in their purchasing decisions. Community involvement is a forward-looking activity for companies that want to be successful in ten or 20 years' time. It is a process of long-term investment, which will enhance the quality of the product and the competitiveness of the company.

Terminations

It is encouraging that so many tour operators spoke in terms of partnership with local communities or local service providers. Many of the smaller specialist operators saw this partnership in terms of a long-term commitment to a destination and the people there, with a strong emphasis on the centrality of good relationships at the heart of tourism, and a fairer distribution of any benefits. Medium-sized operators did also consider long-term relationships to be important. However, many of the more mainstream operators saw 'partnership' only in terms of providing a good-quality service that met the standards of the UK market, and made no mention of community involvement or developing good relationships. This seems to be little more than a new word for 'sub-contracting'. These bigger operators said that they would need so many local partners that they simply opt for the large, usually Western-owned hotels, which they know will already be able to meet their demands for quantity and quality.

Training features on many tour operators' agendas and includes skills development, customer service, product development, understanding the UK market and health, safety and environmental training. However, this was one of the most disappointing results of the questionnaire. One of the main barriers to improving local benefits was identified as lack of capacity or quality of local suppliers and ground agents, and yet the training that operators were offering in this area was limited.

On the whole, where training was offered, it was mainly done by the smaller, specialist operators who were committed to a particular group of people for many years. However, many of these smaller operators said that they were simply too small and could have only limited impact in a destination that they could not afford to provide any training. One even suggested that all operators be encouraged to contribute to a fund in the destination that could help to provide the necessary business training. Finally, developing local partnerships and providing training is often much better than charitable giving in terms of sustainable development. Partnerships and training, by their very nature, are integrated into business activities and their success can be easily be shown to contribute to the overall success of a tour operator in terms of its image, profitability and quality of a product. This is one of the most important areas in which operators could invest more time and effort to make a positive difference.

RECOMMENDATIONS

Principles

These key principles behind developing partnerships and increasing community involvement draw heavily on Tearfund's Operating Principles for community development.

- *Long-term commitment*: A partnership takes time to develop, and both sides need to know that the other is committed to the relationship.
- *Mutual respect*: Although the relationship is likely to have a power imbalance because the UK tour operator will have most of the money, mutual respect is vital if the partnership is to be successful. It acknowledges that both sides have something to bring, and both sides are likely to benefit and be changed in the process. It also includes respecting cultural differences and trying to come to a compromise, as opposed to imposing a Western approach. It may involve making initial contact through someone who is trusted by both sides of the potential partnership.
- *Accountability and transparency*: There needs to be a clear agreement about what any partnership involves, where different responsibilities lie and how the partnership will operate. There should also be clear understanding of what happens when things do not go exactly to plan, with the commitment to rectify any mistakes if possible, as opposed to abandoning a partnership at any sign of trouble. Where possible, decision-making should be a joint process.
- *Integrated into the whole community*: It is important that benefits are widely distributed so that any partnership can be seen to enhance community development and not just the livelihoods of a few people within a community.
- *Training and development*: Any partnership will need to include an element of training and development. This will be based on needs that have been identified together by both sides of the partnership. It will enable the ground agent, service provider or local community to provide a better service for tourists, and will help them maintain control of their lives as tourism develops.
- *Fair price and adherence to labour standards*: As a minimum, any tour operators should pay a good wage for a full-time job and a fair price for any services provided. This could mean paying above the local rate. It will also mean a bare minimum of adherence to international labour standards, but a responsible company should be seeking to implement the highest possible standards in labour, as it does in health and hygiene. They should seek to adhere to the same standards overseas as they do in the UK.

Action

Developing good-quality, long-term partnerships can be time time-consuming if done in a way that respects the other party. However, the initial investment of time will bring dividends in the future in terms of the increased quality of the product, experience for the tourists and benefits to the local community.

Possible activities for tour operators to undertake towards effective partnership with the community are:

- Integrate community involvement goals into the overall company mission and objectives. Develop a clear understanding and articulation of how this fits into the company strategy for providing good-quality holidays. Ensure that there is support at the highest level.
- Appoint a staff member for each destination area who will have responsibility for developing better local partnerships.
- Take a long-term view and consider using some of the money you would have given to charity to invest in training and business development for local communities in the destination. Develop a five or ten-year plan outlining what you hope to achieve.
- Seek local advice on the best way to develop partnerships. Consider working with a local organisation to make the necessary contacts, or with a UK-based group with the necessary expertise and contacts. Develop a clear set of ground rules for the partnership.
- Focus the training input by working with local businesses to identify the barriers they face and the best ways to overcome them. Speak to the local tourism association and consider how you could work together. Support any local training institutions there may be which focus on business development or the hospitality industry. Speak to local government about the issues you face as an operator in using local services and supporting local development. Seek to work with them to support local businesses.
- Take a supply chain perspective and seek opportunities within the supply chain to make a difference and increase the quality of the tourism services you offer.
- Try a pilot project in one or two of the destinations in which you operate and seek your clients' opinions on the service provided and the experience they enjoyed.
- Focus on the poor and investigate how community involvement can integrate them into the tourism industry or provide them with some benefits from it.
- Evaluate your activities regularly to ensure that you are doing the most with your money, and to act to bring improvements if possible. Consider bringing in an independent assessor from time to time.
- Brief the staff in the destinations and in the UK about your community involvement and ensure that they have adequate information with which to brief clients.

RESPONSIBLE TOURISM POLICIES

This stage looks at whether companies have a written responsible tourism policy, the reasons for producing the policy and whether it focuses on the operations of the company, the supply chain or on tourists themselves. This policy may include reference to components mentioned in the previous three parts of the report, namely supporting the local economy, developing partnerships and charitable giving, but is not restricted to these areas of activity. Understanding that responsible tourism involves both companies and tourists, this part concludes with the possible components for a responsible tourism policy for the industry and a code for tourists.

FINDINGS

Do you have a Responsible Tourism Policy

Nearly 50% (32) of those asked claimed to have some form of responsible tourism policy.

What Form does this Policy Take

The responsible tourism policy took a variety of different forms.

Set of Principles within the Company

The most popular type of policy companies had was a set of written principles that underpinned their operations. Some published this in their brochure, others just kept it as an internal document.

Series of Activities

Other operators laid out a list of actions that they would do, and what they would not do.

Aspirations

A few companies had a written set of aspirations i.e. principles that they were aiming for, and what these might look like in practice. One operator even mentioned in their brochure that 'we don't pretend to be getting everything right' but that they are committed to doing as much as they can.

Code for Tourist Behaviour

Many companies said that their responsible tourism policy was a sheet of suggestions for how tourists should behave. Responsibility was therefore shifted away from the operations of the company, on to the behaviour of tourists.

Do you Plan to Produce a Policy in the Future

Of the 33 who did not have a policy, over half of them (17) said they were planning to produce some form of policy in the future.

Why did you Produce your Policy

Companies had produced policies for all sorts of reasons:

- *Integral to the principles of the company*: When this was the case, it was common that tour operators had developed the set of principles right from the start. This was usually the case for smaller specialist operators, who had been established with the aim of promoting development in a region, or whose growth depended on a deep knowledge of a few areas e.g. Tribes Travel, Rainbow Tours.

- *To educate tourists*: The focus of policies on educating tourists is not surprising, considering the earlier results that mentioned unprepared tourists as being a key barrier to bringing more benefits to local people.
- *Way of differentiating themselves*: Some of the smaller operators had produced a policy either to react against mainstream tourism, or as a way of celebrating what they were doing and differentiating themselves. Dragoman wanted a policy as a reaction against the accusations that overland operators cause the most destruction. Discovery Initiatives set up and developed a policy as a reaction against the destruction to the environment of mainstream tourism and many socalled 'ecotourism' initiatives.
- *To integrate the ethos into business*: Some of the tour companies wanted all suppliers and staff to know their policy so that they could ensure that it was implemented right down to ground level. These companies had produced policies in a way that was easy for suppliers and staff to understand and therefore implement.
- *External pressure*: Only three operators mentioned external pressure, from NGOs or from tourists, as a motivating factor for producing a policy. However, when asked if companies were thinking of producing a policy in the future, over half who did not have a policy already, said that they were. Pressure from NGOs or an awareness that clients' expectations were changing were frequently cited as reasons for doing this, even if the clients had not directly approached the companies themselves.

Why have you not Produced a Policy

Integrated into Business

Many of the specialist companies said that their policies were integrated into their operations, that they had only a few staff and that these staff were so involved in the company that they had no need for a written policy. One company previously had a responsible tourism code, but no longer used it.

Time to Explain to Ourists

Again, many of the specialist companies said that a verbal briefing to clients about the issues is better than a written one e.g. Sunvil Africa will spend an average of 2-3 hours overall on the phone to each client, answering their questions, and educating them about the place they are going to.

Lack of Priority

Some companies simply said that it was not a priority, that their clients were not interested and that they were simply in the business to make money.

Appears throughout the Brochure

Finally, a few companies who did not have an explicit policy, mentioned that their values and principles appeared scattered throughout the brochure, and integrated into what they had written.

Are more Clients asking about Responsible Tourism

Despite a recognition by many companies that there is increased interest (especially in the media) in holidays that are more ethical, few companies reported that their clients were asking more about it. Only about 30% (19 out of 61) said that clients were asking more about some of the social, environmental and economic issues in tourism. However, a significant number of the specialist operators said that clients were certainly more interested in the issues when they came back from a holiday and had seen the situations for themselves, and seen the benefits that tourism can bring, and the potential negative effects.

COMMENTARY

Industry Trends

It is increasingly common across all industries for companies to have responsible business policies. Examples include environmental policies of various oil companies, labour standards and ethical sourcing policies of UK supermarkets, a commitment to avoid the use of child labour by textile companies and statements against the use of animal testing by cosmetic companies. Some companies have their practices independently verified and are awarded a mark e.g. the fairtrade mark. Others simply produce a policy for public relations purposes and do little to ensure that it is implemented. In the tourism industry there are numerous schemes and awards, recognising various different aspects of responsible business practice.

British Airways Tourism for Tomorrow Awards have annual awards in six categories including accommodation, tourism organisation and mass tourism. Green Globe certifies for their view of sustainable tourism and allows operators to use one logo if they join the programme and another one if they reach the required standard.

AITO have developed a responsible tourism policy and plan that it will become a condition of membership in the future. Even if some of these schemes could still go further in embracing all aspects of responsible tourism practice, they serve to highlight good practice that is happening at the moment and are encouraging more operators to develop their responsible tourism policies and practices.

Terminations

Many tour operators claim to have some form of responsible tourism policy, although these appear in widely different forms and are aimed at different people. Some are aimed at staff, others at suppliers and others at tourists themselves. Reasons for producing these were to educate tourists, suppliers and staff, as a reaction against the mainstream industry, and because the principles are integral to the operation of the company. Only a few tour operators are up-front about their policies or make them explicit and easy for clients to access. Although the policies may appear in their brochures, many are scattered throughout the brochure so they are difficult to understand fully, and some are so brief as to be virtually meaningless. Some very good and detailed policies do exist, and the best ones include a broad set of principles with details about how these will be implemented in practice right throughout the supply chain e.g. The Imaginative Traveller.

However, over half of the operators asked still have no policies (although half of these said they planned to develop one in the future). It is likely that more and more tourists will be asking for the responsible tourism policies of companies, so there will be a mounting pressure to produce them. However, tourists are increasingly discerning, and will need to see evidence that the policy is not just for show, but is actually implemented on the ground. Companies will need to show evidence of good practice examples where they are behaving responsibly and making a real difference to the lives of people on the ground.

Many tour operators also see themselves as having a strong educational role in helping tourists to understand the people and culture in the destination they will be travelling to. A number of well-developed policies exist in this area, based on work over many years. Sending out a basic code to tourists to encourage them to think about their behaviour is such a well-established practice in some parts of the industry, and it is a relatively straightforward thing to do, that it is surprising that so few operators do it.

RECOMMENDATIONS

Possible Components of a Responsible Tourism Policy for Industry Operations

Many of the principles behind a responsible tourism policy will be similar to the principles involved in setting up partnerships. They have also been covered extensively elsewhere, so as suggested, not attempt to replicate previous work.

What makes a policy meaningful is the details of how it will be put into practice, and below we have offered some suggestions:

- *Support local links*: Use locally-owned accommodation and service providers wherever possible, and support local artisans and craft producers. Favour ground operators who use local transport providers, source food locally and source guides locally. Work with already established local businesses, service providers, co-operatives or associations who favour employment of local people, pay adequate wages, and have good working conditions and employee relations.

- *Clear contract*: Negotiate clear terms and conditions of operation with service providers, recognising the power imbalance that exists and allowing for this while undertaking negotiations.
- *Social and environmental audits*: Extend health and safety audits of hotels to include environmental and social issues, and recommend changes based on your findings.
- *Culture*: Respect the local traditions and culture in the places where you operate, and allow workers and staff to observe their religious and cultural practices.
- *Community partnerships*: Identify community initiatives with which you can form a partnership, and establish what training they will need
- *Charitable giving*: Develop a clear policy on charitable giving and integrate this with your normal business activities and training of local suppliers and service providers.
- *Monitoring*: Monitor your activities regularly to assess their impact and see if there are any areas for improvement.
- *Code for tourists*: Produce a code for tourists in order to encourage responsible behaviour from all those who travel with you. This code may vary between destinations.
- *Training staff*: Train your staff in how to implement the responsible tourism policy.
- *Implement policy through the supply chain*: Make your responsible tourism policy clear and available to service providers with whom you are working, and provide the necessary support and training for them to implement any changes.

TOURISM ATTRACTIONS

The tourism industry includes a number of key elements that tourists rely upon to achieve their general and specific goals and needs within a destination. Broadly categorised, they include facilities, accommodation, transportation, and attractions.

Although an in-depth discussion of each is beyond the scope of this book, there is merit in elaborating upon the importance of tourism attractions as a fundamental element of the tourist experience. Past tourism research has tended to rely more on the understanding of attractions, and how they affect tourists, than of other components of the industry. As Gunn has suggested, 'they [attractions] represent the most important reasons for travel to destinations' (1972:24).

MacCannell described tourism attractions as 'empirical relationships between a tourist, a site and a marker' (1989:41). The tourist represents the human component, the site includes the actual destination or physical entity, and the marker represents some form of information that the tourist uses to identify and give meaning to a particular attraction.

Lew (1987), however, took a different view, arguing that under the conditions of tourist-site-marker, virtually anything could become an attraction, including services and facilities.

Lew chose to emphasise the objective and subjective characteristics of attractions by suggesting that researchers ought to be concerned with three main areas of the attraction:

- *Ideographic*: Describes the concrete uniqueness of a site. Sites are individually identified by name and usually associated with small regions. This is the most frequent form of attraction studied in tourism research.
- *Organisational*: The focus is not on the attractions themselves, but rather on their spatial, capacity, and temporal nature. Scale continua are based on the size of the area which the attraction encompasses.
- *Cognitive*: A place that fosters the feeling of being a tourist. Attractions are places that elicit feelings related to what Relph (1976) termed 'insider' 'outsider', and the authenticity of MacCannell's (1989) front and back regions.

Leiper (1990:381) further added to the debate by adapting MacCannell's model into a systems definition. He wrote that:

A tourist attraction is a systematic arrangement of three elements: a person with touristic needs, a nucleus (any feature or characteristic of a place they might visit) and at least one marker (information about the nucleus).

The type of approach established by Leiper is also reflected in the efforts of Gunn (1972), who has written at length on the importance of attractions in tourism research. Gunn produced a model of tourist attractions that contained three separate zones, including:

- The nuclei, or core of the attraction;
- The inviolate belt, which is the space needed to set the nuclei in a context; and
- The zone of closure, which includes desirable tourism infrastructure such as toilets and information. Gunn argued that an attraction missing one of these zones will be incomplete and difficult to manage.

Some authors, including Pearce (1982), Gunn (1988), and Leiper (1990), have made reference to the fact that attractions occur on various hierarchies of scale, from very specific and small objects within a site, to entire countries and continents. This scale variability further complicates the analysis of attractions as both sites and regions. Consequently, there exists a series of attraction cores and attraction peripheries, within different regions, between regions, and from the perspective of the types of tourists who visit them. Spatially, and with the influence of time, the number and type of attractions visited by tourists and tourist groups may create a niche; a role certain types of tourists occupy within a vacation destination.

Through an analysis of space, time, and other behavioural factors, tourists can be fitted into a typology based on their utilisation and travel between selected attractions. One could make the assumption that tourist groups differ on the basis of the type of attractions they choose to visit, and according to how much time they spend at them. The implications for the tourism industry are that often it must provide a broad range of experiences for tourists interested in different aspects of a region.

A specific destination region, for example, may recognise the importance of providing a mix of touristic opportunities, from the very specific, to more general interest experiences for the tourists in search of cultural and natural experiences, in urban, rural, and back-country settings. Attractions have also been referred to in past research as sedentary, physical entities of a cultural or natural form. Although Gunn acknowledges wildlife as a *foundation* for attractions, it has been clear that wildlife is not simply the foundation of attractions, but an attraction in and of itself.

To a birder, for example, individual species become attractions of the most specific and most sought-after kind. A case in point is the annual return of a single albatross at the Hermaness National Nature Reserve in Unst, Shetland, Scotland. The arrival of this species prompts birdwatching tourists immediately to change their plans in an effort to travel to Hermaness. The albatross has become a major attraction for birder-tourists, while Hermaness, in a broader context, acts as a medium (attraction cluster) by which to present the attraction (bird). Natural attractions can be transitory in space and time, and this time may be measured for particular species in seconds, hours, days, weeks, months, seasons, or years. For tourists who travel with the prime reason to experience these transitory attractions, their movement is a source of both challenge and frustration.

MASS AND ALTERNATIVE TOURISM

Tourism has been both lauded and denounced for its ability to develop and therefore transform regions into completely different settings. In the former case, tourism is seen to have provided the impetus for appropriate long-term development; in the latter the ecological and sociological disturbance to transformed regions can be overwhelming. While most of the documented cases of the negative impacts of tourism are in the developing world, the developed world is certainly not an exception.

Young (1983), for example, documented the transformation of a small fishing-farming community in Malta by graphically illustrating the extent to which tourism development—through an increasingly complex system of transportation, resort development, and social behaviour—overwhelms such areas over time.

These days we are more prone to vilify or characterise conventional mass tourism as a beast; a monstrosity which has few redeeming qualities for the destination region, their people and their natural resource base. Consequently, mass tourism has been criticised for the fact that it dominates tourism within a region owing to its non-local orientation, and the fact that very little money spent within the destination actually stays and generates more income.

It is quite often the hotel or mega-resort that is the symbol of mass tourism's domination of a region, are often created using non-local products, having little requirement for local food products, and owned by metropolitan interests.

Hotel marketing occurs on the basis of high volume, attracting as many people as possible, often over seasonal periods of time. The implications of this seasonality are such that local people are at times moved in and out of paid positions that are based solely on this volume of touristic traffic.

Development exists as a means by which to concentrate people in very high densities, displacing local people from traditional subsistence-style livelihoods (as outlined by Young 1983) to ones that are subservience based. Finally, the attractions that lie in and around these massive developments are created and transformed to meet the expectations and demands of visitors.

Emphasis is often on commercialisation of natural and cultural resources, and the result is a contrived and inauthentic representation of, for example, a cultural theme or event that has been eroded into a distant memory. Admittedly the picture of mass tourism painted above is outlined to illustrate the point that the tourism industry has not always operated with the interests of local people and the resource base in mind. This was most emphatically articulated through much of the tourism research that emerged in the 1980s, which argued for a new, more socially and ecologically benign alternative to mass tourism development. According to Krippendorf (1982), the philosophy behind alternative tourism (AT)—forms of tourism that advocate an approach opposite to mass conventional tourism—was to ensure that tourism policies should no longer concentrate on economic and technical necessities alone, but rather emphasise the demand for an unspoiled environment and consideration of the needs of local people.

This 'softer' approach places the natural and cultural resources at the forefront of planning and development, instead of as an afterthought.

Also, as an inherent function, alternative forms of tourism provide the means for countries to eliminate outside influences, and to sanction projects themselves and to participate in their development—in essence, to win back the decision-making power in essential matters rather than conceding to outside people and institutions.

AT is a generic term that encompasses a whole range of tourism strategies (e.g. 'appropriate', 'eco-', 'soft', 'responsible', 'people to people', 'controlled', 'small-scale', 'cottage', and 'green' tourism), all of which purport to offer a more benign alternative to conventional mass tourism in certain types of destinations (Conference Report 1990, cited in Weaver 1991).

Dernoi (1981) illustrates that the advantages of AT will be felt in five ways:

- There will be benefits for the individual or family: accommodation based in local homes will channel revenue directly to families. Also families will acquire managerial skills.
- The local community will benefit: AT will generate direct revenue for community members, in addition to upgrading housing standards while avoiding huge public infrastructure expenses.
- For the host country, AT will help avoid the leakage of tourism revenue outside the country. AT will also help prevent social tensions and may preserve local traditions.
- For those in the industrialised generating country, AT is ideal for cost-conscious travellers or for people who prefer close contacts with locals.
- There will be benefits for international relations: AT may promote international-interregional-intercultural understanding.

More specifically, Weaver (1993) has analysed the potential benefits of an AT design from the perspective of accommodation, attractions, market, economic impact, and regulation. This more sensitive approach to tourism development strives to satisfy the needs of local people, tourists, and the resource base in a complementary rather than a competitive manner.

Some researchers, however, are quick to point out that as an option to mass tourism, full-fledged alternative tourism cannot replace conventional tourism simply because of mass tourism's varied and many-sided associated phenomena. Instead, it is more realistic to concentrate efforts in attempts to reform the worst prevailing situations, not the development of alternatives. Butler (1990) feels that mass tourism has not been rejected outright for two main reasons. The first is economic, in that it provides a significant amount of foreign exchange for countries; the second is socio-psychological and relates to the fact that many people seem to enjoy being a mass tourist. They actually like not having to make their own travel arrangements, not having to find accommodation when they arrive at a destination, being able to obtain goods and services without learning a foreign language, being able to stay in reasonable, in some cases considerable comfort, being able to eat reasonably familiar food, and not having to spend vast amounts of money or time to achieve these goals.

SUSTAINABLE DEVELOPMENT AND TOURISM

The measurement of development (i.e. a nation's stage of socio-economic advancement) has conventionally been accomplished through the implementation of a number of key economic indicators. Among others, these include variables such as protein intake, access to potable water, air quality, fuel, health care, education, employment, GDP, and GNP. The so-called 'developed' world (countries like Australia, the USA, Canada, and those of Western Europe) therefore is defined by the existence of these socio-economic conditions, whereby those with more are considered more highly developed.

Furthermore, one's level of development, either objectively or subjectively, is often equated or synonymous with one's perceived stage of 'civilisation', whereby progress (usually economic) is a key to the relationship between who is civilised and who is not. The *Oxford English Dictionary* defines civilisation as an 'advanced stage of social development', and civilise as 'bring out of barbarism, enlighten'.

The point to be made is that perhaps our perception of what is developed and what isn't, what is civilised and what isn't, is a matter of debate and one that our more recent approaches to development need to better address. For example, it has been noted that the most developed 20 per cent of the world's population (those in the 'West') are thought to use some 80 per cent of the world's resources with which to achieve development. If it is our goal to have the entire world 'developed' according to this Western paradigm, the planet will be in serious jeopardy. Perhaps in a hundred or two hundred years *Homo sapiens* will look back at Western civilisation as the most barbaric time period in recorded history.

Deming (1996) shares the view that humanity needs to take a good long look at civilisation. She writes that people have an insatiable hunger to see more and more of the planet, and to get closer and closer to its natural attractions.

This behaviour surfaces continually in tourism as the tentacles of the tourist seek to push the fine line that exists between acceptable and unacceptable human-wildlife interactions. For example, animal harassment regularly occurs in Point Pelee National Park in Ontario, Canada, as thousands of birders converge on the spring migration of birds in the park. Despite posted warnings, tourists continue to venture off the designated paths in identifying and photographing species.

Potential benefits derived from an alternative tourism strategy:

Accommodation:

- Does not overwhelm the community.
- Benefits (jobs, expenditures) are more evenly distributed.
- Less competition with homes and businesses for the use of infrastructure.
- A larger percentage of revenues accrue to local areas.
- Greater opportunity for local entrepreneurs to participate in the tourism sector.

Attractions:

- Authenticity and uniqueness of community is promoted and enhanced.
- Attractions are educational and promote self-fulfilment.

- Locals can benefit from existence of the attractions even if tourists are not present.

Market:

- Tourists do not overwhelm locals in numbers; stress is avoided.
- 'Drought/deluge' cycles are avoided, and equilibrium is fostered.
- A more desirable visitor type.
- Less vulnerability to disruption within a single major market.

Economic impact:

- Economic diversity is promoted to avoid single-sector dependence.
- Sectors interact and reinforce each other.
- Net revenues are proportionally higher; money circulates within the community.
- More jobs and economic activity are generated.

Regulation:

- Community makes the critical development/strategy decisions.
- Planning to meet ecological, social, and economic carrying capacities.
- Holistic approach stresses integration and well-being of community interests.
- Long-term approach takes into account the welfare of future generations.
- Integrity of foundation assets is protected.
- Possibility of irreversibilities is reduced.

Deming asks: in the face of global warming, diminishing habitat, and massive extinctions, what can it mean to be civilised? Her response is a plead for limits, both social and ecological, in facing the enemy within: As Pogo said during the Vietnam War, 'We've seen the enemy and it is us.' Suddenly we are both the invading barbarians and the only ones around to protect the city. Each one of us is at the centre of the civilized world and on its edge. Milgrath (1989) talked of values as fundamental to everything we do. He argues that humans have as a central value their personal desire to preserve their lives.

This naturally evolves into a concern and value for other people—a social value. Milgrath suggests that it is inappropriate to elevate the preservation of each human life to a central concern because every person dies and this social preservation can never be realised. He feels instead that we should value the preservation of our ecosystems over society. Beyond the socially oriented values of society, Milgrath says we have given top priority to economic development, the result being that society will not be able to sustain itself over the long term.

Sustainable development has been proposed as a model that can have utility in creating the impetus for structural change within society, one that ventures away from a strictly socio-economic focus to one where development 'meets the goals of the present without compromising the ability of future generations to meet their own needs' (World Commission on Environment and Development 1987:43).

As such, the principles of ecology are essential to the process of economic development, with the aim of increasing the material standards of people living in the world who are impoverished. Even more fundamentally, though, it would seem more inspiring to hope that sustainable development would increase the moral standards of people living everywhere, which might naturally spill over into the realm of economics, which we know is critical to our viability. Tourism's international importance as an engine for economic growth, as well as its potential for growth, makes it particularly relevant to sustainable development. Consequently there is a wealth of literature emerging that is directly related to the sustainability of tourism, however broadly defined.

One of the first action strategies on tourism and sustainability emerged from the Globe '90 conference in British Columbia, Canada. Here, representatives from the tourism industry, government, non-governmental organisations (NGOs), and academia discussed the importance of the environment in sustaining the tourism industry, and how poorly planned tourism developments often erode the very qualities of the natural and human environment that attract visitors.

The conference delegates suggested that the goals of sustainable tourism are:

- To develop greater awareness and understanding of the significant contributions that tourism can make to environment and the economy;
- To promote equity and development;
- To improve the quality of life of the host community;
- To provide a high quality of experience for the visitor; and
- To maintain the quality of the environment on which the foregoing objectives depend.

Although their definition of sustainable tourism development was somewhat non-committal (i.e. 'meeting the needs of present tourist and host region while protecting and enhancing opportunity for the future'), a number of good recommendations were developed for policy, government, NGOs, the tourism industry, tourists, and international organisations.

For example, the policy section contains 15 recommendations related to how tourism should be promoted, developed, defined, in addition to a series of regional, interregional, and spatial and temporal implications. One of the policy recommendations states that 'sustainable tourism requires the placing of guidelines for levels and types of acceptable growth but does not preclude new facilities and experiences'.

From the perspective of financial prosperity and growth, there is an economic rationale for sustainability; as McCool (1995:3) asserts, 'once communities lose the character that makes them distinctive and attractive to nonresidents, they have lost their ability to vie for tourist-based income in an increasingly global and competitive marketplace'. In addition, McCool quotes Fallon in suggesting that sustainability is all about the pursuit of goals and measuring progress towards them.

No longer is it appropriate to gauge appropriate development by physical output or economic bottom lines; these must also be consideration of social order and justice.

McCool feels, therefore, that in order for sustainable tourism to be successful, humans must consider the following:

- How tourists value and use natural environments;
- How communities are enhanced through tourism;
- Identification of tourism's social and ecological impacts; and
- Management of these impacts.

Accordingly, many researchers and associations have initiated the process of determining and measuring impacts. As outlined above, Globe '90 was one of the initial and integral forces in linking tourism with sustainable development.

This was followed by Globe '92 and the move from principles to practice in implementing measures of sustainability in tourism. Even so, it was recognised in this conference that there was much work to be done in implementing sustainable principles in tourism, as emphasised by Roy:

Sustainable tourism is an extension of the new emphasis on sustainable development. Both remain concepts. I have not found a single example of either in India. The closest for tourism is in Bhutan. Very severe control of visitors—2000 per year—conserves the environment and the country's unique socio-cultural identity. Even there, trekking in the high altitudes, I find the routes littered with the garbage of civilization.

Although many examples exist in the literature on tourism and sustainable development, few sustainable tourism projects have withstood the test of time. An initiative that has received some exposure in the literature is the Bali Sustainable Development Project, coordinated through the University of Waterloo, Canada, and Gadjahmada University in Indonesia. This is a project that has been applied at a multisectoral level. Tourism, then, is one of many sectors, albeit a prime one, that drives the Balinese economy. Wall (1993) suggests that some of the main conclusions from his work on the project are as follows:

- Be as culturally sensitive as possible in developing a sustainable development strategy.
- Work within existing institutional frameworks as opposed to creating new ones.
- Multi-sectoral planning is critical to a sustainable development strategy and means must be created to allow all affected stakeholders to participate in decision-making.

The integration of tourism with other land uses in a region has also been addressed by Butler (1993:221), who sees integration as 'the incorporation of an activity into an area on a basis acceptable to other activities and the environment within the general goal of sustainable or long-term development'.

Butler identified complementarity, compatibility, and competitiveness as variables that could be used as a first step in prioritising land uses, where complementarity leads to a higher degree of integration and competitiveness leads to segregation of the activity relative to other land uses. Other models have been more unisectoral in their approach to the place of tourism within a destination region. These have tended to identify a range of indicators that identify a sustainable approach or unsustainable approach to the delivery of tourism.

Examples include Canova's (1994) illustration of how tourists can be responsible towards the environment and local populations; Forsyth's (1995) overview of sustainable tourism and self-regulation; Moscardo *et al.'s* (1996) look at ecologically sustainable forms of tourism accommodation; and Consulting and Audit Canada's (1995) guide to the development of core and site-specific sustainable tourism indicators. These core indicators (e.g. site protection, stress, use intensity, waste management, and so on) must, according to the report, be used in concert with specific site or destination indicators.

This report identifies two categories of this latter group of indicators:

- Supplementary ecosystem-specific indicators (applied to specific biophysical land and water regions), and
- Site-specific indicators, which are developed for a particular site.

Table. Core Indicators of Sustainable Tourism.

Indicator	Specific measures
Site protection	Category of site protection according to IUCN index
Stress	Tourist numbers visiting site (per annum/peak month)
Use intensity	Intensity of use in peak period (persons/hectare)
Social impact	Ratio of tourists to locals (peak period and over time)
Development	Existence of environmental review procedure or control formal controls over development of site and use densities
Waste	Percentage of sewage from site receiving management treatment (additional indicators may include structural limits of other infrastructural capacity on site, such as water supply)
Planning	Existence of organised regional plan for tourist process destination region (including tourism component)
Critical ecosystems	Number of rare or endangered species
Consumer satisfaction	Level of satisfaction by visitors (survey-based)
Local satisfaction	Level of satisfaction by visitors (survey-based)
Tourism contribution to local economy	Proportion of total economic activity generated by tourism

Composite indices	
Carrying	Composite early warning measure of key factors capacity affecting the ability of the site to support different levels of tourism
Site stress	Composite measure of levels of impact on the site (its natural/ cultural attributes due to tourism and other sector cumulative stress)
Attractivity	Qualitative measure of those site attributes that make it attractive to tourism and can change over time

Table. Ecosystem-specific Indicators.

Ecosystem	Sample indicators[a]
Coastal zones	Degradation (percentage of beach degraded, eroded)
	Use intensity (persons per metre of accessible beach)
	Water quality (faecal coliform and heavy metals counts)
Mountain regions	Erosion (percentage of surface area eroded)
	Biodiversity (key species counts)
	Access to key sites (hours' wait)
Managed wildlife	Species health (reproductive success, species parks diversity)
	Use intensity (ratio of visitors to game)
	Encroachment (percentage of park affected by unauthorised activity)
Ecologically unique	Ecosystem degradation (number and mix of sites species, percentage area with change in cover)
	Stress on site (number of operators using site)
	Number of tourist sitings of key species (percentage success)
Urban environments	Safety (crime numbers)
	Waste counts (amounts of rubbish, costs)
	Pollution (air pollution counts)
Cultural sites (built)	Site degradation (restoration/repair costs)
	Structure degradation (precipitation acidity, air pollution counts)
	Safety (crime levels)
Cultural sites	Potential social stress (ratio average income (traditional) of tourists/locals) In season sites (percentage of vendors open year round) Antagonism (reported incidents between locals and tourists)
Small islands	Currency leakage (percentage of loss from total tourism revenues)
	Ownership (percentage foreign ownership of tourism establishments) Water availability (costs, remaining supply)

Some publications have discussed tourism and sustainability from the perspective of codes of ethics. While indicators are variables that are identified and used to measure and monitor tourism impacts, codes of ethics or conduct are lists designed to elicit a change in behaviour of particular stakeholder groups; a form of compliance for acceptable behaviour at a tourism setting.

The *Beyond the Green Horizon* paper on sustainable tourism is a good example of this form of education. To Tourism Concern, sustainable tourism is: tourism and associated infrastructures that, both now and in the future: operate within natural capacities for the regeneration and future productivity of natural resources; recognise the contribution that people and communities, customs and lifestyles, make to the tourism experience; accept that these people must have an equitable share in the economic benefits of tourism; are guided by the wishes of local people and communities in the host areas.

Nothing is measured but 'rules' are stated for the purpose of prompting or reinforcing this appropriate behaviour. The Tourism Industry Association of Canada (1995) joined forces with the National Round Table on the Environment and the Economy in creating a document that demonstrates commitment and responsibility to protecting the environment through cooperation with other sectors and governments at all levels.

Their sustainable tourism guidelines were developed for tourists, the tourism industry, industry associations, accommodation, food services, tour operators, and Ministries of Tourism. Each of these sections contains appropriate guidelines that deal with policy and planning; the tourism experience; the host community; development; natural, cultural, and historic resources; conservation of natural resources; environmental protection; marketing; research and education; public awareness; industry cooperation; and the global village.

A final publication that merits attention in this section is the work of the Federation of Nature and National Parks of Europe (1993). Its comprehensive look at sustainable tourism in Europe's nature and national parks provides good insight into the challenge of implementing sustainability in that part of the world.

Many of the protected areas in Europe are situated in rural working landscapes (e.g. England, Wales, Luxembourg) and must contend with different pressures as compared with some of the larger and less densely populated areas surrounding the protected areas of Australia and New Zealand, Canada, and the United States.

However, Europe also contains many large national parks and biosphere reserves that are maintained accordingly. In both cases (rural and wilderness environments) policy-makers and practitioners are charged with the task of implementing sustainable tourism in these varied settings. The European national parks document recognises that people must be able to improve the quality of their lives, maintain jobs, improve their economy, enjoy their cultures, and promote harmony between cultures. These must be accomplished with an eye to environmental education, political support for the environment, and the protection of heritage values through restorative projects and direct practical help.

Sustainable tourism, however, is not without its critics. Hunter (1995), for example, suggests that the current approach to sustainable tourism development is one that is flawed because it condones the planning and management of tourism in a manner inconsistent with the design of sustainable development. In particular, tourism does not adequately address issues of geographical scale and intersectoral cooperation which are so important to achieving sustainable development.

Furthermore, Macbeth (1994) calls attention to the fact that sustainable tourism is more reactionary than proactive in nature. Macbeth suggests that 'the history of capitalism is full of examples of how reactionary tendencies are easily co-opted by capitalism to sustain its own existence, thus extending the status quo of exploitive relations rather than overthrowing them'. This will continue to occur, according to Macbeth, unless the present form of capitalism is overcome.

McKercher (1993a) feels that tourism is vulnerable to losing sustainability for four main reasons. First, tourism is not recognised as a natural resource-dependent industry; second, the tourism industry is invisible, especially in urban areas; third, tourism is electorally weak, with little support in government; and fourth, there is a distinct lack of leadership driving the industry, which ultimately makes tourism vulnerable to attacks from other land users. McKercher cites the example of resource use in northern Ontario as a case in point. In this region the economy has been dominated politically by the large extractive industries (forestry and mining).

The disaggregated structure of the tourism industry in Ontario's north (predominantly outfitters and lodges) prevents it from having any political decision-making influence at all.

Other critical reviews of tourism and sustainability include Goodall and Cater's (1996) belief that sustainable tourism will probably not be achieved, despite the most committed environmental performance, and Burr's (1995) work illustrating that sustainable tourism development is unlikely to occur unless the people of rural tourism communities work together to make it happen.

There appears to be certain agreement that if sustainability is to occur at all, it must be done at the local level, and perhaps shaped loosely by a broader national or international policy.

The notions of policy and local participation have been examined by Laarman and Gregersen (1994), who feel that sustainable nature tourism policy must include the following three areas: (1) national support and advanced planning; (2) appropriate pricing and revenue policies; and (3) local participation and benefits.

THE MARKETING PROCESS

BACKGROUND TO EXMAR

Professor Malcolm McDonald of Cranfield University School of Management, a world authority on marketing planning, has produced numerous publications on the marketing planning process over the last 10 years. His best selling book, *Marketing Plans - How to prepare them: How to use them*, now in the Fourth Edition, describes *The Ten Steps of the Strategic Marketing Planning Process* as follows:

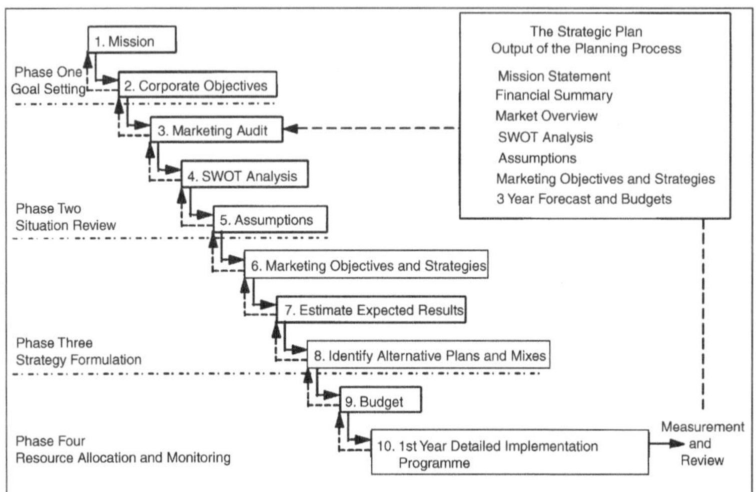

Fig. The Ten Steps of the Strategic Marketing Planning Process

In order to assist companies with the implementation of an effective Strategic Marketing Planning Process many of the techniques were implemented in software programmes. Several prototypes were developed at the Cranfield School of Management, which were widely tested in a variety of commercial environments over a number of years, in order to produce a complete and robust specification of the requirement.

EXMAR

PRODUCT DESCRIPTION

EXMAR is a process, supported by a set of associated services, for developing Strategic Marketing Plans.

It assists companies by:

- Guiding them through a logical marketing planning process
- Prompting and defining key data requirements
- Displaying information graphically to aid understanding of the business
- Providing advice at key stages
- Allowing 'what-if ' analyses
- Automatically outputting the report resulting from the analysis.

There are a number of techniques and methodologies incorporated in EXMAR including:

- Gap Analysis
- SWOT Analysis

- Ansoff Matrix
- Boston Box
- Directional Policy Matrix
- Market Segmentation
- Perceptual Maps
- Porter Matrix
- Objective and Strategy setting.

BENEFITS OF EXMAR

The competitive differentiation derived from EXMAR has been the subject of extensive research by Cranfield School of Management and can be summarised as follows:

- Provides a planning framework which ensures consistency across divisions and each division covers all the key aspects of the planning process
- Takes the 'number crunching' out of marketing analysis
- Gives new insights into the markets particularly through the market segmentation techniques
- Gives powerful graphical display which makes large volumes of data understandable
- Enables easy 'what-if ' iterations as strategy options are explored
- Facilitates team work and multidisciplinary involvement in the marketing planning process
- Improves marketing skills within the company
- Focuses planning on the customer
- Gives a clear vision of markets and the company's position in them
- Adds value to marketing database investment.

IMPLEMENTATION OF THE STRATEGIC MARKETING PLANNING PROCESS USING EXMAR

The successful introduction and implementation of the Strategic Marketing Planning Process within an organisation is dependent on management commitment and high quality process consultancy and training, as well as the EXMAR process support tools. This ensures that key members of staff are familiar with, and trained in, all the marketing processes and integrated techniques that have been developed in conjunction with Cranfield School of Management, and that a first class strategy is produced.

Experience has shown that the most efficient and beneficial method of implementing the Strategic Marketing Planning Process supported by the EXMAR software is to follow the steps shown below:

MARKET MAPPING AND SEGMENTATION WORKSHOP

The objective of the workshop is to produce a structure for the defined market, which clearly identifies the different requirements that customers look to be satisfied. These different requirements can then be used to develop the alternative strategies that need to be implemented to better access the segments and tune the product offers to suit the customer requirements. It should be noted that most organisations do not have access to the information to produce a definitive segmentation structure that is 100% accurate. However most organisations do have sufficient internal knowledge to produce something that is 'roughly right' and a reasonable starting point. Where this is not the case, the process makes it very clear where the information holes are and the importance of that information. If research is required, the process ensures a rigorous and very targeted brief can be produced.

Market Definition

A market is defined in terms of a need that can be satisfied by the products or services customers' view as alternatives. Once this is clear, the boundaries for the segmentation project can be set.

Market Mapping

A market map defines the distribution and value chain between supplier and final user, which takes into account the various buying mechanisms found in a market, including the part played by 'influencers'.

Market maps help focus attention on key decision makers within a market, and identify key target market segments within a market segmentation project. Market channels and the key players within channels can be easily identified with the help of a graphic presentation of a market. A market map can help deliver key customer and consumer insights, and ensures full awareness of the the total market place.

Market Segmentation

Market segmentation is a concept in economics and marketing. A market segment is a sub-set of a market made up of people or organizations with one or more characteristics that cause them to demand similar product and/or services based on qualities of those products such as price or function. A true market segment meets all of the following criteria: it is distinct from other segments, it is homogeneous within the segment; it responds similarly to a market stimulus, and it can be reached by a market intervention. The term is also used when consumers with identical product and/or service needs are divided up into groups so they can be charged different amounts for the services.

The people in a given segment are supposed to be similar in terms of criteria by which they are segmented and different from other segments in terms of these criteria. These can be broadly viewed as 'positive' and 'negative' applications of the same idea, splitting up the market into smaller groups.

Examples:

- Gender

- Price
- Interests
- Location
- Religion
- Income
- Size of Household

While there may be theoretically 'ideal' market segments, in reality every organization engaged in a market will develop different ways of imagining market segments, and create Product differentiation strategies to exploit these segments. The market segmentation and corresponding product differentiation strategy can give a firm a temporary commercial advantage.

Bases for Segmenting Consumer Markets

- Geographic segmentation
- Demographic segmentation
- Psychographic segmentation
- Behavioural segmentation

Geographic Segmentation

The market is segmented just as to geographic criteria- nations, states, regions, counties, cities, neigborhoods, or zip codes. Geo-cluster approach combines demographic data with geographic data to create a more accurate profile of specific

Psychographic Segmentation

Psychographics is the science of using psychology and demographics to better understand consumers.Psychographic segmentation: consumer are divided just as to their lifestyle, personality, values. People within the same demographic group can exhibit very different psychographic profiles.

"Positive" Market Segmentation

Market segmenting is dividing the market into groups of individual markets with similar wants or needs that a company divides into distinct groups which have distinct needs, wants, Behaviour or which might want different products and services. Broadly, markets can be divided just as to a number of general criteria, such as by industry or public versus private. Although industrial market segmentation is quite different from consumer market segmentation, both have similar objectives. All of these methods of segmentation are merely proxies for true segments, which don't always fit into convenient demographic boundaries.

Consumer-based market segmentation can be performed on a *product specific* basis, to provide a close match between specific products and individuals. However, a number of generic market segment systems also exist, *e.g.* the system provides a broad segmentation of the population of the United

States based on the statistical analysis of household and geodemographic data.

The process of segmentation is distinct from positioning. The overall intent is to identify groups of similar customers and potential customers; to prioritize the groups to address; to understand their Behaviour; and to respond with appropriate marketing strategies that satisfy the different preferences of each chosen segment. Revenues are thus improved.

Improved segmentation can lead to significantly improved marketing effectiveness. Distinct segments can have different industry structures and thus have higher or lower attractiveness Once a market segment has been identified, and targeted, the segment is then subject to positioning. Positioning involves ascertaining how a product or a company is perceived in the minds of consumers.

This part of the segmentation process consists of drawing up a perceptual map, which highlights rival goods within one's industry just as to perceived quality and price. After the perceptual map has been devised, a firm would consider the marketing communications mix best suited to the product in question.

Behavioural Segmentation

In Behavioural segmentation, consumers are divided into groups just as to their knowledge of, attitude towards, use of or response to a product:

- *Occasions*: Segmentation just as to occasions.we segment the market just as to the occasions.
- *Benefits*: Segmentations just as to benefits sought by the consumer.
- Users status: nonusers, ex-users, first time users, etc.

Using Segmentation in Customer Retention

The basic approach to retention-based segmentation is that a company tags each of its active customers with 3 values:

1. *Tag No.1*: Is this customer at high risk of canceling the company's service? One of the most common indicators of high-risk customers is a drop off in usage of the company's service. For example, in the credit card industry this could be signaled through a customer's decline in spending on his or her card.
2. *Tag No.2*: Is this customer worth retaining? This determination boils down to whether the post-retention profit generated from the customer is predicted to be greater than the cost incurred to retain the customer. Managing Customers as Investments.
3. *Tag No.3*: What retention tactics should be used to retain this customer? For customers who are deemed "save-worthy", it's essential for the company to know which save tactics are most likely to be successful. Tactics commonly used range from providing "special" customer discounts to sending customers communications that reinforce the value proposition of the given service.

Process for Tagging Customers

The basic approach to tagging customers is to utilize historical retention data to make predictions about active customers regarding:

- Whether they are at high risk of canceling their service
- Whether they are profitable to retain
- What retention tactics are likely to be most effective

The idea is to match up active customers with customers from historic retention data who share similar attributes. Using the theory that "birds of a feather flock together", the approach is based on the assumption that active customers will have similar retention outcomes as those of their comparable predecessor.

Niche Marketing

A niche is a more narrowly defined customer group who seek a distinct set of benefits. Ýdentified by dividing a segment into subsegments,distinct and unique set of needs,requires speciallization, and is not likely to attract too many competitors.

Price Discrimination

Where a monopoly exists, the price of a product is likely to be higher than in a competitive market and the quantity sold less, generating monopoly profits for the seller.

These profits can be increased further if the market can be segmented with different prices charged to different segments charging higher prices to those segments willing and able to pay more and charging less to those whose demand is price elastic.

The price discriminator might need to create rate fences that will prevent members of a higher price segment from purchasing at the prices available to members of a lower price segment.

This Behaviour is rational on the part of the monopolist, but is often seen by competition authorities as an abuse of a monopoly position, whether or not the monopoly itself is sanctioned. Examples of this exist in the transport industry where business class customers who can afford to pay may be charged prices many times higher than economy class customers for essentially the same service.

Ansoff Matrix

To portray alternative corporate growth strategies, Igor Ansoff presented a matrix that focused on the firm's present and potential products and markets.

By considering ways to grow via existing products and new products, and in existing markets and new markets, there are four possible product-market combinations. Ansoff's matrix is shown below:

Table. Ansoff Matrix

	Existing Products	New Products
Existing Markets	Market Penetration	Product Development
New Markets	Market Development	Diversification

Ansoff's matrix provides four different growth strategies:

1. Market Penetration - the firm seeks to achieve growth with existing products in their current market segments, aiming to increase its market share.
2. Market Development - the firm seeks growth by targeting its existing products to new market segments.
3. Product Development - the firms develops new products targeted to its existing market segments.
4. Diversification - the firm grows by diversifying into new businesses by developing new products for new markets.

Selecting a Product-Market Growth Strategy

The market penetration strategy is the least risky since it leverages many of the firm's existing resources and capabilities. In a growing market, simply maintaining market share will result in growth, and there may exist opportunities to increase market share if competitors reach capacity limits. However, market penetration has limits, and once the market approaches saturation another strategy must be pursued if the firm is to continue to grow.

Market development options include the pursuit of additional market segments or geographical regions. The development of new markets for the product may be a good strategy if the firm's core competencies are related more to the specific product than to its experience with a specific market segment. Because the firm is expanding into a new market, a market development strategy typically has more risk than a market penetration strategy.

A product development strategy may be appropriate if the firm's strengths are related to its specific customers rather than to the specific product itself. In this situation, it can leverage its strengths by developing a new product targeted to its existing customers. Similar to the case of new market development, new product development carries more risk than simply attempting to increase market share.

Diversification is the most risky of the four growth strategies since it requires both product and market development and may be outside the core competencies of the firm. In fact, this quadrant of the matrix has been referred to by some as the "suicide cell". However, diversification may be a reasonable choice if the high risk is compensated by the chance of a high rate of return. Other advantages of diversification include the potential to gain a foothold in an attractive industry and the reduction of overall business portfolio risk.

GUIDANCE ON AUDIT PREPARATION

The objective of these two days is to ensure that the data required has been identified in detail and the format of the data is consistent.

DATA COLLECTION AND RESEARCH

The following information needs to be collected and input into EXMAR for each product-market as defined in the Ansoff Matrix. This information is then used to drive the market audit.

For each product-market the following information is required:

- Market size and growth Volume
- Revenue
- Market share

Current figures are requested. Historical data is also useful, as far back as available. If only some of these data items are known, the system will estimate data values where possible. In order for EXMAR to construct the Boston Box and the Directional Policy Matrix, it is necessary to define and gather the following information:

- Market Attractiveness Factors - defined once for the business unit
- MAF scores
- Critical Success Factors
- CSF scores for yourself and important competitors.

Segmentation Verification

Often our clients sell products and services into horizontal segments. In these cases, the product-offer maps onto how the customers run their business, and segments are often hard to identify in a way that will give maximum leverage in the marketing plan. To help solve this problem, we have developed a set of tools and processes for analysing existing and potential customer data, and generating and sizing segments.

CUSTOMER PROFITABILITY AUDIT

This is an optional audit and will develop a more realistic view of Customer/Segment Profitability as opposed to Product Profitability. It is often the case that a few segments generate more than 100% of the profit and it is important to identify which segments are actually profitable.

SOFTWARE TRAINING AND DATA INPUT

Two days of hands on training are provided on the EXMAR software including the use of the extensive help system. Data from your company can be entered into EXMAR at this stage.

Market Audit Workshop

The objective of this workshop is to produce the Market Audit and Trend Analysis, *i.e.* What will happen if we do nothing over the plan period?

For each product-market the following information is analysed:

- Financial performance
- Market share
- Relative strengths and weaknesses
- Competitor strategy
- Relative costs
- Market attractiveness trends
- Opportunities and threats
- Assumptions and sensitivity analysis.

Additionally the portfolio of products and services is analysed using various tools including the Directional Policy Matrix and the Boston Box.

Data Validation

The sensitivity analysis on assumptions, whether they be in terms of relative strength, market growth, or profitability are used to highlight those areas where it is most important to verify the data, as wrong assumptions could lead to inappropriate strategies being developed. This may require highly focused Market Research studies on the particular issues identified.

OBJECTIVES AND STRATEGIES WORKSHOP

The objective of this workshop is to set the overall strategies and those that operate at the product-market level. Objectives are defined as the financial performance and market share required from each product market. Strategies are defined as the set of costed actions required to improve competitive performance in order to reach the objectives. It also includes assigning responsibility for the actions.

The process is iterative and can result for example in the identification of generic problem areas, where one set of actions and investments can affect competitive performance in several productmarkets. These usually provide the best ROI.

Additionally the output of the workshop often results in several scenarios, each with its own investment profile, *i.e.* these are the anticipated results of this level of investment as opposed to a larger or smaller sum. These can highlight the implications of the spread of the investment and resources.

REVIEW OBJECTIVES AND STRATEGIES

This phase of the project involves the Client in performing a 'sanity check' on the strategies. This can be both in terms of the viability of implementation, given the internal processes and constraints on the organisation and investment available, as well as a management review.

PLAN REVIEW AND METRICS WORKSHOP

On completion of the project, a day is set aside to review the Strategic Marketing Plan and to identify key metrics for monitoring the implementation and success of the strategies. For example, if 'service levels' are an important Critical Success Factor, then key performance indicators need to be defined that can be measured, such as 'response times to customer requests' or 'adherence to committed delivery schedules'. If required we can offer our Clients further services to help them design and implement appropriate KPIs in their organisation.

DECIDING WHAT TO BE AND WHAT TO OFFER TO WHOM

In an existing hotel, the developer and architect already may have decided many of the things it is—high-rise or resort, in the business center or on the edge of town, large rooms and baths or smallish, one restaurant or several, wood or marble, with ballroom or not, and so on. Even so, the management team must still consciously examine what they intend the hotel to be and offer to whom. The type of customer originally in mind may not be available now in enough numbers to support the hotel.

Perhaps a competitor has come in and taken away a piece of the market. Perhaps the business center has shifted to another part of the city. Perhaps new customers from Korea or California have replaced the original ones from Europe and the East Coast. Even though the owner has provided a basic envelope within which to operate, there still are options—many things the hotel team can control, many choices to be made on what to offer and to emphasize to various market segments. Is the hotel the place to be seen or the place that guards privacy? Is it better to stress family style or crisp, professional business style? Should the hotel add services, like a Japanese breakfast, to meet the needs of one particular group? Should the team put in meetings express and add more small meeting spaces to tap the short-lead-time corporate meetings market? Should it drop some services the market no longer wants to support?

The answers to what to be and offer are found by studying the marketing situation, which comprises three parts:

1. Strengths and weaknesses,
2. The kinds and numbers of customers available in the marketplace, and
3. The other hotels with whom this hotel competes for these customers.

Careful analysis yields a picture of which segments the hotel is best able to attract and serve. These become the *target markets*—the "to whoms"—and their needs and wants become the "what to be's." The key to successfully deciding what to be and offer to whom is a matter of strategic selection of, focus on, and commitment to a well-defined set of markets for whom the hotel is best suited to compete. Trying to be all things to all potential customers is a guarantee of ineffectiveness.

A good example of focus and targeting is Starwood's W. At risk of turning off a sizeable portion of the business and leisure travel market and leaving families well behind, Starwood focuses tightly on a lifestyle segment of professional and business people, with remarkable success. The talents required to assess the marketing situation, create a data model of the market's segments, calculate a feasible share of each, and select the targets on which to focus are comfort with data, the ability to observe and infer, creativity, patience with detail, comfort with the hypothetical, and an analytic curiosity.

Usually, such analyses are uncomfortably foreign to people with backgrounds in sales, and often to operators as well. It is essential that we teach, motivate, and reward curious, careful, insightful analysis of history and market information—skills that are not natural to those typically attracted to hospitality management. the *target markets*—the "to whoms"—and their needs and wants become the "what to be's."The key to successfully deciding what to be and offer to whom is a matter of strategic selection of, focus on, and commitment to a well-defined set of markets for whom the hotel is best suited to compete. Trying to be all things to all potential customers is a guarantee of ineffectiveness.

A good example of focus and targeting is Starwood's W. At risk of turning off a sizeable portion of the business and leisure travel market and leaving families well behind, Starwood focuses tightly on a lifestyle segment of professional and business people, with remarkable success.

The talents required to assess the marketing situation, create a data model of the market's segments, calculate a feasible share of each, and select the targets on which to focus are comfort with data, the ability to observe and infer, creativity, patience with detail, comfort with the hypothetical, and an analytic curiosity. Usually, such analyses are uncomfortably foreign to people with backgrounds in sales, and often to operators as well. It is essential that we teach, motivate, and reward curious, careful, insightful analysis of history and market information—skills that are not natural to those typically attracted to hospitality management.

SETTING PRICES

Having decided what to be and offer and to whom, the next most important decision is price. Pricing is a critical decision because it determines, first, whether or not the intended customers will purchase, and second, whether they will be satisfied with the value offered and, thus, be willing to return. Third, it determines whether the hotel will be financially healthy enough to maintain itself and reward its employees so customers can once again be satisfied when they do return.

Three factors must come into consideration in pricing—the Three Cs of pricing, if you will: costs, competition, and customers' comfort zones. In F&B, costs drive pricing of menu items and beverages. Drucker says American industry has too much cost-driven pricing, and that it needs more price-driven costing.

Doesn't F&B have the opportunity to build and test menus to discover where price points should be set, and is not the chef challenged to manage ingredients and portion size to deliver the cost and margin structure desired? Yet the cost-driven practice continues.

In rooms, competition is most often the dominant factor. Costs play a role, but changes in variable cost of an occupied room are generally small and rooms' contribution margins are large, typically 65 per cent or better. Moreover, hotel accounting does not measure discounts from a standard price, as do almost all other industries. So there is no visible cost in reducing price to meet competitors. Remember: Any damn fool can cut his price, and some damn fool always will.

Must everyone follow? No. The key is to get in the head of the customer. The truly controlling factor is customer comfort zones, and all too often hotel management leave money on the table because they don't know what those comfort zones are. At what price does the offer attract and deliver value? That is the key question in setting prices.

Price setting requires talent and skill in data gathering and analysis, accounting and building pro formas, interpreting and drawing inferences, and decision making. Do not let salespeople set prices; do not let controllers set prices. Only one person—the GM—can pull together the inputs of sales, control, operations, reservations, and the rest, and make this crucial judgment call. Also, build at least three price scenarios and have the controller and marketing director agree on occupancy impacts. Then run a GOP pro forma on each.

Out of that exercise will come a sense of the best pricing approach to take. Setting prices is the one task the GM cannot delegate, for he or she must live with and be accountable for all that results from this critical decision.

CREATING AWARENESS AND STIMULATING DEMAND

Herein are the typical roles of the marketing department: using sales, communications, and promotions to attract the target markets. But creating awareness is not only marketing's job. Everything the public sees and hears about the hotel—its name or brand, its signs, its restaurants, the public activities of its managers, its charitable support and festivals—all create a meaning, a picture of what this hotel means and offers.

Starwood's W again offers an example: Every element of their presentation expresses the "to whom" they target. In decor, uniforms tone, and attitude, they focus and send a coherent message. It is critical that every department understands the target markets and agrees on the idea, the meaning the hotel intends to have for each of the target customer groups. This is called *positioning;* it's something done not to the product but to the mind of the prospect.

The team should prepare written positioning statements, including a compatible but individual positioning statement for each market segment they intend to target. These statements are the blueprint against which each ad, promotion, and sales call is tested to assure consistent messages are being sent. And those statements should be shared with all employees.When all parts of the hotel are sending a coherent and consistent message of what the name or brand means and what underlying promise is being made, the hotel establishes a clear position in the mind of the prospects—ideally, one that is attractively distinctive from competitors.

Marketers can use a variety of tools to create awareness and stimulate demand—for example, sales blitzes, telemarketing, newspaper ads, Internet sites and ads, partnership alliances, radio ads, and price promotions. The marketing mix is the range and balance of tools selected and resources devoted to each to achieve the hotel's marketing goals.

In most hotels, direct selling is still the primary marketing tool used to create awareness and stimulate demand.There are two parts of effective direct selling: sales skills and sales management. Consider one the weapon, the other the shooter.

Sales skills are not natural; enthusiasm may be natural, liking to meet people may be natural, but selling is a process that anyone can learn and that must be practiced. Make sure your salespeople are taught how to research their prospect, to listen for needs and purposes, to acknowledge that they have heard the prospect, to transform relevant features into benefits and to sell the customer's success, to anticipate objections and prepare responses, to negotiate, to ask for the order, and to thank the customer and facilitate delivery.

Sales management is quite another thing; often the top salesperson does not make the best sales manager. The sales manager must be able to select salespeople; reinforce their training; coach, counsel and motivate them; assign them to prospects and market segments; set goals, manage compensation, review performance; and troubleshoot. He or she must also be the gatekeeper on contracts and rates, making sure that inventory Compensation of salespeople need not be complicated. *First principle:*Tie compensation to goals set in terms of what you want them to do—that is, produce contracts and roomnights.

Don't just set room-night goals; add measures of relationship or share of a specific customer's business. Have salespeople suggest their own goals for the coming year; participation builds commitment. *Second:* Provide them near-term reward and reinforcement, not postponed rewards. Pay out bonuses quarterly.

Third: Build teamwork so that one salesperson supports and encourages another. Add a team bonus multiplier to personal performance measures. *Last:* Separate performance bonuses from overall job appraisal. No one attends to suggestions for performance improvement if he or she has just received a big check for exceeding goal.

Many full-service hotels are overresourced in group sales and under-weighted in transient market tools. Sales efforts should be balanced with other parts of the marketing mix—advertising, publicity, and promotions.

The range of communication options increases geometrically with proliferation of new media—cable television, news magazines and national papers, the Internet, and direct mail and telemarketing. But the eyeballs are not growing apace, meaning the audience for any one medium is steadily shrinking, putting increasing demand on measures of productivity, care in allocating resources, and creativity to get through the clutter. As audiences of prospects become increasingly expensive to reach through advertising, the tools of publicity, the Internet, and direct marketing are increasingly the media of choice.

The Internet is a demanding medium for communication; use professional help to design, maintain, and market the hotel's website as though it were, itself, a product for which awareness must be created and demand stimulated. To draw audience to the site and manage its visibility in search engines are skills beyond the property team. Set specific goals for the site:They might be to attract qualified prospects, to sell services, to provide customer service. Don't just have a site. And measure the experts against those goals.A passive, unmanaged, and undermarketed site is a waste of money.

Promotions can powerfully stimulate demand, but too often, price promotions are resorted to as a last-minute attempt to prop up a weak demand period. Promotions should be planned, justified on a breakeven basis, and used sparingly. Not all promotions need be price promotions; customers invest energy and time in transactions, too: value-added promotions that offer nonmonetary savings can be used to avoid habituating consumers to buying only on sale or shopping only on price. Well-forged alliances for copromotion can increase both productivity and absolute sales volume.

The skills and talents necessary in a comprehensive effort to create awareness and stimulate demand include:

- *In sales:* Initiative; being goal-directed; listening with empathy and imagination; time management; self-confidence.
- *In sales management:* Coaching and counseling; quantitative skills; priority setting, time management, and sense of urgency; leadership and problem solving; ability to manage incentive programmes.
- *In communications:* Ability to write clearly; ability to select, engage, and manage professional creative talents; ability to evaluate and allocate resources among options; comfort with and appreciation of the Internet and the Web.
- *In promotion:* Ability to analyse breakevens; creativity; anticipation; conceiving and selling partnerships and alliances.

MAKING THE HOTEL AVAILABLE

Once a person in one of your target markets is interested in buying, how does he or she reach you? Your hotel's reservations office, the central reservation system, airline global distribution systems, corporate sales offices, and your property sales office are all parts of a distribution network. Travel agents, corporate travel managers and secretaries, meeting planners, and travellers themselves reach your hotel through this network.

Travel industry distribution channels are in chaos by virtue of the shift of travel agencies from commission to fee-for-service models, the rise of the Internet as a consumer's direct booking channel, and online thirdparty intermediaries like Expedia and Travelocity.

Increasingly, the Internet will become your key distribution channel, but in the meantime, you must manage two parallel systems, the traditional central reservation and travel agency channels and the new electronic channels. Are the rooms you want to offer available in both systems, with helpful and upto-date information? Are your prices sensible in each outlet? Making the hotel available is no longer a passive stance but an active part of your marketing.

In other industries, distribution channel revolutions have brought efficiencies that benefit both consumers and suppliers. In the travel distribution revolution now underway, the consumer has benefited, but costs to hotels—the suppliers—have skyrocketed. Since 1993, full-service hotel costs of distribution more than doubled, to $1,377 per occupied room per year in 2002.

Along with these new channels and thirdparty room merchants has come pressure on prices. In the downturn of 2001–2003, this was devastating. Price comparisons are quick and easy for the consumer. Packagers and auction sites unconsciously cultivate the destructive idea that a hotel room is a commodity, as is an airline seat. But hotels are not commodities; each differs in location, features, and benefits. A hotel team must resist the idea that a room is a room is a room, must emphasize their hotel's distinctive positioning, and must resist the urge to simply match the lowest price offered.

For the foreseeable future, both the traditional and Internet-based distribution systems will coexist and have to be managed. This raises a new question:What channels do you want to encourage, and what ones discourage? Conventional wisdom, in recent years, has been to make the hotel's inventory and rates available via as many channels as possible so as to capture from anywhere in the world the last drop of demand for arrival on a given day. Given their sharply differing costs, however, and the difficulty of managing coordinated presence in these new and overlapping channels, the time may be coming for a new strategy. One possibility is to starve undesirable channels with limited information and access while being fully open and transparent to others. Another approach might be to price differentially among channels to reflect their different costs. A large Hawaiian resort group is already doing that by explaining to consumers what comparative options and costs are. Other chains advertise a guarantee that the lowest price will be found on their own website, which is a low-cost channel for them.

Reservations, revenue, and channel management constitute the fastest-changing part of hotel management today. Channel management requires a comfort with and interest in technology and systems, and a knack for problem solving, anticipating, and risk taking.

CLOSING, CONFIRMING, AND MANAGING REVENUE

How one commits space—a room, meeting space, ballroom, or even a restaurant table— and at what price—determines the revenues and financial health of the hotel and determines the customer's expectation of value.

Revenues must be managed to optimize financial returns and customer satisfaction— that is, the customer's willingness to return. No one department controls the tools of revenue management. They are shared among salespeople, catering and banqueting managers, front desk agents, reservation agents, and so on. To manage properly requires frequent and open conversation between managers, good forecasting, skillful selling by customer contact people, and an appreciation of each week's goals and targets for the hotel. Poor forecasting, inflexible inventory policies, and conflicting approaches by different departments with whom the customer deals can undo all the best advertising, selling, and promotion.

Through the same forecasting disciplines, hotel teams manage their revenues to maximize the productivity of the hotel and assure its financial health. Revenue management tools and increasingly affordable yield systems can have a major and salutory effect on the financial health of the hotel.

Another part of revenue management is incentives for reservations upselling, conversion of callers, and average rate increases, and for front desk agents upselling. In the same way, F&B staff should be viewed as salespeople and given training on suggestive selling. Inventory policies for tier price quotes by forecast levels of occupancy, for stay-through restrictions, for same-rate substitutions and upgrading to clear demand inventory categories— all these are tools through which reservation and revenue managers optimize the RevPAR performance of the hotel.

It is in the area of revenue management that chains, especially multibrand management companies, have achieved significant advantage over independent hotels and franchisees that do not participate in cluster or regional revenue management.

Decisions on pricing are still the domain of the property GM, but with a centralized expert staff collecting data and forecasting, the advice and guidance available has brought yield and RevPAR premiums to the chain member properties.

Revenue management requires attention to detail and analytic and forecasting skills; tolerance for ambiguity and comfort with change; and managing, training, leading, and motivating reservations agents. This is one of the most critical and dynamic areas of hotel management, one with which every aspiring general manager or director of sales and marketing should take pains to become familiar.

PREPARING TO DELIVER AND DELIGHT

A marketer of a product can count on the factory quality-control system to deliver a consistent product for sale. When the sale is closed, the customer takes the product away and uses it. In a service business, however, the product is human Behaviour, and the customer uses the product in the hotel. Because we are humans, both customers and employees, our interactions are never the same one time to the next. The job of the marketer is to help employees understand what the customer will want, need, and expect, and to sell employees on doing their job with enthusiasm.

In a full-service hotel, the conference services department embodies this preparing idea as its primary function. Conference service managers are the essential group business brokers between sales and operations. Conference services people can create loyal and repeat meeting planners; the job requires empathy, attention to detail, willingness to work unusual hours, action orientation, internal relationship building, and persuasiveness.

Preparing the hotel to fully satisfy and regularly make customers happy is as much a marketing task as attracting customers in the first place.What makes marketing hospitality services harder than marketing a tangible product is that for every market segment there must be two marketing programmes, one directed externally to customers, the other internally to employees.

RETAINING CUSTOMERS

The key to both financial health and market leadership is retaining a higher proportion of customers than do any of your competitors. Retain more customers than others do, and over time your costs drop—because of efficiency, lower advertising and selling costs, better forecasting—and your occupancy and rates rise. Numerous studies validate the high correlation between profit leadership and customer retention

Frequent-stay rewards are often mistaken for retention programmes. They are not. Rewards can motivate returns only as long as the customer values the points or airline miles or whatever. But they do not create loyalty.They are valuable only insofar as they give employees the opportunity to come to recognize and satisfy the guest, and insofar as they give the marketing department information on who the customer is and where he or she is coming from.

Retaining customers takes more than just doing the job well. Guests and customers must come to know they are valued. Management must build relationships—the tie that binds regardless of a new hotel opening in the market or a hot promotional offer from across the street. Relationships are built on recognition and familiarity, on trust, and on appreciation.Thus, guest and customer retention must be a planned and creative activity that involves both sides of the relationship— the customers and the employees. It takes more than just smiling and trying hard. Among the talents and skills needed are analytic skills, curiosity, direct marketing planning, and management of data retrieval and direct marketing service providers.

MEASURING SATISFACTION AND EVALUATING PERFORMANCE

If the purpose of the business is, in part, to keep customers, does a financial statement of rate, occupancy, revenue, expense, and profit give enough information? No. Also needed is a scorecard of customer satisfaction, of how likely customers are to return or tell others about your good hotel. That scorecard is the guest satisfaction survey. Accounting statements tell of the hotel's financial health; a guest satisfaction scorecard tells of its reputation's health. The scorecard also helps management spot changes in expectations.

Customers are not the same from one visit to the next. Experience with a new hotel, perhaps even in another city, may raise a customer's standards. To measure satisfaction, one needs quantitative skills for tracking, analysing, and reporting data, and the ability to manage the logistics of repetitive distribution, collection, and processing. The information helps management figure out what the hotel needs to be and to offer next in order to remain competitive and keep customers. Note, now, the return to the first step of the marketing process.

2

The Demand for Recreation and Tourism

Understanding why human beings engage in recreational and tourism activities is an increasingly important and complex area of research for social scientists. Historically, geographers have played only a limited part in developing the literature on the behavioural aspects of recreational and tourists' use of free time, tending to have a predisposition towards the analysis of aggregate patterns of demands using quantitative measures and statistical sources. This almost rigid demarcation of research activity has, with a few exceptions, meant that behavioural research in recreation and tourism has only recently made any impact on the wider research community, with notable studies applying spatial principles to the analysis of recreational and tourism behaviour.

Within the recreational literature, the geographers' contributions have often been subsumed into social science perspectives, such as sociology, psychology and planning, so that the spatiality and placefulness of their contribution has been implicit rather than explicit. For this reason, this chapter discusses some of the key behavioural issues associated with recreation and tourism demand followed by an analysis of the major data sources which researchers use, emphasising how the geographer has used and manipulated them to identify the patterns, processes and implications of such activity.

Within the literature on recreation and tourism, there is a growing unease over the physical separation of the theoretical and conceptual research that isolates behavioural processes and spatial outcomes, and fails to derive generalisations applicable to understanding tourism in totality. According to Moore *et al.* (1995:74) there are common strands in the 'relationships between the various motivating factors applicable to both leisure and tourism'; and as Leiper (1990) argued, tourism represents a valued category of leisure, where there is a degree of commonality between the factors motivating both tourist and recreational activities and many of the needs, such as relaxation or being with friends, can equally be fulfilled in a recreational or tourism context.

Although there is some merit in Leiper's (1990) approach, grouping leisure into one amorphous category assumes that there are no undifferentiated attributes which distinguish tourism from leisure. As Pigram and Jenkins (1999:19) confirm, 'the term recreation demand is generally equated with an individual(s) preferences or desires, whether or not the individual has the economic and other resources necessary for their satisfaction'.

In this respect, it is the preference-aspiratio-desire level, reflected in behaviour or participation in activities. It is interesting to note that Leiper's (1990) approach has a great deal of validity if one recognises that some tourism motivations may in fact differentiate tourism from leisure experiences, just as the reverse may be true, and that ultimately the particular range of motives associated with a tourism or recreational activity will be unique in each case despite a range of similarities. For this reason, the following discussion examines recreational demand, emphasising many of the explanations commonly advanced in the recreational literature followed by a discussion of the tourism context and the issues raised, bearing in mind the need to compare and contrast each literature base in the light of the arguments advanced by Moore *et al.* (1995) and Leiper (1990).

RECREATIONAL DEMAND

Human activity related to recreation and tourism is a function of an individual's or group's willingness or desire to engage in such pursuits. Yet understanding this dimension in recreation and tourism requires a conceptual approach which can rationalise the complex interaction between the desire to undertake leisure activities, however defined, and the opportunities to partake of them. As Coppock and Duffield (1975:2) argued: 'the success of any study of outdoor recreation depends on the synthesis of two contrasting elements: the sociological phenomenon of leisure or ... that part of leisure time which an individual spends on outdoor recreation [and tourism] and ... the physical resources that are necessary for the particular recreational activities.'

In other words, Coppock and Duffield (1975) ackno-wledged the need to recognise the interrelationship between human demand as participation or a desire to engage in recreation and tourism, and the supply of resources, facilities and opportunities which enable such demand to be fulfilled. The concepts of demand and supply have largely been developed and applied to conventional market economies, where the individual has a choice related to the consumption of recreation and tourism. According to Smith (1989:45):

Recreation geographers use the work [demand] in at least four different ways. The most traditional sense is a neoclassical definition: demand is a schedule of the quantities of some commodity that will be consumed at various prices.... A second definition of demand is that of current consumption ... [which] is of limited utility to recreation planners because it tells nothing about trends in participation or about current levels of unmet need. Demand is also used to refer to unmet need. This is sometimes referred to as latent demand. ... Finally, demand is used to describe the desire for a psychological experience. In contrast, Patmore (1983:54) acknowledges, 'leisure is far more easily recognised than objectively analysed ... the difficulties are only in part conceptual: equally important are the nature and limitations of available data', which this section will seek to explain in a recreation context. According to Pigram (1983) there is a general lack of clarity in the use of the term *demand* in the recreational literature.

One can distinguish between demand at a generic level, where it refers to an 'individual's preferences or desires, whether or not the individual has the economic or other resources necessary for their satisfaction' reflecting behavioural traits and preference for certain activities. At another level, there are the specific activities or participation in activities often expressed as visitation rates and measured to reflect the actual observed behaviour.

One factor that prevents observed demand equating with participation is the concept of latent demand (the element which is unsatisfied due to a lack of recreational opportunities). Knetsch (1969) identified the mismatch and confusion between participation and demand, arguing that one cannot simply look at what people do and associate it with what people want to do, so ideally any analysis of demand should also consider why people do not participate, and examine ways of overcoming such obstacles by the provision of new resources as well as understanding social and cultural barriers. As Pigram and Jenkins (1999:20) argued, 'In the real world, recreation demand rarely equals participation.

The difference between aggregate demand and actual participation (or expressed, effective, observed, revealed demand) is referred to as latent demand or latent participation-the unsatisfied component of demand that would be converted to participation if conditions of supply of recreation opportunities were brought to ideal levels'. Attempting to summarise the factors which influence the decision to participate in recreation led Pigram (1983) which highlights the complex range of variables that affect the process.

Most research has examined effective demand which is actual participation rather than latent demand, and the geographers' contribution has largely been related to the spatial and temporal expression of demand in relation to supply (i.e. demand at specific sites). This is very much resource specific, and dates back to the geographical tradition of resource identification, use and analysis which can be traced to at least the 1930s. However, Coppock and Duffield (1975) also distinguish between passive recreation and active recreation, thereby beginning to differentiate between different forms of demand.

While passive recreation is by far the most important type numerically, it is difficult to study due to its diffuse and often unorganised nature. Coppock and Duffield (1975:40) argued that Active recreation in the countryside differs from passive recreation in a number of ways. Not only are participants a minority of those visiting the countryside for outdoor recreation, but they are generally younger and differ in respect of a number of socio-economic characteristics: they often depend on particular (and sometimes scarce) recreational resources in the countryside ... yet as with passive recreation, information about such activities is scanty. This illustrates the necessity of trying to measure recreational demand together with gauging the types of factors which can facilitate and constrain recreational demand. But what motivates people to engage in recreational activities?

Argyle (1996) argues that part of the reason why people undertake leisure and recreational activities can be found in the process of socialisation and personality traits, where childhood influences such as parents and peers are forms of social influence and learning that affect future activity choice. In fact, nearly half of adult leisure interests are acquired after childhood, and personality factors influence preferences towards specific forms of recreation. However, understanding the broader psychological factors which motivate individuals to undertake forms of recreation is largely the remit of psychologists, being an intrinsic form of motivation (i.e. something one is not paid to undertake).

Crandall's list of motivations:

- Enjoying nature, escaping from civilisation
  - To get away from civilisation for a while
  - To be close to nature
- Escape from routine and responsibility
  - Change from my daily routine
  - To get away from the responsibilities of my everyday life
- Physical exercise
  - For the exercise
  - To keep in shape
- Creativity
  - To be creative
- Relaxation
  - To relax physically
  - So my mind can slow down for a while
- Social contact
  - So I could do things with my companions
  - To get away from other people
- Meeting new people
  - To talk to new and varied people
  - To build friendships with new people
- Heterosexual contact
  - To be with people of the opposite sex
  - To meet people of the opposite sex
- Family contact
  - To be away from the family for a while

  - To help bring the family together more
- Recognition, status
  - To show others I could do it
  - So others would think highly of me for doing it
- Social power
  - To have control over others
  - To be in a position of authority
- Altruism
  - To help others
- Stimulus seeking
  - For the excitement
  - Because of the risks involved
- Self-actualisation (feedback, self-improvement, ability utilisation)
  - Seeing the results of your efforts
  - Using a variety of skills and talents
- Achievement, challenge, competition
  - To develop my skills and ability
  - Because of the competition
  - To learn what I am capable of
- Killing time, avoiding boredom
  - To keep busy
  - To avoid boredom
- Intellectual aestheticism
  - To use my mind
  - To think about my personal values

A simplistic approach to recreational motivation is to ask recreationalists what actually motivates them. Crandall (1980) outlined 17 factors from leisure motivation research, derived from a synthesis of previous studies in this field, while Kabanoff (1982) identified a similar list of factors. It is apparent that relaxation, the need for excitement and self-satisfaction are apparent, though Argyle (1996) argues that specific motivations are evident in particular forms of recreation.

Torkildsen (1992:79), however, posits that homeostasis is a fundamental concept associated with human motivation where people have an underlying desire to maintain a state of internal stability. Human needs, which are 'any lack or deficit within the individual either acquired or physiological', disturb the state of homeostasis. At a basic level, human needs have to be met where physiological theory maintained that all human behaviour is motivated. This leads to one of the most commonly cited studies in relation to recreation and tourism motivation-Maslow's hierarchy of human needs.

MASLOW'S HIERARCHY MODEL OF HUMAN NEEDS

Within the social psychology literature on recreation and tourism, Maslow's (1954) needs hierarchy remains one of the most commonly cited theories of motivation. It follows the principle of a ranking or hierarchy of individual needs, based on the premise that self-actualisation is a level to which people should aspire.

Maslow argued that if the lower needs in the hierarchy were not fulfilled then these would dominate human behaviour. Once these were satisfied, the individual would be motivated by the needs of the next level of the hierarchy. In the motivation sequence, Maslow identified 'deficiency or tension-reducing motives' and 'inductive or arousal-seeking motives', arguing that the model could be applied to work and non-work contexts.

Despite Maslow's research shaping much of the recreation and tourism demand work, how and why he selected five basic needs remains unclear, though its universal application in recreation and tourism appears to have a relevance with regard to understanding how human action is related to understandable and predictable aspects of action compared to research which argues that human behaviour is essentially irrational and unpredictable.

While Maslow's model is not necessarily ideal, since needs are not hierarchical in reality because some needs may occur simultaneously, it does emphasise the development needs of humans, with individuals striving towards personal growth.

Therefore, Maslow assists in a recreational (and tourism context) in identifying and classifying the types of needs people have. Tillman (1974) summarised some of the broader leisure needs of individuals within which recreational needs occur, and these may include the pursuit of:

- New experiences (i.e. adventure);
- Relaxation, escape and fantasy;
- Recognition and identity;
- Security (freedom from thirst, hunger or pain);
- Dominance (to control one's environment);
- Response and social interaction (relating and interacting with others);
- Mental activity (to perceive and understand);
- Creativity;
- A need to be needed;
- Physical activity and fitness.

A different perspective is offered by Bradshaw (1972), who argued that social need is a powerful force, explaining need by classifying it as normative, felt, expressed and comparative need.

Mercer (1973), Godbey (1976) and McAlvoy (1977) extended Bradshaw's argument within a recreational context, modifying the four categories of need by adding created, changing and false needs. Normative needs are based on value judgements, often made by professionals who establish that what they feel is appropriate to the wider population. Felt needs, which individuals may have but not necessarily express, are based on what someone wants to do and is a perceived need.

Expressed needs relate to those needs and preferences for existing recreational activities which are often measured but can only be a partial view of demand, since new recreational opportunities may release latest demand. Comparative needs are apparent where existing provision for the general population is compared with special groups (e.g. the elderly, ethnic minorities or disabled) to establish if existing provision is not fulfilling the needs of the special group.

Created needs may result from policy-makers and planners introducing new services or activities which are then taken up by the population. A false need is one that may be created by individuals or society, and which is not essential and may be marginal to wider recreational needs. Changing needs, however, are a recognition of the dynamic nature of human needs which change through time as individuals develop and their position in the life cycle changes.

Thus what is important at one point in the life cycle may change through time as an individual passes through four key stages (Ken and Rapoport 1975):

- Youth (school years);
- Young adulthood;
- Establishment (extended middle-age);
- Final phase (between the end of work and of life).

Other researchers (e.g. Iso-Ahola 1980; Neulinger 1981) prefer to emphasise the importance of perceived freedom from constraints as a major source of motivation. Argyle (1996) synthesises such studies to argue that intrinsic motivation in leisure relates to three underlying principles:

- Social motivation;
- Basic bodily pleasures (e.g. eating, drinking, sex and sport);
- Social learning (how past learning explains a predisposition towards certain activities).

One useful concept which Csikszentmihalyi (1975) introduced to the explanation of motivation was that of flow. Individuals tend to find a sense of intense absorption in recreational activities, when self-awareness declines, and it is their peak experience - a sense of flow - which is the main internal motivation.

The flow is explained as a balance resulting from being challenged and skill which can occur in four combinations:

- Where challenge and skill are high and flow results;
- Where the challenge is too great, anxiety results;
- If the challenge is too easy, boredom may occur;
- Where the challenge and skill level is too low, apathy may result.

But this does not mean that everyone always seeks recreational activities which provide forms of high arousal. Some recreational activities may just fulfil a need to relax, being undemanding and of low arousal. As Ewert and Hollenhurst (1989) reported, those who engaged in outdoor recreational sports with a high-risk factor (i.e. whitewater rafting) viewed the sport as providing a flow experience, and the study predicted that as their skill level improved they would increase the level of participation and risk.

Yet even though this occurred the internal motivation of the group remained unchanged, where low and high arousal seem to be juxtaposed. Thus levels of arousal vary from time to time, a factor which can be used by adventure tourism operators to manage the adventure experience and increase the level of satisfaction of participants. Recreation may also lead to an enhanced self-image, where the identity becomes a basis for motivation because recreational activities can lead to a sense of belonging to a particular and identifiable group. Some activities may also require the development of special skills and enhanced self-esteem. Where recreational activities require a degree of competency, Bandura (1977) proposed that perception of one's ability to perform the skill is a motivator and may result in self-efficacy, a form of self-confidence and judgement of one's ability.

In spite of the significance of motivation, it is apparent that no single theory or even a clear consensus exists in relation to recreation. Instead, 'in theories of motivation need is seen as a force within the individual to gain satisfactions and completeness. There appear to be many levels and types of need, including the important needs of self-actualisation and psychological growth'.

An understanding of needs and intrinsic motivation and some of the ideas implicit in studies of recreational motivation may offer a range of insights into why people engage in recreational activities. But not only is it necessary to understand why people engage in recreation, but also what factors or barriers may inhibit them from participating. Torkildsen (1992) outlines the influences on leisure participation in terms of three categories: personal, social and circumstantial, and opportunity factors. These influences are also of value in understanding some of the constraints on recreation.

BARRIERS TO RECREATION

Within the wider literature on recreation and leisure, a specialist research area has developed, focused on constraints, namely those factors, elements or processes which inhibit people from participating in leisure activities. From the diverse range of studies published, two forms of constraint have been identified: intervening constraints, namely those which intervene between a preference and participation, and antecedent constraints, which influence a person's decision not to undertake an activity.

Although the constraints on recreation and leisure literature can be dated to the 1960s, the 1980s saw a range of studies published, a number of which have set the research agenda in recent years. In the initial formulation, Crawford and Godbey (1987) proposed that constraints were associated with intrapersonal, interpersonal and structural constraints. In the subsequent reformulation of their thinking, Crawford *et al.* (1991) proposed a hierarchical process model, with their three types of constraint integrated. As a consequence of their model, they proposed, which indicates that:

- Participation in leisure is a negotiation process, where a series of factors became aligned in a sequence;
- The order in which constraints occur leads to a 'hierarchy of importance', where intrapersonal constraints are the most powerful in sequence ending with no structural constraints;
- That social class has a strong influence on participation and non-participation leading to a hierarchy of social privilege, i.e. social stratification is a powerful conditioning factor and may act as a constraint.

Table. Influences on Leisure Participation.

Personal	**Social and circumstantial**	**Opportunity factors**
Age	Occupation	Resources available
Stage in life cycle	Income	Facilities - type and quality
Gender	Disposable income	Awareness
Marital status	Material wealth and goods	Perception of opportunities
Dependants and ages	Car ownership and mobility	Recreation services
Will and purpose in life	Time available	Distribution of facilities
Personal obligations	Duties and obligations	Access and location
Resourcefulness	Home and social environment	Choice of activities
Leisure perceptions	Friends and peer groups	Transport
Attitudes and motivation	Social roles and contacts	Costs: before, during, after
Interests and preoccupations	Environment factors	Management: policy and support
Skill and ability - physical, social and intellectual	Mass leisure factors	Marketing
Personality and confidence	Education and attainment	Programming
Culture born into	Population factors	Organisation and leadership
Upbringing and background	Cultural factors	Social accessibility
		Political policies

This research has provided a framework for further evaluations of constraints (e.g. Samdahl and Jekubovich 1997, and subsequent criticisms by Henderson 1997). In fact, subsequent research by Jackson *et al.* (1993) suggested that the real key to understanding leisure constraints was embedded in the negotiation process: namely how an individual will proceed with experiencing an activity even when constraints are apparent. Ultimately, Pigram's (1983) model helped to frame the context in which participation may occur, and the way that process may be affected by underlying constraints on one's participation.

It is against this background that one can appreciate the use of leisure time and leisure space in different cultures and among groups where leisure time in a western conception is inappropriate. For example, in a fascinating review of poor rural women's leisure experiences in Bangladesh by Khan (1997), it is evident that 'the conventional approach to leisure studies which has a myopic view of leisure as free or non-obligatory time' is meaningless due to blurring of boundaries between free or non-work time and obligatory activities which are often cumbersome and all-encompassing in everyday life. At an empirical level, a range of notable studies have highlighted the prevailing constraints to recreation.

For example, Kay and Jackson's (1991) notable study of 366 British adults' recreational constraints identified:

- 53 per cent who cited money as the main constraint;
- 36 per cent who felt lack of time was the main limitation;
- Conflicts with family or work, transportation problems and health concerns as other contributory factors.

A study in Alberta which surveyed 1,891 people asked respondents to rate 15 possible barriers to a desired activity, and the results highlighted social isolation, accessibility, personal reasons (lack of confidence or skill), costs, time and facilities as the main constraints. It has been proposed that such constraints have a specific ordering in terms of importance, with the most significant constraints being interpersonal ones, followed by structural ones (e.g. lack of time or money).

Yet such arguments have been queried by Shaw *et al.* (1991), who found that in a survey of 14,674 Canadians, of 11 constraints, only lack of energy and ill-health were associated with a lower rate of participation. Therefore, barriers may be negotiable or solvable, as Kay and Jackson (1991) suggest.

Patmore (1983) summarises the main physical barriers to recreation in terms of:

- Seasonality;
- Biological and social constraints;
- Money and mobility;
- Resources and fashions; with the availability of time also being a major constraint.

Coppock and Duffield (1975:8) recognised the principal variations which exist in terms of demand due to variable uses of leisure time budgets by individuals and groups in relation to the day, week and year.

Both Coppock and Duffield (1975) and Patmore (1983) use similar data sources (e.g. the UK's Pilot National Recreation Survey (British Travel

Association and Univeristy of Keele 1967 and 1969) and sociological studies of family behaviour in the pioneering study by Young and Wilmott (1973)) to examine time budgets, variations in demand and constraining factors. One of the most important distinctions to make is that 'the weekend thus represents a large increase in the time that can be committed to leisure pursuits, which in turn affects the weekend time budget'.

Yet when one looks beyond the day and week to the individuals and groups concerned, a wider range of influences emerge which are important in explaining recreation patterns. Argyle (1996) highlights the fact that one of the main reasons for examining constraining and facilitating factors is to understand 'how many people engage in different kinds of leisure, how much time they spend on it, and how this varies between men and women, young and old, and other groups'. This is because some groups such as 'women, the elderly and unemployed face particular constraints which may affect their ability to engage in leisure and recreational activities which people do because they want to, for their own sake, for fun, entertainment or self-improvement, or for goals of their own choosing, but not for material gain'.

SEASONALITY

Patmore (1983:70) argued that 'one of the most unyielding of constraints is that imposed by climate, most obviously where outdoor activities are concerned. The rhythms of the seasons affect both the hours of daylight available and the extent to which temperatures are conducive to participant comport outdoors.' This is reflected in the seasonality of recreational activity which inevitably leads to peaks in popular seasons and a lull in less favourable conditions. Patmore (1983) identified a continuum in recreational activities from those which exhibit a high degree of seasonality to those with a limited degree of variation in participation by season.

The first type, which is the most seasonal, include outdoor activities often of an informal nature which are weather dependent. The second, an intermediate group, is transitional in the sense that temperature is not necessarily a deterrent since a degree of discomfort may be experienced by the more hardened participants (e.g. when walking and playing sport).

The final group is indoor activities which can be formal or informal, and have virtually no seasonality. In addition, the physical constraints of season, climate and weather inhibit demand by curtailing the periods of time over which a particular resource can be used for the activity concerned, although resource substitution (e.g. using a man-made ski slope instead of a snow-clad one) may assist in some contexts, but often the man-made resource cannot offer the same degree of excitement or enjoyment.

ACCESS TO RECREATIONAL OPPORTUNITY

Argyle (1996) observed that while many studies emphasised lack of money as a barrier to engaging in recreational activities, Coalter (1993) found that it had little impact on participation in sports. In fact, Kay and Jackson (1991) also acknowledged that money or disposable income was a barrier to undertaking activities which were major consumers of money (drinking and eating socially) whereas it had little impact on sport which was comparatively cheap.

Income, occupation and access to a car combined have a significant impact on participation, and as Patmore (1983:78) succinctly summarised, 'those with more skilled and responsive occupations, with higher incomes, with ready access to private transport and with a longer period spent in full-time education tend to lead a more active and varied leisure life, with less emphasis on passive recreations both within and beyond the home'. It is the car which has provided the greatest degree of personal mobility and access to a wider range of recreational opportunities in time and space since the 1960s in many developed countries (and earlier in some cases such as the USA and Canada).

For example, most car-owning households in UK studies have twice the propensity to participate in sport and recreation than non-car-owning households. Even so, Martin and Mason (1979:62) observe that 'one of the paradoxes of leisure is that while time and money are complementary in the production of leisure activities, they are competitive in terms of the resources available to the individual. Some leisure time and some money to buy leisure goods and services are both needed before most leisure activities can be pursued.'

GENDER AND SOCIAL CONSTRAINTS

The influence of gender on recreation remains a powerful factor influencing participation, a feature consistently emphasised in national surveys of recreational demand. As Argyle (1996:44) argues, 'there is an influential theory about this topic, due to a number of feminist writers, that women have very little or no leisure, because of the demands of domestic work and the barriers due to husbands who want them at home ... [and] that leisure is a concept which applies to men, if it is regarded as a reaction to or contrast with paid work'. Thus women with children appear to have less time for recreation, while those in full- and part-time employment have less time available than their male counterparts.

These general statements find a high degree of support within the recreational literature, with gender differences in part explained by the male free time occurring in larger blocks and in prime time.

Even so, studies by Talbot (1979) explore this theme in more detail. Rodgers (1977) documents the wide discrepancy in male:female participation in sport as a form of recreation within a European context where for every 100 females engaging in sport, there were 188 male participants in Britain, 176 in Spain, 159 in France, 127 in Belgian Flanders, 127 in Norway, 116 in the Netherlands and 111 in former West Germany.

While definitions and the variations in data sources may in part explain the variability, the presence of a gender gap is prominent. Age also exerts a strong influence on participation in recreation, with Hendry *et al.* (1993) describing adolescence as the peak time of leisure needs. Therein lie two key explanations of participation and constraints.

Stages in the life cycle present a useful concept to explain why women with young children appear to have fewer opportunities for recreation than adolescents. Likewise, physical vigour and social energy are traditionally explained in terms of a decline in the later stages of adulthood resulting in a decline in active recreation throughout later life. The Greater London Recreation Survey of 1972 (Greater London Council 1976) identified some of these traits in that:

- Activities exist where participation markedly declined by age (e.g. energetic sports like football);
- Activities occur with sustained participation through the life cycle (e.g. tennis and indoor swimming);
- Some activities exist where participation increased as a person got older (e.g. golf and walking).

In fact these results not only illustrate the importance of age (and to a degree gender), but also the need to consider the significance of the life cycle in relation to changes or 'triggers' (Patmore 1983). One such trigger is retirement, and while it is sometimes interpreted as a stressful life event, Long (1987) found that for 58 per cent of male retirees there was no change in their leisure activities, while 8 per cent undertook education, 3 per cent developed an interest in photography and 3 per cent partook of sport.

What Argyle (1996:63) emphasises from studies of retirement are that 'people carry on with the same leisure as before, though they are more passive and more house-bound, and do not take up much new leisure'.

CASE STUDY: THE GEOGRAPHY OF FEAR IN RECREATION AND LEISURE SPACES: GENDER-BASED BARRIERS TO PARTICIPATION

Since the 1980s there has been a growing interest in the role of fear, personal safety and the spatial implications in the urban environment. There has also been an accompanying interest in the gender dimensions of personal safety, which has important implications within an urban environment in relation to the use of public leisure resources such as open space and urban parks.

In fact, the concern with such issues may be traced to the changes in the discipline of geography 'and transformative developments both resulting from, and contributing to, a number of new and competing philosophies with the social sciences'. In relation to leisure and recreation geography, this transformation effect can be related to the concern with gender relations and theoretical perspectives associated with the new cultural geography as a mechanism to conceptualise and theorise leisure space. One of the central tenets of this approach is embodied in Green *et al.*'s (1990:311) comment where 'A significant aspect of the social control of women's leisure is the regulation of their access to public places, and their behaviour in such places'. These critical perspectives have only recently begun to emerge in tourism geography, where empirical, logical-positivist approaches to personal safety have paid little attention to gender and public places.

In conceptual terms, the analysis of the geography of fear, particularly the implications for gender, is a good illustration of the participation issues for particular groups of women. The application of this perspective to recreational and leisure spaces in the city reveals the male domination of public leisure space. The new cultural geographies have seen leisure and recreational geographers move away, albeit slowly, from a positivist paradigm and the model-building era as new perspectives were conceptualised and theorised. The rise of feminist perspectives in leisure studies by geographers is a notable development, with the impetus provided by landmark studies by feminist leisure studies.

One of the principal problems with the emergence of a new cultural geography is epitomised in Sharmar-Smith and Hannam's (1994:13) comments: 'Place is a deceptively simple concept in geographical thought. We want to make it difficult, uneasy.' Herein lie many of the criticisms of the new cultural geography: one must have a sound grounding in social theory, cultural studies and a knowledge of the new tenets underpinning the debates.

One consequence is that 'the new cultural geography as it has been referred to since the early 1990s demonstrates that space, place and landscape - including landscapes of leisure and tourism - are not fixed but are in a constant state of transition as a result of continuous, dialectical struggles of power and resistance among and between the diversity of landscape providers, users and mediators'. This means that the focus is on agency rather than structure, criticising earlier geographical studies of leisure and recreation which did not problematise space or recognise the human element in the landscape.

This perspective - and one has to recognise it is only one perspective in geographical research - emphasises the diversity, differences and nuances in cultural phenomena which is the antithesis of logical positivist geographical thought that searches for certainty, coherence and generalisations in relation to patterns, forms and processes of spatial phenomena.

As a consequence the new interest in leisure and tourism as cultural phenomena in the 'post-positivist geography [is such] that the new cultural geography has emerged and become merged with sociological and cultural studies analyses which are now combining to investigate the multiplicity of behaviours, meanings, consumption trends and identities constructed in and through leisure and tourism', and this case study focuses on the sexuality dimension.

Given the growing interest in feminism within the leisure constraints literature, and the concern with constraints to participation, it is timely to focus on the issue of fear, derived from Madge's survey of Leicester's urban park system.

IMPLICATIONS FOR SOCIAL EXCLUSION

Urban parks are estimated to be used by 40 per cent of the British population on a regular basis, but critics argue that urban parks as a recreational resource are being avoided by the general public. This is particularly acute for certain groups of the population (e.g. women, children and ethnic groups), where fear acts as a constraint on use. This adds a new dimension to the recreational constraints literature. Explanations of the growing neglect of urban parks within the UK have been related to a decline in public spending, from 54 per cent of leisure budgets in 1981 to 1982 to 44 per cent in 1991 to 1992, although these statistics need to recognise greater financial efficiencies derived from contracting out park services.

In the 1990s there was growing evidence that urban parks were not perceived as peaceful sanctuaries for recreational and leisure pursuits among the wider population. Burgess *et al.*'s (1988a) innovative Greenwich Open Space Project documented the dimensions of fear. Dimensions included antisocial behaviour among teenagers and vandalism that reduced local enjoyment and participation.

Similar concerns of insecurity, fear and use of parks and open spaces have also been recorded in Australia, and North America. Additional research shows how women, black people, the elderly and the gay community may be excluded from using urban space as freely as other subgroups of the population. As Burgess *et al.* (1988a: 472) remarked in the Greenwich context: 'many people expressed feelings of insecurity and vulnerability in open spaces, reflecting fears of personal attack and injury.

Among the Asian community, these feelings are exacerbated by the growth in incidence of racially motivated attacks in public open spaces.' The outcome, as Madge (1997:238) recognised, was that 'This fear, which reflects structural inequalities in society, is translated into spatial behaviour which usually involves a reluctance to occupy certain public spaces at certain times of the day'.

For the geographer, it is the spatial manifestation of that fear and its implications for recreational resource use. Although the evolution and development of Leicester's urban parks are reviewed later, it is worth observing the socio-demographic context of Madge's study prior to outlining the principal findings.

Leicester, located in the East Midlands in the UK, is a medium-sized city with a population of 272,000 people. What is notable is its diverse ethnic mix: 72 per cent of the population are white, 24 per cent are Asian, 2 per cent Afro-Caribbean, 2 per cent Chinese and other 'ethnic groups'.

Despite the city's urban-industrial development, it is widely acknowledged that the city has an enviable distribution of open space. By 1994, Leicester City Council was responsible for over 1200 ha of open space, which comprised 20 per cent of the total city area. This is a significant level of provision within an international context, and certainly enhances the city's green and open feel as a British city.

In this context, Madge's (1997) analysis of the geography of fear was timely. The sampling framework, namely face-to-face interviews with Leicester residents at on-street locations sought to derive a sample of city-wide park and open space use, with some 535 respondents interviewed. From the survey, ten main constraints emerged which influenced park use.

In order of importance these were:

- Fear
- Weather
- Lack of time due to work
- Family constraints
- Lack of transport
- Lack of interest
- Limited awareness of facilities available
- Housework
- Distance of parks/too far away
- Physically unable to get to the parks.

Some 43 per cent of respondents attributed fear as a 'very important' factor constraining their use of parks. The gender difference was striking with 75 per cent of women compared to 50 per cent of men stating fear was a major constraint on park use. This is in line with Westover's (1985) finding in North America, where 90 per cent of female respondents felt unsafe if alone in parks. Studies of victimisation in Leicester (e.g. Willis 1992) recognise that women have a greater sense of insecurity due to their vulnerability to crime.

When ethnicity was examined, Asian groups expressed higher levels of fear compared with white and Afro-Caribbean groups reflecting victimisation statistics, racial abuse and attacks in the urban environment. In terms of age, those over 45 expressed the greatest levels of fear. As Madge (1997:241) rightly acknowledged: 'The result of fear of crime is, however, concrete: the elderly are less likely to use public parks for recreation.'

In terms of causes of fear, Madge (1997) observed that the main causes of fear of park use were: anxieties related to actual or potential bodily harm (e.g. mugging, sexual attack, loitering people, gangs of youths, dogs and racial attack). Women's fears were greatest in relation to fear of sexual attack by men. These findings reflected the prevailing levels of fear of sexual violence which women in Leicester harbour, particularly the high level of sexual harassment which was rarely reported (Women's Equality Unit 1993). In fact 77 per cent of female respondents were fearful of sexual attacks in parks, a much higher figure than in similar surveys in Edinburgh and Seattle. Fear of racial attack was also much higher for Afro-Caribbean and Asian groups than for white groups. The implications of these findings are reflected in the behaviour and use of parks. Women tended to avoid large open spaces, unlit areas and those areas with dense undergrowth and trees. The onset of nightfall also elevated fear of using such places, especially if they were alone. As Madge suggested, 'Fear is a significant factor structuring the use of public parks in Leicester. The intensity and cause of fear varied with social traits of gender, ethnicity and age and affected spatial behaviour regarding use of parks. The geography of fear is mediated through a set of overlapping social, ideological and structural power relations which become translated into spatial behaviour.'

The findings of Madge's study highlight how a new constraint on leisure behaviour has specific gender, ethnic and social ramifications for recreational resource use. Although Madge (1997) criticises the existing recreational literature for neglecting this issue, fear is a more profound issue in urban environments than has hitherto been the case in recreational research.

While Hoyles (1994) argued for a greater feminisation of public space, and Madge (1997) argued for increased informal surveillance to encourage public participation and use of parks and open spaces, creating safer parks is deeply embedded in more complex notions of creating safe cities. Koskela and Pain (2000) point to the problems and failures of designing out fear from the urban environment, given the extent to which fear of crime pervades city spaces.

In a review of urban public space in Tokyo and New York, Cybriwsky (1999) recognised the growth in the surveillance of public spaces to improve security which could lead to a return to private spaces and attempts to modify social behaviour in recreational spaces. This is a feature which Giddens (1990:20) recognised whereby 'surveillance is a means of levering the modern social world away from traditional modes of social activity'.

Indeed, Koskela and Pain (2000:279) argued that 'Geographers and planners should take greater account of the complexity of fear. ... Places have some influence on fear, but perhaps of equal or greater significance is the ways in which fear shapes our understanding, perception and use of space and place.'

This is certainly a truism in the case of recreational use of urban parks in Madge's (1997) findings which have a wider application to urban recreational resource use in the developed world. A great deal of progress will need to be made in addressing fear of crime and recreational and leisure spaces in urbanised societies until Koskela and Pain's (2000:274) analysis that 'Green urban spaces and woodlands are commonly perceived as dangerous places and feelings of insecurity often have a deterrent effect on women's use of them' is no longer a valid assessment.

- The geography of fear is an important factor shaping participation by certain social groups in recreational activities.
- The problem of fear affects certain groups' participation patterns (e.g. the elderly and women) more than others.

- The creation of safer recreational open spaces is more problematic since it will involve greater surveillance, monitoring and control of informal leisure spaces.
- The new cultural geography, particularly the geography of gender, provides invaluable insights to explain how women's leisure space is embedded in notions of fear, constraints on the use of urban space and the resultant inequalities.

RESOURCES AND FASHIONS

While models of participation and obstacles to recreation have attempted to predict the probability of people participating in activities, using variables such as age, sex, marital status and social variables (e.g. housing tenure, income and car ownership), predictions decline in accuracy when attempting to identify individual activities (e.g. golf). What such recreational models often fail to acknowledge is the role of choice and preference given a range of options. In this respect, geographical proximity to recreational resources and access to them is a major determinant. This is demonstrated by Burton (1971), who found that in Britain, people were three times as likely to use a recreational resource if they lived between half and three-quarters of a mile away, a feature emphasised by Patmore (1983) and Page *et al.* (1994) in research on urban parks.

This shows that the proximity to a recreational resource increased the propensity for use at a swimming pool, yet for leisure centres where attendees used cars to visit them, the distance-decay function had a less rapid decline in attendance in relation to distance. Outside urban areas, the occurrence of recreational resources are more varied in their spatial distribution, and recreational opportunities need to be closely examined in relation to demand and supply. To provide a number of detailed insights into the patterns of recreation in different countries, and how demand is influenced and constrained, a number of national recreational patterns are examined followed by a case study of regional demand.

MEASURING RECREATIONAL DEMAND

Most geographers acknowledge the continued lack of suitable data on recreational demand, as Patmore (1983:55) explains: Prior to the 1960s sources were scattered and fragmentary, and lacked any coherent basis. The studies undertaken for the American Outdoor Recreation Resources Review Commission and published in 1962 gave the impetus for work in Britain. Two wide-ranging national surveys were carried out later in the latter part of that decade: the Pilot National Recreation Survey ... and the Government social survey's Planning for Leisure.... These surveys remain unique at national level.

Although such surveys also have a number of limitations - they were 'one-off' studies, the methods of data collection did not allow comparability of the data for each survey, and the results are often dated on publication due to the time required to analyse the results - they were a starting point for analysing demand. Yet since 1972 no major survey specifically focusing on leisure has been undertaken in the UK, although the General Household Survey (GHS), which normally occurs every four years, has included a number of questions on leisure.

PROBLEMS AND METHODS OF MEASURING RECREATIONAL DEMAND

When seeking to understand their recreational habits, asking individuals questions about their recreational habits using social survey techniques remains the most widely used approach. A landmark study by Rowntree and Lavers (1951) of *English Life and Leisure* provides a good illustration of the early use of a diverse range of research methods and sources to construct patterns of participation in leisure and recreation in post-war Britain. Even so, researchers recognise that precision is needed to identify participation, non-participation and the frequency of each.

For this reason, questions on surveys need to follow the type of format used on the GHS, to provide both a temporal and quantitative measure of demand.

Patmore (1983:57) cites the GHS, which begins by asking respondents: 'What ... things have you done in your leisure time ... in the four weeks ending last Sunday?' Survey data rarely record all the information a researcher seeks (e.g. respondents' recall ability may not accurately record the full pattern), or respondents have a different understanding of a term to that intended by the researcher. As a result, a variety of survey techniques are necessary to derive a range of complementary and yet unique insights into recreation demand.

Within the recreation literature, three techniques have primarily been used:

- A continuous record of recreation activities of a sample population for a given time period which involves respondents keeping a diary of activities (the time budget approach) (Zuzanek *et al.*'s (1998) cross-national survey of Dutch and Canadian use of time is a good source to consult).
- Questionnaire surveys which require respondents to recall activities either in the form of an individual case study, which are detailed and sometimes contain both qualitative and quantitative questions and which are inevitably small-scale due to the time involved in in-depth qualitative interviews.
- Questionnaire surveys which are large scale, enabling subsamples to be drawn which are statistically significant. Such surveys may be derived using simple and unambiguous questions which focus on a specific recreation activity or one that covers the entire spectrum of leisure activities (e.g. the GHS which surveyed 17,574 people in 1993 in Great Britain aged 16 and over). To illustrate how these techniques have been used and the way such data have been analysed, the time

budget approach and national surveys of recreational activities are now examined.

According to Coppock and Duffield (1975:5), 'recreation takes place in that portion of people's lives in which they are free (within constraints) to choose their activities, that is, their leisure time, [and] how they spend their time (time-budgets) is of paramount importance in any attempt to establish recreational demand, since it determines where recreational activities are possible'.

Therefore, time budget analysis is a vital tool in analysing demand. Time budgets provide a systematic record of a person's use of time. They describe the duration, sequence and timing of a person's activities for a given period, usually of between a day and a week. When combined with the recording of the location at which activities occur, the record is referred to as a space time budget. Time budget studies provide for the understanding of spatial and temporal behaviour patterns which may not be directly observable by other research techniques either because of their practicality or their intrusion into individual privacy. Such studies are often undertaken through the use of detailed diaries which are filled in by participants.

However, this method has not been widely used in comparison with more traditional survey techniques due to the difficulty for individuals of accurately keeping records. For example, in 1966 and 1974 to 1975 the British Broadcasting Corporation used its Audience Research Department to recruit people to keep a diary for a full week with half-hour entries. Yet even in such a short time span, diarists' willingness to record information accurately declined towards the end of the week.

However, pioneering research by Glyptis (1981a) used a diary technique which examined a sample of 595 visitors to the countryside. Respondents kept a diary record spanning three days and five evenings, recording the dominant pursuit in half-hour periods. While respondents identified up to 129 different leisure activities, each cited an average of 11. The value of the study was that through the use of cluster analysis to statistically analyse the sample and to group the population for more detail of this technique), it identified the leisure lifestyles of respondents with distinct groupings, where people of different social classes engaged in similar activities. The value of such research is in the identification of factors beyond simplistic analogies of demand determined by biological, social and economic factors.

INTERNATIONAL PERSPECTIVES

The most useful survey of national surveys of leisure time and the recreational activities undertaken may be found in Cushman *et al.* (1996a) which reviews international data on leisure and the existence of cross-national comparative research. It is also useful since the origins and role of participation surveys are reviewed, a feature subsequently updated by Parker (1999) in the UK context.

THE UNITED KINGDOM

Since the publication of Patmore's (1983) detailed review of data sources for analysing leisure and recreation patterns in the UK, Veal (1992) updated the situation pointing to the GHS and the role of the Australian Commonwealth government in commissioning the first National Recreation Participation Survey in Australia in 1985 to 1986.

This section examines demand at the national level in a number of countries to provide comparisons. However the most up-to-date and accessible source which documents these issues in the UK is the Office of Population and Censuses (OPCS) Social Trends.

The 1999 edition compiles data from a wide variety of sources and examines:

- Use of time for leisure and other activities showing that men in full-time employment had around two more hours of free time than women in full-time employment.
- Participation in home-based leisure activities in the period 1977 to 1997 indicated that watching television remained the most important pastime, while other activities vary by age and sex (i.e. gardening is more popular among men aged 25 years or more).

Table. Participation in Home-based Leisure Activities: by Gender, in Great Britain 1977-97.

	1977	1987	1996-97
Males			
Watching TV	97	99	99
Visiting/entertaining friends or relations	89	94	95
Listening to radio	87	89	90
Listening to records/tapes/ CDs	64	76	79
Reading books	52	54	58
DIY	51	58	58
Gardening	49	49	52
Dressmaking/needlework/ knitting	2	3	3
Females			
Watching TV	97	99	99
Visiting/entertaining friends or relations	93	96	97
Listening to radio	87	86	87
Listening to records/tapes/ CDs	60	71	77

Reading books	57	65	71
DIY	22	30	30
Gardening	35	43	45
Dressmaking/needlework/ knitting	51	47	37

Note: Percentage in each age group participating in each activity in the four weeks before interview.

- Day visits form a popular activity in terms of leisure time and derived from the 1998 UK Day Visits Survey examined round trips from home to locations in the UK. Between 1994 and 1998, leisure day visits increased by 15 per cent, rising to 5.9 billion in 1998. The two most commonly cited reasons for day visits were to drive out for a drink to a restaurant or public house, or to visit friends and relatives. In terms of gender, males were more likely to go out for a drink than females while females would tend to visit friends and relatives more than males.
- In terms of tourism, Blackpool Pleasure Beach was the UK's most popular tourist attraction (7.1 million visits in 1998), with the British Museum the second most popular (5.6 million visits in 1998).
- In 1998, 56 million holidays of four nights or more were taken by British residents, a rise of 36 per cent on 1971. The number of domestic holidays taken fell slightly in the of consumption of high forms of culture (e.g. visiting museums, exhibitions and concert halls).

Table. Participation in the Most Popular Sports, Games and Physical Activities: by Gender and Age, in the UK 1996-97

	16-19	**20-24**	**25-34**	**35-44**	**45-54**	**55-64**	**65 and over**	**All aged 16 and over**
Males								
Walking	57	57	50	53	51	50	37	49
Snooker/pool/ billiards	54	45	29	19	13	9	5	19
Cycling	36	24	19	18	12	8	5	15
Swimming	18	17	17	20	10	7	5	13
Soccer	47	28	17	10	2	1	-	10
Females								
Walking	45	43	44	45	49	43	25	41
Keep fit/yoga	29	28	24	20	14	12	6	17
Swimming	23	21	26	22	14	12	5	16
Cycling	14	11	10	12	7	4	2	8
Snooker/pool/ billiards	24	17	6	3	1	-	-	4

Table. Day Visits from Home: by Gender and Main Activity, 1998.

Great britain	Percentages		
	Males	Females	All
Eat/drink	21	15	18
Visit friends	14	19	17
Walk/hill-walk/ramble	16	14	15
Shop	9	15	12
Entertainment	5	7	6
Indoor sport	7	4	5
Outdoor sport	8	3	5
Hobby/special interest	4	5	5
Drive/sightsee	3	3	3
Swimming	2	3	3
Leisure attraction	2	2	2
Watching sport	2	1	2
Cycling/mountain biking	3	1	2
Informal sport/games	2	2	2
Other	2	5	3
All visits	100	100	100

Table. Holidays Abroad: by Destination.

	1971	1981	1991	1998
Spain	34.3	21.7	21.3	27.5
France	15.9	27.2	25.8	20.2
United states	1.0	5.5	6.8	7.0
Greece	4.5	6.7	7.6	5.3
Italy	9.2	5.8	3.5	4.0
Portugal	2.6	2.8	4.8	3.6
Irish republic	-	3.6	3.0	3.5
Turkey	-	0.1	0.7	3.0
Netherlands	3.6	2.4	3.5	2.7
Cyprus	1.0	0.7	2.4	2.6
Belgium	-	2.1	2.1	2.3
Germany	3.4	2.6	2.7	1.8
Malta	-	2.6	1.7	1.3

Austria	5.5	2.5	2.4	1.3
Other countries	19.0	13.7	11.8	13.9
All destinations (=100%)				
(thousands)	4,201	13,131	20,788	32,306

1990s, compensated by overseas trips. The most popular destination remained Spain in 1998, with Europe the dominant destination for British holidaymakers. The USA remains the most popular non-European destination.

- In 1998, people aged 65 or more were the least likely to go on holiday, with those aged 45 to 54 years of age the most likely to take a holiday overseas.
- In terms of sporting activities, men are consistently more likely than women to participate in sport. In 1996 to 1999, 71 per cent of men and 57 per cent of women participated in at least one sporting activity in the four weeks prior to being interviewed for the GHS.

POLAND

Poland is an interesting example, given the new roles for recreation in the post-communist state, since market reforms and ideological change has led to new roles for leisure post-1989. Although one consequence of austerity programmes to deal with budget deficits, a number of pre- and post-communist data sources exist to reconstruct leisure participation. The government Central Statistical Office (GUS) collects the majority of data.

Jung (1996) noted that over the period between 1972 and 1990, participation trends showed:

- Listening to the radio and watching television remained the dominant activities in terms of participation.
- Former communist culture activities, such as going to the cinema, theatre and opera declined in importance from over half of the population in 1972 to under one-third by 1990.
- Economic and political reforms in the 1980s may account for a sharp decline in participation

More detailed time budget studies have been examined by Olszewska (1989), and Jung (1996) highlighted a number of key global influences upon leisure participation: a growing media influence on mass culture, outbound travel by the Polish population (and inbound tourism), despite the withdrawal of state social subsidies for holiday travel. The electronic mass media also had an impact on leisure consumption. In the post-communist era, problems associated with the commercialisation of leisure and a growing polarisation of wealth, less economic security, rising unemployment and increasing rates of crime provide a new context for leisure participation.

HUNGARY

Fukaz (1989) examined the Csepel project undertaken in Hungary, which in 1969 sampled 400 blue-collar workers in one of the country's largest metal factories. Further in-depth interviews were undertaken in the period 1969 to 1972, 1975 to 1979 and 1979 to 1982, to collect time budget data as well as in-depth case studies. The longitudinal nature of the survey up to 1982 allows changes to be charted through time, and a simulation sample in 1985 (not using the original 1969 workers) provided a further in-depth case study. While the Csepel project is not representative of the Hungarian population, macro-economic changes in Hungarian society are reflected in the lifestyles of the population and these are reflected in the Csepel sample. Over the period 1969 to 1985, hours of work in Hungary were reduced from 48 to 40 hours a week, which is often argued by researchers as a pre-condition for the expansion of leisure.

But in Hungary the reduction in official hours of work was accompanied by increases in overtime working and the growth of second jobs. Fukaz (1989:41) argued that 'as Hungary's economy developed, the prestige of leisure appears to have grown.... Only 6.4 per cent in 1976 and 3.9 per cent in 1979 preferred work to leisure on Saturdays'. Yet the evidence from the Csepel study indicates that 'the main obstacles to a growth and enrichment of leisure in Hungary are not rooted in inadequate leisure education, or in a weakening or absence of leisure values. Rather, the barriers have been erected by objective material and financial conditions. The latter have discouraged individuals from using reductions in official work time to enhance their leisure' preferring to use the time in some cases for pecuniary reward.

In terms of leisure activities undertaken by the Csepel workers, these were largely related to passive forms of recreation. The most popular activities were watching television and just relaxing, though seasonal variations exist, with winter leisure being home-based but urban work patterns tend to dominate leisure in present-day Hungary. The growth of second home ownership has also characterised weekend and vacation leisure time for those families with access to such resources.

These three examples of recreational demand show that the patterns of leisure activities for each population exhibit a common range of characteristics, in terms of the predominance of passive activities, and the constraints of urban living which largely structure the time budgets of those in employment due to weekday work commitments. In other words, the patterns of demand highlighted in the three national surveys point to the existence of factors which facilitate and constrain recreational activities in each particular context.

Even so, it is important to recognise the current criticisms and concerns with national participation surveys observed by Cushman *et al.* (1996b: 12) as 'Recently surveys have had a "bad press" from academics, particularly in light of the growing popularity - and indeed orthodoxy - of qualitative research methods in the field'. As a result, qualitative researchers point to the shortcomings, limitations and somewhat outmoded approach of quantitative 'positivist' research methods. However, so far the discussion of demand has focused on national patterns, and therefore attention now turns to the regional level to examine the contribution the geographer can make to the analysis of demand within a regional geographic framework.

THE REGIONAL DEMAND FOR LEISURE AND RECREATION

Within the studies of national recreational demand reviewed in the previous section, it is clear that the analyses of geographical patterns of demand were relatively scant, given the tendency for national studies to lack a regional dimension. It is the spatial variations in demand which are of interest to the geographer, and a number of studies have been undertaken which utilise the geographer's spatial analytical approach to examine demand patterns.

North-West England is one such area which has seen a significant contribution made to understanding the scale and nature of regional recreational demand including evidence in Rodgers' (1969) insights from the *Pilot National Recreation Survey*, Rodgers' (1977) contribution to leisure in the North-West and Rodgers and Patmore's (1972) *Leisure in the North-West*.

The North-West of England is an interesting region with a variety of socioeconomic contrasts ranging from the urban decline apparent in inner-city areas through to a range of country districts with high levels of prosperity akin to South-East England.

What Rodgers (1993) explored was the changing political climate for leisure provision at national level, namely the rolling back of the frontiers of the state and changing social philosophy that active and creative leisure pursuits deserved to 'be promoted as widely as possible, with the support of public funding and subsidy, to an increasing emphasis on the concept that the provision of recreation is simply another service industry best left to the operation of the market for most efficient delivery at least cost'.

This marks a shift in political ideology: that leisure is no longer a significant welfare service to be delivered to all sectors of the population at free or subsidised prices due to the contribution it makes to enhanced quality of life. Thus the move to a market-driven approach requires local authorities as the principal planners of community-based leisure provision to recognise the existence of leisure markets which comprise different forms of recreational demand in time and space. Local leisure markets are diverse, where a multitude of factors may affect their composition.

For example, those where unemployment, social stress due to environmental factors and low rates of population growth exist may offer little commercial opportunity for the private sector despite real leisure needs. Yet if left to the market, such needs may not be served adequately due to the apparent lack of prosperity or ability of individuals to pay for a resource that poor people view as a luxury item when they cannot always command the financial resources to meet basic needs. Thus, at a regional level, a detailed district-by-district assessment of the market is necessary to show which areas and markets may still require local authority support to avoid gross inequalities in access and provision from developing any further.

Rodgers (1993) used two principles to underpin an analysis of leisure markets:

- A significant proportion of demand is age-related, and changes through time will affect future needs;
- Aocio-economic well-being is a powerful determinant of the volume and pattern of demand in the present and the future.

By combining these factors in an overall assessment, Rodgers (1993) was able to develop a typology of districts and their ability to support a market-based approach to leisure provision.

In terms of age-related markets, Rodgers (1993:119-20) identified four groups:

- The teenage-young adult, who is active and a major generator of recreational demand, especially active pursuits. Within the North-West, this group exhibits an almost universal decline;
- The family phase (aged 25 to 44 years), with a distinctive set of leisure interests;
- A post-family phase (aged 45 to 60 years), where active recreational interests are in decline but an interest in general leisure activities is strong;
- The elderly, with a significant range of passive leisure interests.

By analysing forecast population growth in each of these groups, Rodgers (1993:125) concluded that for planning future leisure provision the following characteristics needed to be incorporated into any geographical assessment of demand:

- A common feature of districts in the region is the absence of growth, except in the family phase. Rates of growth of 4 per cent above the national average are apparent in the age group 25 to 44 years for 1981 to 1991. The opportunities for market-driven provision include fitness training, outdoor pursuits in the countryside, water-sports and ten-pin bowling.
- In the post-family phase, growth rates are less than the national average, with a degree of localised growth in the industrial towns of Greater Manchester, West Lancashire and districts of North Cheshire though not in Merseyside. The most prominent activities are bowls, fishing, dance, keep fit and walking which are likely to have little appeal for private sector operators.
- The youth market exhibits a clear decline, except for areas where planned growth exists (e.g. new towns), with rates above the national average for Merseyside and parts of inner Manchester. In the period 1981 to 1991 a decline of 13 to 17 per cent exists in most districts, with the exception of Cheshire and West Lancashire.
- Among the elderly, trends are complex, but no patterns of growth are evident in traditional retirement areas.

- A number of extremes exist in subregional patterns of demand, with weaknesses in Merseyside which stretches beyond the inner-city districts. In East Cheshire (e.g. Congleton, Crewe and Nantwich) a profile of demand akin to the affluent South-East of England exists with different subgroupings of demand in other areas.

One of the most significant contributory factors to the size and nature of demand is clearly related to socio-economic contrasts. Social well-being is, according to Rodgers (1993:126), 'a strong influence on both the volume and structure of leisure demand and on the relative roles of public and commercial provision in meeting it'. Using the Department of the Environment (DoE) Social Deprivation Index, which derives negative indices based on unemployment, overcrowding, single-parent and pension households, housing quality and ethnic origin, Rodgers (1993) ranked the districts in the North-West on this composite measure of social stress and also included levels of car ownership.

The results were used to identify a range of geographically based leisure markets which were strong or weak in terms of demand, particularly in relation to their capacity to pay for recreational activities in a market-driven local leisure economy.

- Approximately 12 districts are in the top left quadrant, which represent areas of prosperity with comparatively little unemployment, high levels of car ownership and income generation and low levels of social stress.

  These districts exhibit some strength in demand despite a drop in numbers of people aged 13 to 24 years, while growth in the family and post-family sectors exists. These districts have the most appeal to commercial providers. Rodgers (1993:127) suggests that 'for large sections of the community and for many recreations a blend of private-sector and voluntary body provision, with local authorities acting largely with a market philosophy, might offer an effective formula. The case for massive direct subsidy is relatively weak, against the stronger conflicting claims of less fortunate areas' in the allocation of scarce public sector resources for recreation. Even so, pockets of target groups exist (e.g. housewives, the young and active elderly) who would benefit from some subsidy of their activities. In the north-west of the region, problems of access to recreational resources also exist in largely rural districts.
- A grouping which occupies the bottom right corner scores low on prosperity while the age-related markets show a major decline. This reflects the limited growth in a single age category and districts of population loss (e.g. Merseyside and some of the textile towns). Both the absolute numbers and spending power of the population are declining, where the case of recreational provision for social reasons is essential due to the concentration of disadvantaged groups (e.g.

the unemployed, the poor, single-parent families, the elderly and ethnic minorities). Dependence upon state benefits underpins the case for public subsidy for provision due to the multiple deprivation existing in such areas.

- A further six districts such as Hyndburn and Rochdale score high on low prosperity indices, with selective growth in family and post-family groups with a strong ethnic dimension. The welfare case for provision is also apparent in this category.
- The remaining districts exhibit relatively prosperous populations with limited growth potential, with limited justification for public funding of their recreational services.

While Rodgers (1993) admits the allocation of scarce public resources raises controversial decision-making choices, it does illustrate the value of a spatial analytical approach to recreation, if a wide range of data and factors are taken into account. In other words, this case study illustrates the geographer's ability to synthesise a wide range of complex data sources and concepts to derive a series of spatially contingent generalisations and groupings of the population for a region as diverse as North-West England.

Using concepts from social geography (e.g. social well-being and deprivation) and combining demographic data from districts across the region, the geographer is able to highlight the challenge for regional and local planners in the allocation of declining absolute public sector resources for recreational provision.

Regional analysis epitomises the geographer's interest in places, and differences and similarities in both time and space. The greatest contribution geographical research has made is to the site-specific studies of demand, most notably site surveys. For this reason, the remaining focus of this section on recreation examines recreation site surveys.

THE SPATIAL ANALYSIS OF DEMAND AT THE MICRO LEVEL

Within the growing literature on geographical studies of recreation in the 1960s and 1970s, site surveys have become the most documented. As Glyptis (1981b: 277) indicated, 'numerous site surveys - mostly set in the format devised by Burton (1966) ... established the characteristics of visitors and their trips.

Social profiles, trip distances, modes of transport and the duration, purpose and frequency of visits are well documented.' Glyptis (1981b) also noted that the 1980s were ripe for behavioural analysis which had been neglected in relation to site surveys. While reviews of site surveys are too numerous to list, novel research methods which examine the behaviour rather than the socio-economic characteristics of recreationalists have remained less common in the published literature, although some reports have probed this area. Glyptis' (1981b) analysis of one 242 ha site - Westwood Common, Beverley near Hull (UK) - is one such example.

By employing participant observation methods to examine an undulating grassland area of common pasture land 13 km from the urban area of Hull, the spatial distribution of site use by recreationalists was observed and analysed. The main recreational activities observed at the site were sitting, sun-bathing, walking, picnicking, informal games and staying inside one's car. On a busy Sunday in summer, up to 2,000 visitors came to the site. Using dispersion maps, observational mapping permitted the visitor distributions to be located in time and space while length of stay (using car registration data) and maps of use for different days and times complemented traditional social survey methods to analyse visitor behaviour. The site features, access points, availability of parking and location of landscape features and facilities permit a more detailed understanding of site use. Glyptis (1981b) used observations on five days in August and September between 11 a.m. and 6 p.m. to collate data. Visitor arrivals at the site during the weekend occurred between 12 noon and 2 p.m., and peak use occurred at 4.30 p.m., with the majority of visitors spending one to two hours on site.

The gradual increase in intensity of use by time of day varied by activity, with informal games and picnicking declining after Sunday lunch and walking increasing throughout the afternoon. Local users also displayed a preference to use the site at off-peak times, with increased patterns of dispersion and clumping through time. This reflects access roads, with visitors parking close to (within 15 yards) the site they visited. Visitors were also recorded going to landmarks and facilities (e.g.viewpoints) as well as buying refreshments (e.g. from mobile vans), with the density of use increasing through the day rather than the distribution.

Glyptis (1981c) devised a simple model to explain the dynamics of visitor dispersion. Thereafter, as the pace of arrivals slows, a degree of infilling and consolidation occurs. Then as people depart, dispersion occurs, with a more irregular pattern of distribution arising, although it may be affected by new arrivals in the afternoon who intensify the pattern. What Glyptis (1991:119) recognised was that even though 'sites clearly experience an increase in visitor density, visitor dispersion in a spatial sense remains fairly constant, even with space to spare and no restrictions on public access'.

Using nearest neighbour analysis, Glyptis (1981c) was able to measure the distances between groups of visitors, and that comfortable levels of tolerance exist for visitors in terms of proximity to other people, although the amount of personal space which recreationalists require may vary between different cultures. In fact, Glyptis (1991:119) remarked that 'as levels of use increase on a given day, the percentage occupancy of space actually decreases: visitors only ever use about a fifth of the space available to them, and at times of heaviest use they choose to occupy even less. In other words, site carrying capacity changes continually.'

This study also highlighted the significance of recreation sites with multiple uses, where a variety of recreational needs are capable of being met and, as Burton's (1974) survey of Cannock Chase, Staffordshire (UK) found, individual sites cannot be viewed in isolation: there are relationships between them and understanding them is vital to site management. Glyptis (1981c) highlighted a certain degree of consistency in visitor use of a site, explaining the patterns as a function of the resource base, visitor use and behavioural factors. It may be possible to accommodate or reduce capacity through simple modifications as 'the geographer is well placed to examine fundamental aspects of ... recreation, to diagnose issues in site management, and to propose solutions' (Glyptis 1981b: 285). Therefore, having outlined many of the factors and dimensions of recreational demand at a variety of spatial scales from the national, regional and local level, the discussion now turns to tourism demand.

TOURISM DEMAND

One of the fundamental questions tourism researchers consistently seek to answer is: Why do tourists travel? This seemingly simple proposition remains one of the principal challenges for tourism research. D.G. Pearce (1995a: 18) expands this proposition by asking 'What induces them to leave their home area to visit other areas? What factors condition their travel behaviour, influencing their choice of destination, itineraries followed and activities undertaken?' Such questions underpin not only issues of spatial interaction, but also lead the geographer to question:

- Why tourists seek to travel;
- Where they go;
- When they go and how they get there.

These basic issues have spatial implications in terms of the patterns of tourism, where tourism impacts will occur and the nature of management challenges for destinations which may attract a 'mass market' or be seeking to develop tourism from a low base. In other words, an understanding of tourism demand is a starting point for the analysis of why tourism develops, who patronises specific destinations and what appeals to the client market.

However, geographers are at a comparative disadvantage in answering some of the principal questions associated with tourism demand since 'geographers have not been at the forefront of this research which has been led by psychologists, sociologists, marketers and economists. Some of these researchers have touched on such issues as the potential significance of variations in motivation on destination choice'.

However, tourist behaviour and the analysis of motivation has not traditionally been the logical positivist and empirical approach of traditional forms of spatial analysis on tourism with some exceptions. The area of tourist behaviour has a more developed literature within the field of social psychology than geography, and the emphasis in this section is on the way such approaches assist in understanding how tourist behaviour may result in the spatial implications for tourism. The precise approach one adopts to the analysis of tourism demand is largely dependent upon the disciplinary perspective of the researcher. Geographers view demand in a uniquely spatial manner as 'the total number of persons who travel, or wish to travel, to use tourist facilities and services at places away from their places of work and residence', whereas in this context demand 'is seen in terms of the relationship between individuals' motivation [to travel] and their ability to do so' with an attendant emphasis on the implications for the spatial impact on the development of domestic and international tourism.

In comparison, the economist emphasises 'the schedule of the amount of any product or service which people are willing and able to buy at each specific price in a set of possible prices during a specified period of time. Psychologists view demand from the perspective of motivation and behaviour', while Uysal (1998) reviewed the wider context of tourism demand.

In conceptual terms, there are three principal elements to tourism demand:

- *Effective or actual demand* comprises the number of people participating in tourism, commonly expressed as the number of travellers. This is most commonly measured by tourism statistics which means that most official sources of data are measures of effective demand.
- *Suppressed demand* is the population who are unable to travel because of circumstances (e.g. lack of purchasing power or limited holiday entitlement) which is called potential demand. Potential demand can be converted to effective demand if the circumstances change. There is also deferred demand where constraints (e.g. lack of tourism supply such as a shortage of bedspaces) can also be converted to effective demand if a destination or locality can accommodate the demand.
- *No demand* is a distinct category for the population who have no desire to travel.

According to Cooper et al. (1993:16) the demand for tourism may be viewed in other ways using a number of other concepts:

- *Substitution of demand* where the demand for a specific activity is substituted by another activity;
- *Redirection of demand* where the geographical distribution of tourism is altered due to pricing policies of competing destinations, special events or changing trends and tastes.

Therefore, it is apparent that the analysis of tourism demand as an abstract concept remains firmly within the remit of tourism economics.

However, the factors which shape the tourist decision-making process to select and participate in specific forms of tourism is largely within the field of consumer behaviour and motivation.

TOURIST MOTIVATION

According to Moutinho (1987:16), motivation is 'a state of need, a condition that exerts a push on the individual towards certain types of action that are seen as likely to bring satisfaction'. In this respect Cooper *et al.* (1993:20) rightly acknowledge that 'demand for tourists at the individual level can be treated as a consumption process which is influenced by a number of factors. These may be a combination of needs and desires, availability of time and money, or images, perceptions and attitudes'.

Not surprisingly, this is an incredibly complex area of research and it is impossible within a chapter such as this to overview the area in depth. Nevertheless, P. Pearce's (1993) influential work in this field outlined a 'blueprint for tourist motivation', arguing that in an attempt to theorise tourist motivation one must consider the following issues:

- The conceptual place of tourism motivation;
- Its task in the specialism of tourism;
- Its ownership and users;
- Its ease of communication;
- Pragmatic measurement concerns;
- Adopting a dynamic approach;
- The development of multi-motive perspectives;
- Resolving and clarifying intrinsic and extrinsic motivation approaches.

To date no all-embracing theory of tourist motivation has been developed which has been adapted and legitimised by researchers in other contexts. This is largely due to the multidisciplinary nature of the research issues identified above and the problem of simplifying complex psychological factors and behaviour into a set of constructs and ultimately a universally acceptable theory that can be tested and proved in various tourism contexts. As a result, Cooper *et al.* (1993:20) prefer to view the individual as a central component of tourism demand to understand what motivates the tourist to travel. Their research rightly acknowledges that:

No two individuals are alike, and differences in attitudes, perceptions and motivation have an important influence on travel decisions [where] attitudes depend on an individual's perception of the world. Perceptions are mental impressions of ... a place or travel company and are determined by many factors which include childhood, family and work experiences. However, attitudes and perceptions in themselves do not explain why people want to travel. The inner urges which initiate travel demand are called travel motivators.

If one views the tourist as a consumer, then tourism demand is formulated through a consumer decision-making process, and therefore one can discern four elements which initiate demand:

- *Energisers of demand*: Factors that promote an individual to decide on a holiday;
- *Filterers of demand*: Which means that even though motivation may prevail, constraints on demand may exist in economic, sociological or psychological terms;

- *Affecters*: Which are factors that may heighten or suppress the energisers that promote consumer interest or choice in tourism;
- *Roles*: Where the family member involved in the purchase of holiday products and the arbiter of group decision-making on choice of destination, product, and the where, when and how of consumption.

These factors underpin the tourist's process of travel decision-making although it does not explain why people choose to travel.

HIERARCHY MODEL AND TOURIST MOTIVATION

Within the social psychology of tourism there is a growing literature which has built upon Maslow's work (discussed earlier in relation to recreation) to identify specific motivations beyond the concept of needing 'to get away from it all' pioneered by Grinstein (1955), while push factors motivating individuals to seek a holiday exist, and pull factors (e.g. promotion by tourist resorts and tour operators) encourage as attractors.

Ryan's (1991:25-9) analysis of tourist travel motivators (excluding business travel) identifies the following reasons commonly cited to explain why people travel to tourist destinations for holidays, which include:

- A desire to escape from a mundane environment;
- The pursuit of relaxation and recuperation functions;
- An opportunity for play;
- The strengthening of family bonds;
- Prestige, since different destinations can enable one to gain social enhancement among peers;
- Social interaction;
- Educational opportunities;
- Wish fulfilment;
- Shopping.

From this list, it is evident that while all leisure involves a temporary escape of some kind, 'tourism is unique in that it involves real physical escape reflected in travelling to one or more destination regions where the leisure experience transpires ... [thus] a holiday trip allows changes that are multi-dimensional: place, pace, faces, lifestyle, behaviour, attitude.

It allows a person temporary withdrawal from many of the environments affecting day to day existence' (Leiper (1984) cited in D.G. Pearce (1995:19). Within most studies of tourist motivations these factors emerge in one form or another, while researchers such as Crompton (1979) emphasise that socio-psychological motives can be located along a continuum, Iso-Ahola (1980) theorised tourist motivation in terms of an escape element complemented by a search component, where the tourist is seeking something.

However, Dann's (1981) conceptualisation is probably one of the most useful attempts to simplify the principal elements of tourist motivation into:

- Travel as a response to what is lacking yet desired;
- Destination pull in response to motivational push;

- Motivation as fancy;
- Motivation as classified purpose;
- Motivation typologies;
- Motivation and tourist experiences;
- Motivation as definition and meaning.

This was simplified a stage further by McIntosh and Goeldner (1990) into:

- Physical motivators;
- Cultural motivators;
- Interpersonal motivators;
- Status and prestige motivators.

On the basis of motivation and using the type of experiences tourists seek, Cohen (1972) distinguished between four types of travellers:

- The organised mass tourist, on a package holiday, who is highly organised. Their contact with the host community in a destination is minimal.
- The individual mass tourist, who uses similar facilities to the organised mass tourist but also desires to visit other sights not covered on organised tours in the destination.
- The explorers, who arrange their travel independently and who wish to experience the social and cultural lifestyle of the destination.
- The drifter, who does not seek any contact with other tourists or their accommodation, preferring to live with the host community.

Clearly, such a classification is fraught with problems, since it does not take into account the increasing diversity of holidays undertaken and inconsistencies in tourist behaviour.

Other researchers suggest that one way of overcoming this difficulty is to consider the different destinations tourists choose to visit, and then establish a sliding scale similar to Cohen's (1972) typology, but which does not have such an absolute classification.

In contrast, Plog (1974) devised a classification of the US population into psychographic types, with travellers distributed along a continuum from psychocentrism to allocentrism. The psychocentrics are the anxious, inhibited and less adventurous travellers while at the other extreme the allocentrics are adventurous, outgoing, seeking new experiences due to their inquisitive personalities and interest in travel and adventure.

D.G. Pearce (1995) highlights the spatial implications of such conceptualisations, that each tourist type will seek different destinations which will change through time. However, criticisms by P. Pearce (1993) indicate that Plog's model is difficult to use because it fails to distinguish between extrinsic and intrinsic motivations without incorporating a dynamic element to encompass the changing nature of individual tourists.

P. Pearce discounts such models, suggesting that individuals have a 'career' in their travel behaviour where people 'start at different levels, they are likely to change levels during their life-cycle and they can be prevented from moving by money, health and other people. They may also retire from their travel career or not take holidays at all and therefore not be part of the system'.

These are:

- A concern with biological needs;
- Aafety and security needs;
- Relationship development and extension needs;
- Special interest and self-development needs;
- Fulfilment or self-actualisation needs.

Cooper *et al.* (1993:23) argue that 'the literature on tourism motivation is still in an immature phase of development, it has been shown that motivation is an essential concept behind the different patterns of tourism demand'. From the existing literature on tourist motivation, the problems of determining tourist motivation may be summarised as follows:

- Tourism is not one specific product, it is a combination of products and experiences which meet a diverse range of needs.
- Tourists are not always conscious of their deep psychological needs and ideas. Even when they do know what they are, they may not reveal them.
- Tourism motives may be multiple and contradictory (push and pull factors).
- Motives may change over time and be inextricably linked together (e.g. perception, learning, personality and culture are often separated out but they are all bound up together) and dynamic conceptualisations such as P. Pearce's (1993) leisure ladder are crucial to advancing knowledge and understanding in this area.

Having examined some of the issues associated with what motivates tourists to travel, attention now turns to the process of measurement and recording tourist demand using statistical measures.

TOURISM STATISTICS

Ritchie argued that 'an important part of the maturing process for any science is the development or adaptation of consistent and well-tested measurement techniques and methodologies which are well-suited to the types of problems encountered in practice'. In this context, the measurement of tourists, tourism activity and the effects on the economy and society in different environments is crucial to the development of tourism as an established area of study within the confines of social science.

Burkart and Medlik (1981) provide a useful insight into the development of measurements of tourism phenomena by governments during the 1960s and their subsequent development through to the late 1970s.

While it is readily acknowledged by most tourism researchers that statistics are a necessary feature to provide data to enable researchers, managers, planners, decision-makers and public and private sector bodies to gauge the significance and impact of tourism on destination areas, Burkart and Medlik (1981:74) identify four principal reasons for statistical measurement in tourism:

- To evaluate the magnitude and significance of tourism to a destination area or region;
- To quantify the contribution to the economy or society, especially the effect on the balance of payments;
- To assist in the planning and development of tourism infrastructure and the effect of different volumes of tourists with specific needs;
- To assist in the evaluation and implementation of marketing and promotion activities where the tourism marketer requires information on the actual and potential markets and their characteristics.

Consequently, tourism statistics are essential to the measurement of the volume, scale, impact and value of tourism at different geographical scales from the global to the country level down to the individual destination. Yet an information gap exists between the types of statistics provided by organisations for and the needs of users.

The compilation of tourism statistics provided by organisations associated with the measurement of tourism has established methods and processes to collect, collate and analyse tourism statistics (World Tourism Organisation (WTO) 1996), yet these have been understood by only a small number of researchers and practitioners.

Thus this section attempts to demystify the apparent sophistication and complexity associated with the presentation of statistical indicators of tourism and their value to spatial analysis, since geographers have a strong quantified methods tradition, which is reflected in the use and reliance upon such indicators to understand spatial variations and patterns of tourism activity.

All too often, undergraduate and many postgraduate texts assume a prior knowledge of tourism statistics and they are only dealt with in a limited way by most tourism texts, and where such issues are raised they are usually discussed in over-technical texts aimed at a limited audience (e.g. Frechtling 1996). A commonly misunderstood feature which is associated with tourism statistics is that they are a complete and authoritative source of information (i.e. they answer all the questions posed by the researcher).

Other associated problems are that statistics are recent and relate to the previous year or season, implying that there is no time lag in their generation, analysis, presentation and dissemination to interested parties. In fact, most tourism statistics are 'typically measurements of arrivals, trips, tourist nights and expenditure, and these often appear in total or split into categories such as business or leisure travel'.

Furthermore, the majority of published tourism statistics are derived from sample surveys, with the results being weighted or statistically manipulated to derive a measure which is supposedly representative of the real-world situation. In reality, this often means that tourism statistics are subject to significant errors depending on the size of the sample. The statistical measurement of tourists is far from straightforward, and Latham (1989) identifies a number of distinctive and peculiar problems associated with the tourist population:

- Tourists are a transient and highly mobile population, making statistical sampling procedures difficult when trying to ensure statistical accuracy and rigour in methodological terms.
- Interviewing mobile populations such as tourists is often undertaken in a strange environment, typically at ports or points of departure or arrival where there is background noise which may influence responses.
- Other variables, such as the weather, may affect the responses.

Even where sampling and survey-related problems can be minimised, one has to treat tourism statistics with a degree of caution because of additional methodological issues that can affect the results. For example, tourism research typically comprises:

- Pre-travel studies of tourists' intended travel habits and likely choice of destination (intentional studies);
- Studies of tourists in transit to provide information on their actual behaviour and plans for the remainder of their holiday or journey (actual and intended studies);
- Studies of tourists at the destination or at specific tourist attractions and sites, to provide information on their actual behaviour, levels of satisfaction, impacts and future intentions (actual and intended studies);
- Post-travel studies of tourists on their return journey from their destination or on-site experience or once they have returned to their place of residence (post-travel measures).

In an ideal world, where resource constraints are not a limiting factor on the generation of statistics, each of the aforementioned approaches should be used to provide a broad spectrum of research information on tourism and tourist behaviour. In reality, organisations and government agencies select a form of research which meets their own particular needs. In practice, most tourism statistics are generated with practical uses in mind and they may usually, though not exclusively, be categorised as follows:

- Measurement of tourist volume, enumerating arrivals, departures and the number of visits and stays;
- Expenditure-based surveys which quantify the value of tourist spending at the destination and during the journey;
- The characteristics and features of tourists to construct a profile of the different markets and segments visiting a destination.

However, before any tourism statistics can be derived, it is important to deal with the complex and thorny issue of defining the population - the tourist. Therefore, how does one define and differentiate between the terms *tourism* and *tourist*?

The terms *travel* and *tourism* are often interchanged within the published literature on tourism, though they are normally meant to encompass 'the field of research on human and business activities associated with one or more aspects of the temporary movement of persons away from their immediate home communities and daily work environments for business, pleasure and personal reasons'.

These two terms tend to be used in differing contexts to mean similar things, although there is a tendency for the United States to continue to use the term 'travel' when in fact they mean tourism. Despite this inherent problem which may be little more than an exercise in semantics, it is widely acknowledged that the two terms are used in isolation or in unison to 'describe' three concepts:

- The movement of people;
- A sector of the economy or an industry;
- A broad system of interacting relationships of people (including their need to travel outside their communities and services that attempt to respond to these needs by supplying products).

From this initial starting point, one can begin to explore some of the complex issues in arriving at a working definition of the terms *tourism* and *tourist*. In a historical context, Burkart and Medlik (1981:41) identify the historical development of the term *tourism*, noting the distinction between the endeavours of researchers to differentiate between the concept and technical definitions of tourism. The concept of tourism refers to the 'broad notional framework, which identifies the essential characteristics, and which distinguishes tourism from the similar, often related, but different phenomena'.

In contrast, technical definitions have evolved through time as researchers modify and develop appropriate measures for statistical, legislative and operational reasons implying that there may be various technical definitions to meet particular purposes. However, the concept of tourism, and its identification for research purposes, is an important consideration in this instance for tourism statistics so that users are familiar with the context of their derivation.

While most tourism books, articles and monographs now assume either a standard definition or interpretation of the concept of tourism, which is usually influenced by the social scientists' perspective (i.e. a geographical, economic, political, sociological approach or other disciplines), Burkart and Medlik's (1981) approach to the concept of tourism continues to offer a valid assessment of the situation where five main characteristics are associated with the concept.

- Tourism arises from the movement of people to, and their stay in, various destinations.
- There are two elements in all tourism: the journey to the destination and the stay including activities at the destination.
- The journey and the stay take place outside the normal place of residence and work, so that tourism gives rise to activities which are distinct from those of the resident and working populations of the places, through which tourists travel and in which they stay.
- The movement to tourist destinations is of a temporary, short-term character, with the intention of returning home within a few days, weeks or months.
- Destinations are visited for purposes other than taking up permanent residence or employment remunerated from within the places visited (Burkart and Medlik 1981:42).

Furthermore, Burkart and Medlik's (1981) definition of tourism as a concept is invaluable because it rightly recognises that much tourism is a leisure activity which involves a discretionary use of time and money, and recreation is often the main purpose for participation in tourism.

But this is no reason for restricting the total concept in this way and the essential characteristics of tourism can best be interpreted to embrace a wider concept.

All tourism includes some travel but not all travel is tourism, while the temporary and short-term nature of most tourist trips distinguishes it from migration. Therefore, from the broad interpretation of tourism, it is possible to consider the technical definitions of tourism.

TECHNICAL DEFINITIONS OF TOURISM

Technical definitions of tourism are commonly used by organisations seeking to define the population to be measured, and there are three principal features which normally have to be defined:

- Purpose of travel (e.g. the type of traveller, be it business travel, holiday-makers, visits to friends and relatives or for other reasons).
- The time dimension involved in the tourism visit, which requires a minimum and a maximum period of time spent away from the home area and the time spent at the destination. In most cases, this would involve a minimum stay of more than 24 hours away from home and less than a year as a maximum.
- Those situations where tourists may or may not be included as tourists, such as cruise passengers, those tourists in transit at a particular point of embarkation/departure and excursionists who stay less than 24 hours at a destination (e.g. the European duty-free cross-channel day-trip market).

Among the most recent attempts to recommend appropriate definitions of tourism was the World Tourism Organisation (hereafter WTO) International

Conference of Travel and Tourism in Ottawa in 1991 which reviewed, expanded and developed technical definitions, where tourism comprises 'the activities of a person travelling outside his or her usual environment for less than a specified period of time and whose main purpose of travel is other than exercise of an activity remunerated from the place visited', where 'usual environment' is intended to exclude trips within the areas of usual residence and also frequent and regular trips between the domicile and the workplace and other community trips of a routine character, where 'less than a specified period of time' is intended to exclude long-term migration, and 'exercise of an activity remunerated from the place visited' is intended to exclude only migration for temporary work.

The following definitions were developed by the WTO:

- International tourism: consists of inbound tourism.
- Visits to a country by non-residents and outbound tourism residents of a country visiting another country.
- Internal tourism: residents of a country visiting their own country.
- Domestic tourism: internal tourism plus inbound tourism (the tourism market of accommodation facilities and attractions within a country).
- National tourism: internal tourism plus outbound tourism (the resident tourism market for travel agents and airlines) (WTO, cited in Chadwick 1994:66).

In order to improve statistical collection and improve understanding of tourism, the United Nations (UN) (1994) and the WTO (1991a) also recommended differentiating between visitors, tourists and excursionists (day trippers).

The WTO (1991a) recommended that an international tourist be defined as: 'a visitor who travels to a country other than that in which he/she has his/her usual residence for at least one night but not more than one year, and whose main purpose of visit is other than the exercise of an activity remunerated from within the country visited'; and that an international excursionist (e.g. cruise ship visitors) be defined as 'a visitor residing in a country who travels the same day to a country other than which he/she has his/her usual environment for less than 24 hours without spending the night in the country visited and whose main purpose of visit is other than the exercise of an activity remunerated from within the country visited'.

Similar definitions were also developed for domestic tourists, with domestic tourists having a time limit of 'not more than six months' (WTO 1991a; UN 1994).

Interestingly, the inclusion of a same-day travel, 'excursionist' category in UN/WTO technical definitions of tourism makes the division between recreation and tourism even more arbitrary, and there is increasing international agreement that 'tourism' refers to all activities of visitors, including both overnight and same-day visitors (UN 1994:5).

Given improvements in transport technology, same-day travel is becoming increasingly important to some countries, with the UN (1994:9) observing, 'day visits are important to consumers and to many providers, especially tourist attractions, transport operators and caterers'. Chadwick (1994) moves the definition of tourists a stage further by offering a typology of travellers (tourists) which highlights the distinction between tourists (travellers) and non-travellers (non-tourists) which is summarised.

It is also useful because it illustrates where technical problems may occur in deciding which groups to include in tourism and which to exclude. From this classification of travellers, the distinction between international and domestic tourism needs to be made. Domestic tourism normally refers to tourists who travel from their normal domicile to other areas within a country. In contrast, international tourism normally involves a tourist leaving their country of origin to cross into another country which involves documentation, administrative formalities and movement to a foreign environment.

DOMESTIC TOURISM STATISTICS

D.G. Pearce (1995a) acknowledges that the scale and volume of domestic tourism worldwide exceeds that of international tourism, though it is often viewed as the poorer partner in the compilation of statistics. For example, most domestic tourism statistics tend to underestimate the scale and volume of flows since certain aspects of domestic tourist movements are sometimes ignored in official sources. The 'visits to friends and relatives, the use of forms of accommodation other than hotels (for example, second homes, camp and caravan sites) and travel by large segments of a population from towns to the countryside are not for the most part included'.

This is supported by the WTO, who argue that 'there are relatively few countries that collect domestic travel and tourism statistics. Moreover some countries rely exclusively on the traditional hotel sector, thereby leaving out of account the many travellers staying in supplementary accommodation establishments or with friends and relatives'. Therefore, the collection of domestic tourism statistics requires the use of different data sources aside from the more traditional sources such as hotel records which identify the origin and duration of a visitor's stay.

To assist in the identification of who to include as a domestic tourist, the WTO (1983) suggests the following working definition: 'any person, regardless of nationality, resident in a country and who travels to a place in the same country for not more than one year and whose main purpose of visit is other than following an occupation remunerated from within the place visited.'

Such a definition includes domestic tourists where an overnight stay is involved and domestic excursionists who visit an area for less than 24 hours and do not stay overnight. In fact, Latham (1989:66) points to the variety of definitions which exist aside from those formulated by WTO and the following issues complicate matters further:

- *Purpose of visit*: All countries using this concept define a domestic tourist as one who travels for a purpose other than to perform a remunerated activity.
- *The length of trip and/or distance travelled*: Certain definitions state that travellers should, for example, be involved in an overnight stay and/or travel a prescribed minimum distance.
- *Type of accommodation*: For practical reasons, some countries restrict the concept of domestic tourism to cover only those persons using commercial accommodation facilities (after Latham 1989:66).

Problems in applying WTO definitions may also reflect an individual country's reasons for generating such statistics, which may not necessarily be to contribute to a better understanding of statistics *per se*. For example, WTO (1981) identified four uses of domestic tourism statistics:

- To calculate the contribution of tourism to the country's economy, whereby estimates of tourism's value to the Gross Domestic Product is estimated due to the complexity of identifying the scope of tourism's contribution.
- To assist in the marketing and promotion of tourism, where government-sponsored tourism organisations seek to encourage its population to take domestic holidays rather than to travel overseas for a discussion of this activity among Pacific Rim countries).
- To aid the regional development policies of governments which harness tourism as a tool for area development where domestic tourists in congested environments are encouraged to travel to less developed areas and to improve the quality of tourism in different environments.
- To achieve social objectives, where socially oriented tourism policies may be developed for the underprivileged which requires a detailed understanding of the holiday-taking habits of a country's nationals.

Regional and local tourist organisations also make use of such data to develop and market destinations and different businesses within the tourism sector. But how is domestic tourism measured?

Burkart and Medlik (1981) argue that two principal features need to be measured: first, the volume, value and characteristics of tourism among the population of the country; second, the same data relating to individual destinations within the country. The WTO (1981, cited in Latham 1989) considers the minimum data requirements for the collection of domestic tourism statistics in terms of arrivals and tourist nights in accommodation classified by:

- Month;
- Type of grade of accommodation establishment;
- Location of the accommodation establishment and overall expenditure on domestic tourism.

Latham (1989) argues that it is possible to generate additional data from such variables including length of stay, occupancy rate and average expenditure. Many countries also collate supplementary information beyond the minimum standards identified by WTO, where the socioeconomic characteristics of tourists are identified, together with their use of tourist transport and purpose of visit, though the cost of such data collection does mean that the statistical basis of domestic tourism in many less developed countries remains poor.

The methods used to generate domestic tourism statistics are normally based on the estimates of volume, value and scale derived from sample surveys due to the cost of undertaking large-scale surveys of tourist activities. The immediate problem facing the user of such material is the type of errors and degree of accuracy which can be attached to such data. For example, Latham (1989) identifies the following sample surveys which are now used to supplement data derived from hotel records:

- *Household surveys,* where the residents of a country are interviewed in their own home to ascertain information of tourist trips for the purpose of pleasure. A useful example of a pan-European study is the EC Omnibus study. Even so, little progress has been made internationally to collate common data on household surveys since the OECD's attempt in 1967 to outline the types of data which national travel surveys should collect.
- *Destination surveys,* where high levels of tourist activity occur in a region or resort. Such studies frequently compile statistics on accommodation usage, sample surveys of visitors and may be linked to existing knowledge derived from household surveys.
- *En route surveys,* where tourists are surveyed en route to examine the characteristics and features of tourists. Although it is a convenient way to interview a captive audience depending upon the mode of transport used, the results may not necessarily be as representative without a complete knowledge of the transport flows for the mode of tourist transport being surveyed.

The problem of incomplete questionnaires or non-response may occur where such surveys require a respondent to post the form back to the surveyor.

INTERNATIONAL TOURISM STATISTICS

The two principal organisations which collate data on international tourism are the World Tourism Organisation (WTO) and the Organisation for Economic Cooperation and Development (OECD). In addition, international regional tourism organisations such as the Pacific Asia Travel Association and the ASEAN Tourism Working Group also collect international tourism statistics. Page (1994b) reviews the major publications of the first two organisations in relation to international tourism, noting the detailed contents of each.

In the case of the WTO, the main source is the *Yearbook of Tourism Statistics*, which contains a summary of the most salient tourism statistics for almost 150 countries and territories. In the case of the OECD, their *Tourism Policy and International Tourism* (referred to as the 'Blue Book') is less comprehensive, covering only 25 countries, but it does contain most of the main generating and receiving areas. While the main thrust of the publication is government policy and the obstacles to international tourism, it does expand on certain areas not covered in the WTO publication.

In contrast to domestic tourism, statistics on international tourism are normally collected to assess the impact of tourism on a country's balance of payments, though as Withyman (1985:69) argued: Outward visitors seem to attract less attention from the pollsters and the enumerators. Of course, one country's outward visitor is another country's (perhaps several countries) inward visitor, and a much more welcome sort of visitor, too, being both a source of revenue and an emblem of the destination country's appeal in the international market. This has meant that governments have tended to be generally more keen to measure inward than outward tourism, or at any rate, having done so, to publish the results.

This statement indicates that governments are more concerned with the direct effect of tourism on their balance of payments. Yet such statistics are also utilised by marketing arms of national tourism organisations to base their decisions on who to target in international campaigns. The wider tourism industry also makes use of such data as part of their strategic planning and for more immediate purposes where niche markets exist. Even so, Shackleford (1980) argued that the collection of tourism statistics should be a responsibility of the state to meet international standards for data collection (WTO 1996). However, it is increasingly the case that only when the economic benefits of data collection can be justified will national governments continues to compile tourism statistics.

Where resource constraints exist, the collection and compilation of tourism statistics may be impeded. This also raises important methodological issues related to what exactly is being measured. As Withyman (1985:61) argued: 'In the jungle of international travel and tourism statistics, it behoves the explorer to step warily; on all sides there is luxuriant growth. Not all data sources are what they appear to be - after close scrutiny some show themselves to be inconsistent and often unsuitable for the industry researcher and planner.'

The key point Withyman (1985) recognises is the lack of comparability in tourism data in relation to what is measured (e.g. is it visitor days or visitor nights?) and the procedures and methodology used to measure international tourism. Frechtling (1976) concluded that the approaches taken by national and international agencies associated with international tourism statistics were converging towards common definitions of trip, travel and traveller. Yet the principal difficulty which continues to be associated with this is whether business travel should be considered as a discrete activity in relation to tourism. Chadwick (1994:75) notes that 'the consensus of North American opinion seems to be that, despite certain arguments to the contrary ... business travel should be considered part of travel and tourism'. While BarOn (1984) examines the standard definitions and terminology of international tourism as used by the UN and WTO, research by Ngoh (1985) is useful in that it considers the practical problems posed by such definitions when attempting to measure international tourism and find solutions to the difficulties. Latham (1989) suggests that the main types of international tourism statistics collated relate to:

- Volume of tourists;
- Expenditure by tourists;
- The profile of the tourist and their trip characteristics.

As is true of domestic tourism, estimates form the basis for most statistics on international tourism since the method of data collection does not generate exact data. For example, volume statistics are often generated from counts of tourists at entry/exit points (i.e. gateways such as airports and ports) or at accommodation. But such data relate to numbers of trips rather than individual tourists since one tourist may make more than one trip a year and each trip is counted separately. In the case of expenditure statistics, tourist expenditure normally refers to tourist spending within a country and excludes payments to tourist-transport operators.

Yet deriving such statistics is often an indirect measure based on foreign currency estimates derived from bank records, from data provided by tourism service providers or more commonly from social surveys undertaken directly with tourists. Research by White and Walker (1982) and Baretje (1982) directly questions the validity and accuracy of such methods of data collection, examining the main causes of bias and error in such studies. According to Edwards (1991:68-9), 'expenditure and receipts data apart, tourist statistics are usually collected in one of the five following ways':

- Counts of all individuals entering or leaving the country at all recognised frontier crossings, often using arrival/departure cards where high-volume arrivals/departures are the norm. Where particularly large volumes of tourist traffic exist, a 10 per cent sampling framework is normally used (i.e. every tenth arrival/ departure card). Countries such as New Zealand actually match the arrival/departure cards, or a sample, to examine the length of stay.
- Interviews carried out at frontiers with a sample of arriving and/or departing passengers to obtain a more detailed profile of visitors and their activities within the country. This will often require a careful sample design to gain a sufficiently large enough sample with the detail required from visitors on a wide range of tourism data including places visited, expenditure, accommodation usage and related items.

- Selecting a sample of arrivals and providing them with a self-completion questionnaire to be handed in or posted. This method is used in Canada but it fails to incorporate those visitors travelling via the United States by road.
- Sample surveys of the entire population of a country including travellers and non-travellers, though the cost of obtaining a representative sample is often prohibitive.
- Accommodation arrivals and nights spent are recorded by hoteliers and owners of the accommodation types covered. The difficulty with this type of data collection is that accommodation

As a government-sponsored survey which began in 1961, the International Passenger Survey now covers all ports of entry/exit to the UK. It is based on a stratified random sample of tourists arriving and departing from the UK by air and sea. According to Latham (1989:64), IPS' four principal aims are:

- To collect data for the travel account (which acts to compare expenditure by overseas visitors to the UK with expenditure overseas by visitors from the UK) of the balance of payments;
- To provide detailed information on foreign visitors to the UK, and on outgoing visitors travelling overseas.
- To provide data on international migration.
- To provide information on routes used by passengers as an aid to aviation and shipping authorities.

owners have no incentive to record accurate details, particularly where the tax regime is based on the turnover of bed-nights.

The final area of data collection is profile statistics, which examine the characteristics and travel habits of visitors. For example, the UK's International Passenger Survey (IPS) is one survey that incorporates volume, expenditure and profile data on international tourism.

METHODOLOGICAL ISSUES

Latham (1989) reviews the major types of questionnaire/social survey type of data collection used for tourism statistics. He reports that among state-sponsored tourism research in the United States, conversion studies are a popular method to examine and evaluate advertising campaigns and visitor surveys, to assess a sample of visitors to individual states. The use of other methods of data collection are also discussed (e.g. diary questionnaires, participant observation and personal interviews). Yet few studies consider the issue of sampling, sample design and the sources of error which may arise from such surveys.

In fact the lack of research on the reliability of the estimate from a sample survey (the standard error) is rarely discussed in most tourism surveys. In many cases, large tourism surveys focus on the logistics of drawing the sample and the bias which may be reflected in the results. Therefore, any tourism survey will need to pay careful attention to the statistical and mathematical accuracy of the survey, especially the survey design and the effect it may have on the results, a feature which is discussed in great detail by Ryan (1995). Ryan (1995) provides an excellent review of survey design, questionnaire design, sampling and also an insight into the statistical techniques to use for different forms of tourism data. As a result it serves as an important reference point for issues of methodology and the technical issues associated with the statistical analysis of tourism data. Without reiterating the excellent features of Ryan's findings, it is appropriate to consider some of the main accuracy problems associated with the collection of domestic and international tourism statistics.

PROBLEMS OF ACCURACY

Ryan (1995) argues that errors in data collection can lead to errors in data analysis. Among the most frequently cited problems associated with domestic and international tourism statistics are:

- The methods by which the data are collected, which are influenced by administrative, bureaucratic and legislative factors in each country;
- Sample sizes which are too small and lead to unacceptable sampling errors and in some instances where the sample design is flawed;
- The procedures for collecting tourism statistics are not adhered to by the agency collecting the data.

In addition, Edwards (1991:68) argues that a 'fourth potential reason - arithmetic mistakes and data processing errors - only occasionally produce significant errors'. In fact, Edwards (1991:68) supports the cause of 'tourist statisticians [who] are both knowledgeable and conscientious, but are having to work with tools which they know could produce inaccurate or misleading data', concluding that for any set of tourist data, potential sources of error obviously depend on the method of collection employed. This, in turn, tends to be largely determined by the legislative and administrative framework and by the financial and manpower resources available.

In the case of tourist expenditure and receipts data, organisations such as the International Monetary Fund (IMF) issue guidelines for the compilation of balance of payments statistics. But errors may occur where leakage results from tourist services paid for in overseas bank accounts and in extreme cases, where a black market exists in currency exchange. Edwards (1991) suggests that a regular programme of interviews with departing tourists and returning residents may assist in estimating levels of expenditure.

Despite the apparent problems which may exist with tourism statistics, Edwards (1991:72) argues that data on arrivals and nights spent for most destinations outside of Europe appear reasonably reliable. Within Europe, data for both inbound and outbound travel are fairly satisfactory for the UK. Greece, Portugal, Spain and [the former] Yugoslavia all appear to have usable frontier arrivals data. The most serious problems are in core continental

European countries such as France, Germany, Italy and the Netherlands for which there are no adequate volumetric measures of travel in either direction. Accommodation arrivals and nights data are clearly gross understatements for many European countries ... often expenditure and receipts data appear better indicators. Outside Europe, the major problems are also in relation to high volume land flows, as between Canada and the USA (in both directions), from the USA to Mexico and from Hong Kong to China.

Therefore, in view of these potential constraints, Edwards (1991) advocates that researchers should compile a range of data from different sources which will not only highlight the deficiencies in various sources, but also extend the existing baseline data. Although Edwards (1991) provides guidelines for comparative tourism research using a range of data for different countries, trends in tourism data remain one of the main requirements for travel industry organisations.

Edwards (1991:73) lists key issues to consider in examining tourism trends (i.e. Have arrivals or accommodation data been changed in coverage or definition? Have provisional data for earlier years been subsequently revised? Has the reliability of the data changed and how are changing tastes in travel products affecting the statistics?). Even so, the analysis of trends remains the fundamental starting point for most research studies in tourism. Having considered the issues associated with how tourism statistics are generated, attention now turns to the ways in which geographers analyse such statistics, and variations in tourism activity at different scales.

PATTERNS OF TOURISM

D.G. Pearce's (1995a) seminal study on the geographer's analysis of tourism patterns offers an excellent synthesis reflecting his international contribution to the methodological development of spatial analysis of tourism. By using geographical methodologies and concepts, D.G. Pearce (1995a) uses statistical sources and primary data on tourist activity patterns to analyse the processes and patterns associated with the dynamics of domestic and international tourist activity. This section can only provide a limited evaluation of the geographer's approach to analysis of the presentation of spatially oriented insights on modern-day tourism demand.

The WTO provides the main source of data for international tourism, collated from a survey of major government agencies responsible for data collection. While most international tourists are expressed as 'frontier arrivals' (i.e. arrivals determined by means of a frontier check), arrival/ departure cards (where used) offer additional detail to the profile of international tourists, and where they are not used periodic tourism surveys are often employed. WTO statistics are mainly confined to all categories of travellers, and in some cases geographical disaggregation of the data may be limited by the collecting agency's use of descriptions and categories for aid of simplicity (e.g. rest of the world) rather than listing all categories of arrivals.

In terms of the growth of international travel, documents the expansion of outbound travel with constant growth in the 1960s in an age of discovery of outbound travel for many developed nations. The late 1960s saw international travel expanded by new technology in air travel (e.g. the introduction of the Boeing 747 jumbo jet and the 737 as well as the DC10) which led to rapid growth until the oil crisis in the early 1970s.

Growth rates varied in the 1980s, with 'shock waves' to the upward trend being caused by events such as the Gulf Crisis, but international travel has maintained strong growth rates, often in excess of 5 per cent per annum. In contrast, international receipts from travel have outperformed arrivals, with consistent rates of growth (with the exception of the oil crisis and Gulf Crisis) of 10 to 20 per cent which is indicative of the powerful economic effect of tourism for countries. However, China is the notable success story in terms of growth in receipts while a number of European destinations (e.g. the Netherlands and Belgium) have retained the volume of arrivals but their ranking of expenditure has dropped.

As the world's largest tourism markets by expenditure, the USA and Germany have retained their prominence in the top two rankings, whereas Japan has increased its importance as an outbound high spending market as have a number of other Pacific Rim nations such as Taiwan, Singapore and South Korea until the 1997 Asian financial crisis (Hall and Page 2000). As a result of the growth of major outbound growth and travel within the Pacific Rim region, a case study of the outbound South Korean market is now examined.

CASE STUDY: TOURISM DEMAND IN EAST ASIA PACIFIC: THE CASE OF THE SOUTH KOREAN OUTBOUND MARKET AND ACTIVITY PATTERNS IN NEW ZEALAND

Prior to the Asian financial crisis, Korea represented one of the major outbound markets in the Asia-Pacific region. Outbound travel grew from 484,000 in 1985 to 725,000 in 1988 to 3.1 million in 1994, which quadrupled in a six-year period up to 1994. By 1995, outbound travel had reached 3.8 million, representing 9 per cent of the national population of 45 million.

Within New Zealand, inbound Korean arrivals increased consistently between 1989 and 1995 as the fastest growing market and remained the focus of industry attention until the Asian financial crisis (New Zealand Tourism Board 1995), despite any substantive and detailed research to consider the needs, aspirations and impact of this market in New Zealand.

Holiday travel has remained a major reason to visit, while females outnumbered males in holiday travel by 54.4 per cent: 45.66 per cent in 1994 and VFR by 63.5 per cent: 36.5 per cent, highlighting the trend towards housewives comprising the majority of outbound female visitors. Male visitors dominated in the purpose of visiting in relation to business travel (91 per cent), to attend a convention (87.7 per cent) and official travel (91.3 per cent).

The age profile of the most common outbound Korean tourist was the 31 to 40 age group followed by the 21 to 30 age group, with a significant proportion of 'honeymooners' and single female office workers. According to the 1994 Nationals Overseas Travel Survey, shopping was a major leisure activity for Korean tourists, with an average spends of US$413 per person on purchases such as cosmetics, alcoholic beverages, electronic goods, clothing and toys. McGahey (1996) observed that 40 per cent of these purchases were for gifts.

THE KOREAN INBOUND MARKET IN NEW ZEALAND

According to New Zealand's International Visitor Survey (New Zealand Touri7sm Board 1995), the Korean market was estimated to have generated NZ$225 million of spending at 1995 prices, equating to an average spend of NZ$2253 per person of NZ$345 a day, the highest amount for any inbound market. In the 12 months ended March 1996, Koreans comprised 8 per cent of New Zealand's international visitor market, increasing from 2,018 in 1987 to 4,184 visitors in 1990 to 61,583 in 1994. The significance of this market was reflected in the New Zealand Tourist Board's (1995) optimistic forecasts for a further doubling of visitor arrivals over the next five years and a target of 114,000 arrivals. However, the size of the impact of the Asian financial crisis on Korea can be illustrated by the 78 per cent drop in Korean visitors to New Zealand in December 1997 compared with the previous year, with there being an expected 75 per cent drop in arrivals from South Korea in 1998 over the previous year.

In contrast to the age profile of the entire Korean tourist outbound market, the main age group of visitors to New Zealand was dominated by the visitors aged 45 to 64 years, predominately those aged 55 to 64. Yet among those visitors aged under 24 years, females outnumber males as unmarried office workers or tertiary level students are more likely to travel than their male counter-parts, since the former enjoy relatively more leisure time.

Since group travel tends to predominate among the inbound Korean market, the length of stay in New Zealand was conditioned by two key factors. First, it is a medium long-haul destination, and second, Korean holiday entitlement was still limited to under ten paid days a year and is not available in one block. Therefore, the maximum length of stay for most outbound Korean tourists was less than one week. According to research (New Zealand Tourism Board 1995), Korean tourists perceived the main appeal of visiting New Zealand as its unspoiled natural phenomena such as hot springs in Rotorua and volcanic areas such as Mount Tongariro.

This reflects the limited spatial activity patterns which most inbound Korean tourists were likely to experience, typically including arrival and departure through Auckland International Airport, with time spent in Auckland, Rotorua, Waitomo Caves, Taupo and returning to Auckland. The following results report the findings of a survey to understand the interrelationship between the time constraints of Korean inbound travel and the spatial distribution of such visitors beyond the limited knowledge base derived from the 442 Korean tourists included in the New Zealand International Visitor Survey of 1995/1996.

KOREAN TOURISTS' ACTIVITY PATTERNS IN NEW ZEALAND

Using a time budget methodology, a survey in July 1996 was employed to produce a systematic record of a person's use of time over a given period to hereby understand the sequence, timing and duration of the tourist's activities in relation to the location of the activities. The technique provides a systematic record of a person's use of time over a given period, typically for a short period ranging from a single day to a week.

One of the fundamental assumptions in using this research method is that tourist behaviour and activities are the result of choices, a point illustrated by Floor (1990). D.G. Pearce (1987a) argues that there has been a comparative neglect of tourist activities by tourist researchers, compounded by the lack of available data. Where questionnaire surveys have addressed such issues, the results have often failed to provide a comprehensive assessment of tourist activities, both formal/informal and the relative importance of each.

Thrift (1977) provides an assessment of three principal constraints on tourists' daily activity patterns, which are:

- *Comparability constraints* (e.g. the biologically based need for food and sleep);
- *Coupling constraints* (e.g. people need to interact and undertake activities with other people);
- *Authority constraints* (e.g. where activities are controlled, not allowed or permitted at a certain point in time).

Thus both Chapin (1974) and Thrift (1977) identify choices and constraints which will influence the specific activities and context of tourists' daily activities. The use of time budgets via diaries to record tourists' activity patterns has been employed in a number of contexts as research by Gaviria (1975), Cooper (1981), P.L. Pearce (1981), D.G. Pearce (1986) and Debbage (1991) indicates. Methodological issues raised by these studies highlight the problem of selecting appropriate temporal measures to record tourists' activities.

P.L. Pearce (1981) used three main time periods (morning, afternoon and evening) with Gaviria (1975) selecting quarter-hour periods and Cooper (1981) using five time sequences. While the recording of activities by time is a demanding activity for tourists, D.G. Pearce (1986) argues that the main methodological concerns for such surveys are the type of technique to be used; the period to be covered; and the type of sample selected. In addition, Chapin (1984) argues that such studies may choose to use three main survey techniques, which are:

- *A checklist technique,* where respondents select the list of activities they engage in from a pre-categorised list;

- *The yesterday technique,* where subjects are asked to list things they did the previous day, where and when they did them;
- *The tomorrow technique,* where participants keep a diary on what they do, where and when they undertake them.

Although time budget studies may still be viewed as experimental in tourism research, they do offer great potential to gain a detailed insight into tourist activity patterns.

THE SURVEY

During three weeks in July 1996, a time budget survey was developed using the 'yesterday technique' and the time sequencing technique advocated by P.L. Pearce (1981) as part of a more detailed survey of inbound Korean tourists. The complete survey was designed to be completed by Korean tourists during their tour of the North Island of New Zealand and four sites were selected as distribution points for the surveys during the tourists' initial familiarisation point of their tour in Auckland and Rotorua. Two major hotels and two Korean restaurants were selected to provide a degree of close contract with Korean tourists in a familiar environment. Due to the highly organised nature of the Korean itineraries, a one-page diary was distributed at the key sites over a three-week period.

One immediate problem facing the use of the budget approach was in soliciting responses. While a Korean researcher approached the respondents on a random basis, it was essential to keep the survey to one A4 page to encourage participation.

As a result, only time-budget questions could be included and key demographic data were omitted (a separate survey by the authors was undertaken examining demand issues among Korean tourists which did consider the profile of visitors). However, from participant observation conducted during the data collection, it is apparent that the sample of 78 tourists who were prepared to participate in the time budget exercise were typical of the Korean tourist then visiting New Zealand, being largely aged 31 to 50, being of middle-class status, earning between NZ$40,000 and $60,000 a year and undertaking a multi-destination product.

ACTIVITY PATTERNS OF KOREAN TOURISTS

According to D.G. Pearce (1995a), few data are collected to examine circuit tourism which this market is following, since they adhere to a predetermined circuit pattern. Data exist in a New Zealand context on the touring patterns of international tourists which builds on Forer and Pearce's (1984) innovative study of coach tours by nights spent at key nodes and inter-regional flows.

Forer and Pearce (1984) established the Auckland to Rotorua and Taupo axis by examining tour group itineraries for package tours. While it is apparent that a great deal of continuity and similarity exists in terms of the Korean tour group itineraries which follow a series of linear routes, activity patterns of the tour groups and their specific time budgets remain largely unresearched. One immediate feature which emerges from the 78 completed schedules is that the activity patterns of the visitors closely follow the tour itineraries.

The respondents were undertaking three commonly used itineraries developed by tour companies which comprised:

- *Itinerary* 1: Auckland to Rotorua and return to Rotorua (12 tourists).
- *Itinerary* 2: Auckland to Rotorua and Waitomo Caves and return to Auckland (39 tourists).
- *Itinerary* 3: Auckland to Rotorua and Waitomo Caves to Taupo and return to Auckland.

Both itinerary 1 and 2 record only a limited amount of free time, being the shortest tour schedules among inbound visitors to New Zealand. The typical itinerary commences at 07:00 and finishes at 18:00 to 19:00 hours, with sightseeing comprising the major activity (30 to 32 per cent), undertaken over two nights and three days.

During the 53 to 59-hour period, respondents spent their time:

- Sleeping (33 per cent);
- Touring (30 per cent);
- Free time (14 per cent);
- Transfers (12 per cent);
- Eating/meals (11 per cent).

On the basis of these results, three types of Korean tourists could be identified based on time budget research by Ashworth and Dietvorst (1995):

- *Organised sightseeing oriented visitors,* who comprise the large majority of visitors, with a city tour in a chartered coach during the day, interspersed with shopping before or after meals and a limited amount of free time spent walking around attractions and taking photographs. Evenings were spent at the accommodation base to rest after the day's activities.
- *Shopping and conviviality oriented tourists,* where shopping activities were conducted near to the accommodation base in the morning. The age profile of this group was younger (typically under 40 years of age), in search of specialist markets, tourist attractions and not venturing far from the accommodation base. In the evening, this group spent their leisure time at a wide variety of fun-related facilities (e.g. at a pub, gambling at the Casino in Auckland or at a night-club). In Rotorua, this group spent most of their free time at Korean pubs in the central tourist district.
- *Health and sports oriented tourists,* comprising the majority of the senior group (aged 50-plus) and a number of business travellers who pursued largely 'private' leisure activities. While no 'typical' activity patterns could be discerned during the day, with some preferring walking or going shopping, the time spent on these activities was much less than the two former groups. In the afternoons, sports

activities dominated (e.g. golf and fishing) and in the early evening they frequented health facilities followed by relaxation for the remaining part of the evening.

While the results from the Korean case study indicate that removal of travel restrictions in 1989 has significantly increased outbound travel, there were significant 'pull' factors promoting Korean travel to New Zealand (e.g. immigration policy, no-visas agreement, new air services and 15,000 Korean residents living in Auckland promoting VFR traffic) which can be related to the motivational literature and the unique attractions available in New Zealand. The analysis of tourist activity patterns shows that in urban areas, Korean visitors do not venture far from their accommodation base. This limits the flow and distribution of visitors, with a tendency for bunching and concentration at key nodes around Auckland, Rotorua and Taupo.

Concerns over a saturation of tourists at key attraction sites accentuates the problem of managing the geographical patterns of this short and concentrated experience of New Zealand tourism. Many attractions are unable to cope with the arrival of large numbers of tour groups simultaneously, as this highly organised and almost regimented form of tourism is posing significant strains on the visiting infrastructure.

In this respect, a spatial analysis of activity patterns and time budgets illustrates not only the shape of existing demand, determined by tour operators and group leaders, but also the geographical interaction and time constraints under which these tourists visit New Zealand have clear spatial implications for the type of tourism experience they require in time and space.

- Developing tourism from new markets in East Asia Pacific highlighted the fickle nature of tourism as an economic activity: a currency crisis led the Korean outbound market to New Zealand to decline dramatically.
- Packaged tourist itineraries have a strong influence on the activity patterns of tourist groups. This conditions the geographical patterns of consumption in time and space for tour groups.
- Even within tour groups, time budget research identified the diversity of motivations in relation to the reasons for undertaking a tour.
- Within urban areas, the Korean visitor has a tightly defined spatial search area which constrains the flow and distribution of their activities in time and space.
- Specific research tools such as time budget surveys, when linked to spatial patterns of activity, can yield a great deal of important information for tourism planners and commercial operators about the tourists' use of time and space.

PATTERNS OF DOMESTIC TOURISM

According to the WTO, domestic tourism is estimated to be up to ten times greater in volume than international tourism and yet comparatively little research has been undertaken on this neglected area of tourism activity. D.G. Pearce (1995a: 67) argues that this may be attributed 'to the less visible nature of much domestic tourism, which is often more informal and less structured than international tourism, and a consequent tendency by many government agencies, researchers and others to regard it as less significant'.

This problem of neglect is compounded by a paucity of data, since it is not a straightforward matter of recording arrivals and departures. It requires an analysis of tourism patterns and flows at different spatial scales to consider spatial interaction of tourists between a multitude of possible origin and destination areas within a country as well as a detailed understanding of inter-regional flows.

Where government agencies and other public sector organisations undertake data collection of domestic tourism 'the results are not often directly comparable, limiting the identification of general patterns and trends'. For this reason, the innovative research undertaken by D.G. Pearce (1993b) is worthy of attention here since it comprises one of the few systematic analysis of domestic tourism in a country, which in this case is New Zealand.

As D.G. Pearce (1995a: 67) rightly acknowledges, 'there are still few examples of comprehensive inter-regional studies where the analysis is based on a complete matrix of both original and destination regions ... [since] few appropriate and reliable sets of tourism statistics exist which might be used to construct such a matrix'. Nationwide surveys are undertaken which are weighted to reflect the population base. One of the few comprehensive studies which yielded an origin-destination matrix is the somewhat dated New Zealand Domestic Travel Survey (NZDTS), established in 1983 (New Zealand Tourism Board 1991a) and recently updated.

THE NEW ZEALAND DOMESTIC TOURISM SURVEY

Domestic tourism data are harder to collect than those for international visitors, simply because no frontiers are crossed or formal registers required. Domestic travel estimates can thus only be made by factoring up from representative surveys of the population. As with all surveys, sample size and representativeness are critical, so that a manageable (and affordable) sample size of a thousand or so will give reasonably accurate figures for national trends but is useless at a regional level. The domestic travel surveys of the 1980s carried out by the NZTP were based on a sample of 12,000 interviews.

This gave confidence limits of +/" 0.9 per cent at the 95 per cent level and so was extremely reliable for national estimates. Even so, the authors of the research noted that potential error limits increase very quickly as sample sizes reduce and particular care should be taken in interpreting results for small subgroups of the sample. They went on to remind us that when a large proportion is being sampled and the sample result is projected, the sampling error is magnified also, and that a sampling error may run into very large numbers when expressed as a projection, even though, expressed as a percentage, it may appear to be quite small. The implication of this is that even regional statistics derived from a national survey may be quite inaccurate.

In 1999, New Zealanders are estimated to have made 16.6 million trips with at least one night away, comprising a total of 52.9 million nights; they spent NZ$4.1 billion on overnight trips. In addition, they made 44.3 million day trips of more than 40 km each way and spent a further NZ$2.8 billion on them (Forsyte Research 2000). As well as easily equalling the expenditure of international tourists, albeit in local currency, domestic travellers provide the essential base for most tourism infrastructure.

These domestic tourism figures were derived from a major 1999 study carried out by Forsyte Research on contract to the former Public Good Science Fund. The primary focus of the research was to determine the direct economic impact of domestic tourism in New Zealand. A secondary objective was to measure domestic travel patterns for both overnight and day trips for 1999, to a level that allowed regional analysis.

This was the first study of its scale since the last of the domestic travel survey series, noted above, carried out by AGB McNair in 1989/90 and the first to measure day trips in addition to overnight trips. Prior to this, the only recent research was a pilot survey carried out by Simmons (1997). The Forsyte sample was substantial, at 17,037, and provides high-grade data.

In all, almost 70 per cent of domestic travel in New Zealand was to the North Island, or within it. Canterbury, and then Otago, were the major destinations in the South Island. Regional flows, in net person nights, show a more interesting picture. The North Island is a net exporter of some two and a half million person nights to the South. Within the North Island, Auckland and Wellington are the main deficit regions, exporting a total of almost nine million person nights. The major beneficiaries are Northland, Waikato and the Bay of Plenty. In the South Island, the main beneficiaries are Otago and Nelson, followed by Marlborough and the West Coast. Canterbury is the only deficit region.

About half of all travel (46 per cent) is for holidays and leisure, with an average duration of 3.8 nights, and one-third (35 per cent and 2.9 nights) for visiting friends and relatives; a further 12 per cent is business travel, with an average stay of 2.5 nights. Of course, the economic impacts will not fall in direct proportion to the type of travel. Accommodation used is, overwhelmingly, the private home of a friend or relative or a borrowed second home. Motels are the commonest form of commercial accommodation with a total of 14 per cent; hotels attract only 7 per cent, many of whom would be business travellers (Forsyte Research 2000; Hall and Kearsley 2002).

Overall patterns of expenditure are split between the two islands broadly proportionately to visitor numbers, but the average amount spent per night varies considerably by region, with Wellington and Auckland the highest and

Northland, Gisborne and Marlborough the lowest. As a result, Auckland has the largest total receipts at over NZ$700 million, followed by Waikato, Wellington and Canterbury. In total, the North Island receives almost NZ$2.8 billion and the South NZ$1.29 billion.

Even the least earning region, Gisborne, receives nearly NZ$47 million, although in Gisborne's case there is a small net outflow. In terms of regional flows of income, the North Island is an exporter of money, to the value of NZ$212 million, to the South. Auckland shows the largest net deficit by far ("NZ$453 million). In the South Island, every region is a net beneficiary, so that domestic tourism is a major economic sector and a powerful agent of income redistribution on a regional basis. In aggregate, a quarter of all expenditure is on accommodation and just over a quarter is on food.

Shopping of all types consumes one-fifth of expenditure, while transport, recreation and alcohol account for about 10 per cent each. Business travel is getting on for three times the cost of other trips per night, and is heavily weighted towards travel and accommodation costs when compared with other sectors, both proportionately and in real terms. VFR travel is slightly more demanding of travel expenditure than are holidays, but accommodation costs, not surprisingly, are considerably less.

The analysis of behavioural issues in recreational and tourism research indicates that 'in behavioural terms then, there seems little necessity to insist on a major distinction between tourism and leisure phenomena. Therefore, it should follow that a greater commonality between the research efforts in the two areas would be of advantage' although different social theoretical approaches exist towards the analysis of recreation and tourism phenomena. As a result, Moore *et al.* (1995:79) conclude that 'there is little need, if any, to take a dramatically different approach to the behavioural analysis of tourism and leisure'.

One needs to view each activity in the context of the everyday life of the people involved to understand how each is conceived. There is a clear distinction within the literature between what motivates recreationalists and tourists, and comparative studies of similar groups of people and the similarities and differences between these motivations has yet to permeate the research literature. While geographers have focused on recreational and tourist behaviour in relation to demand issues, the analysis has largely been quantitative, site specific, and has not adapted a comparative methodology to examine the recreation-tourism continuum.

3

Attitudes and Job Evaluation

JOB ANALYSIS AND JOB DESCRIPTION

Job analysis is the systematic process of gathering information regarding the duties required of a job and the human characteristics necessary to successfully perform those duties. The work products of job analysis are job descriptions, which describe the job, and job specifications, which describe what kind of person to hire for the job. Job analysis can be described as the foundation of human resource management because it the basis for so many HR programmatic activities.

Job analysis is used for:

- *Recruitment:* Provides information about the nature of the job to guide recruitment activities
- *Selection:* Provides information on the knowledge, skills, and abilities required of persons that can successfully perform the job
- *Training Provides:* information regarding the tasks to be performed and the skills and knowledge required in order to guide the development of training programmes
- *Performance Evaluation:* Provides information on the level of proficiency of various tasks that are required in order to develop performance standards
- *Compensation:* Provides information necessary to evaluate the internal worth of the job to the organization and to compare it with jobs in the relevant job market in order to determine appropriate wage and benefit levels
- *EEO compliance:* Forms the basis for determining whether employment practices and decisions are job-related

The SPHR should be familiar with a number of concepts regarding the process of job analysis. Discussed in the following sections are:

- Job analysis process
- Job analysis information requirements
- Data collection methods

- Writing job descriptions and job specifications
- Competencies and the future of job analysis

The Job Analysis Process

Job analysis can be described as a six-step process as follows:

1. *Determine the purpose for conducting job analysis:* The purpose should be clearly linked to organizational success and the organizational strategic plan. A frequent reason for conducting job analysis projects is that jobs are much more dynamic than ever before. Technology and the demands of a competitive environment frequently change the nature of the job requiring reevaluation. Rapid organizational growth often means new types of jobs requiring job descriptions. High turnover or low job satisfaction might be other indicators of the need for job analysis projects. High turnover might indicate that jobs are not properly priced in relation to the external job market. Because job analysis drives compensation decisions, old job analysis results might need to be updated. Low job satisfaction is often the result of boring or repetitive jobs. Job analysis can identify new ways to design jobs to make them more interesting and challenging.
2. *Identify the jobs to be analyzed:* After the purpose is identified, it provides some indication as to which jobs should be included in the job analysis. Often, however, time and resource constraints limit the total number of jobs that can be included in the process. For example, if the organization as a whole is experiencing turnover, that data should be analyzed to determine the particular departments in which the problem seems to be the worst. That analysis indicates the direction for the project. The same is true if the organization is growing or experiencing significant change in only certain areas. Those are the jobs that are most appropriate for job analysis.

   When a large number of employees encumber the same job, a determination must be made as to how many of the positions will be included in the project. Statistical sampling might be appropriate if the number is large.

   This is also the time in the project in which communication with both employees and managers begins to take place. They should be advised as to the purpose of the project and provided a general overview of the process.
3. *Review relevant background data:* Efficient and effective job analysis often builds from previous work and data that are already corrected. A review of current job descriptions and organizational charts provides basic information with which to begin the project. Analysis of workflow assists in understanding the responsibilities of the job and how it fits into the total work process.

4. *Plan and execute the job analysis project:* Planning is the key to successful projects. The appropriate data-gathering methodologies must be determined and an action plan developed as to project activities and milestones. Data collection methods are covered in the next section.
5. *Write the job description and job specifications:* After the data are collected and analyzed, they must be turned into the written work outputs, job descriptions, and job specifications. Before these documents are finalized, they should be reviewed with a representative sample of both the affected employees and their managers. If modifications to the documents are required, they should be made and the appropriate final approvals obtained.
6. *Periodic review:* It is good HR practice to engage in a planned process of periodic review of job descriptions and job specifications. Many organizations use a revolving process, reviewing a portion of the organization each year so that the entire organization is reviewed in a cycle—usually three, four, or five years. During the review, managers in that portion of the organization under review are required to verify the accuracy of the job descriptions and job specifications. If managers indicate job descriptions are out of date, those descriptions are included in the job analysis review. In addition, a random sample of jobs is also included for review.

Job Analysis Information Requirements

The job analysis process requires the collection of sufficient information to fully understand the job, its functions, and how it fits in both the workflow and organizational structure of the organization to produce the job description and job specifications.

The following information is representative of the types of data collected during the job analysis process:

- *Work activities:* Information must be collected on the tasks performed by the job and what is to be accomplished (work outputs). The data should include how, why, and when the activity is performed.
- *Worker activities:* These data include worker behaviours such as decision-making, communicating, and performing physical actions such as lifting heavy weights.
- *Machines, tools, and equipment:* Data here include information regarding the types of equipment that are used in the job. This might include computers, safety equipment, machines, and other devices that facilitate accomplishment of the work.
- *Job-related tangible and intangibles:* Information is required on the types of materials used and the products made or services rendered. In addition, information is needed on the type of knowledge dealt with (chemistry or accounting, for example).

- *Performance standards:* Information is needed about requirements for productivity and quality required for successful performance of the job. Work standards, production records, and so forth are collected.
- *Job context:* A wide variety of information is collected here. Examples include reporting relationships, type of employees supervised (if any), working conditions, financial incentives, and types of contacts the job has with other jobs and the purposes of those contacts.
- *Human requirements:* These include job-related knowledge and skills such as education, training, credentials, and work experience. In addition, information is needed on required personal attributes such as aptitudes, physical characteristics, and personality.

Data Collection Methods

Information regarding the tasks performed and the human characteristics needed to successfully perform them can be gathered in many ways.

The most common are as follows:

1. *Observation:* The observer watches the individual that is performing the job and takes notes as to what is occurring. The advantage of such an approach is that the individual doing the job analysis sees for him or herself exactly what is being done. However, there are several disadvantages. The first is that this method might be appropriate only for what are referred to as short-cycle jobs; that is, those that are repetitive in nature and in which the full range of job responsibilities is repeated at relatively short intervals. Otherwise, the observer is liable to miss some of the tasks that are essential to the job. Observation cannot really capture work that is not observable, such as decision-making, thinking, and analysis. Another issue is time. Observation methods are very time-consuming, and, thus, expensive to do. Some types of observation methods are

- *Time and motion studies:* These are normally performed by industrial engineers and involve determining the most efficient way to perform a particular task and the normal time required to do so. Time and motion studies can be used to not only develop job descriptions and job specifications, but also to develop piece rate compensation programmes.
- *Work sampling:* This process involves statistically sampling what is being done by the worker during random periods of the day. These are recorded and analyzed. This method is typically more efficient than continuous observation and is most appropriate for repetitive jobs.
- *Critical incidents:* Critical incidents are the recordation of positive and negative job performance. Critical incidents can be used to develop the job description and job specifications and also to develop the associated performance standards.

- *Employee logs:* The employee can observe him or herself by completing a diary or log, recording exactly what is being done at periodic intervals during the day. In addition to the obvious interruption of work, other issues associated with this method are that the employee might often forget to record activities and might indicate what he or she thinks should be done as opposed to exactly what is being done.

2. *Interviews:* The job analyst can interview the employee inquiring as exactly what activities are engaged and what knowledge, skills, and abilities are required. To cover all aspects of the job and provide a basis for analysis, good practice is to develop a standardized and structured interview protocol that is used in all interviews. Interviews provide in-depth information and might be appropriate when there are only a few persons occupying the job or when the data can be used to develop a survey instrument to be given to a larger number of employees. The disadvantage of using interviews is that they are very staff-intensive and can be costly.
3. *Questionnaires and checklists:* Surveys can be developed and given to a large number of employees. This is an efficient way of gathering data when a large number of individuals occupy the same job and when the employees are widely dispersed geographically. In addition, data gathered in this method can often be statistically analyzed.

   However, questionnaires are only as good as the questions they ask. Poorly developed questionnaires do not yield the data required to accurately prepare job descriptions and specifications. In addition, some employees might not have the literacy skills to properly complete the questionnaire, and others might purposefully answer the questions inaccurately. There are numerous off-the-shelf questionnaires and checklists that can be purchased from vendors or that are available from governmental agencies. Some of the more frequently used ones are:

   - *Position analysis questionnaire:* This is a specialized checklist, usually referred to as PAQ, which analyzes the job in six dimensions based on responses to nearly 200 questions. It can be used both for job analysis and job evaluation. The dimensions analyzed are
     i. Information input
     ii. Mental processes
     iii. Work output
     iv. Relationships with other persons
     v. Job context
     vi. Other job characteristics

- *Function job analysis:* Referred to as FJA, this is a comprehensive approach to job analysis that incorporates the goals of the organization, what workers do to achieve those goals, level and orientation of what the workers do, performance standards, and training content. The FJA evaluates the function of the job in three classifications: data, people, and things.
- *Management position description questionnaire:* This instrument is similar to the PAQ, but has been developed specifically to describe managerial jobs.
- *O Net Online:* This is a resource provided by the Department of Labour. It is a huge database, providing standardized job descriptions for a large number of jobs and incorporates the DOL's Dictionary of Occupational Titles.
- *Computer-based systems:* A huge number of computer-based job analysis systems can be obtained from a variety of vendors. These systems frequently contain large databases of descriptive statements that can be used to describe various tasks, based on responses to questions. These systems can often dramatically decrease the time required for job analysis and can facilitate decentralization of the process to management.
- *Multiple methods:* It is often good practice to use multiple methods of data collection. For example, interviews can often be used to develop a basic understanding of the job under evaluation and can be used to develop a questionnaire used to capture data from many employees. The data can then be analyzed and entered into another system prior to developing the job descriptions and job specifications. This often provides a deeper understanding of the job and more defensible job description and job specifications should either be an issue in a complaint process being heard before a third party.

  Job analysis data collection is extremely important in regard to compliance with the Americans with Disabilities Act. Analysis of the data must reveal what the essential functions (as opposed to marginal functions) of the job are. The essential functions, as previously discussed, are those that a disabled individual must be able to perform to be considered qualified for the job. Disqualification of an individual based on an inaccurate determination of the essential functions of the job might be a violation of the ADA.

Job Descriptions and Job Specifications

Job descriptions are written documents that describe the functions and working conditions of a job. Job specifications are the human characteristics necessary to successfully perform the job. Job specifications are typically a subsection of a job description. In general, federal law does not require job descriptions. One exception is employees that handle or dispose of certain types of hazardous chemicals.

However, job descriptions are desirable for a number of reasons:

- They assist employers in complying with the Americans with Disabilities Act and Fair Labour Standards Act as discussed earlier.
- They assist in compliance with antidiscrimination laws that require employment practices and decisions be job-related as they define the job.
- They assign work and document work assignments.
- They help clarify the mission through the types of work assigned.
- They provide the basis for developing training and performance evaluation programmes.

  Job descriptions should use action verbs to specifically describe the essential functions and duties. These descriptions should be logical, concise, and specific as to exactly what is to be done by the employee. It contains the following components, which are typically included in job descriptions:

- Identification section This section provides general information regarding the job including the job title, where the position is located in terms of geography, the department in which the job is located, whether the job is exempt or nonexempt under the Fair Labour Standards Act, the pay grade of classification of the job, the EEOC classification required for the EEO-1 report, and whether the job is included in the bargaining unit. In addition, this section often includes a job code or other identifying number used for identification in the human resource information system (HRIS). The HRIS might permit or require the entry of skill codes that identify the type of skills used in the job. If so, those codes are often placed in the identification section. Finally, the section might include information regarding the name of the individual that wrote the job description and job specifications and the name of the manager that approved them. The amount of information placed in this section depends on the needs of the organization and might range from merely identifying the job to a rather extensive section with large amounts of identifying information.
- Position summary This section is a concise statement indicating what the job does, why it exists, and what makes it different from other jobs. The statement is generally only one or two sentences.
- Essential functions This section is the meat of the job description and specifies clearly what the major functions of the job are. This is the most important section of the job description and the most difficult and time-consuming to write.

- Nonessential functions This section lists other duties of the job that are minor in nature. For the purposes of the ADA, these are the duties that could potentially be assigned elsewhere in the organization as a reasonable accommodation.
- Job specifications As previously stated, job specifications are normally included within the job description. This section should list the knowledge, skills, and abilities that a job incumbent should possess to perform the job successfully. Such characteristics as experience, education, and physical abilities are included in this section if they are requirements of the job. For example, "B.S. degree in biology," "two years of directly related experience," and "able to lift 100 pounds above the shoulders" are examples of explanatory statements that might be used in this section.
- Working conditions This section describes the environment in which the work is performed. Such issues as exposure to weather, fumes, heat or cold, noise, and so forth should be described in this section. If the job is not performed in a difficult environment, the conditions under which the work is performed should still be described. For example, "the work is performed in an office environment with no disagreeable conditions" might be appropriate in those situations.
- Disclaimers Many organizations put a variety of disclaimers in this section. These statements often include information that the management reserves the right to change the nature of the job and that the job description does not describe all tasks and responsibilities of the job. The purpose of these statements is to clarify that the employee might be required by management to perform other tasks. Often employers include this concept in a statement under the functions section using the terminology "other duties as assigned." However, the courts find this a bit problematic, especially if placed in the essential functions section, because the essential functions have to be clearly defined. A disclaimer section at the end of the job description is preferable. A final disclaimer often used is a statement to the effect that the job description does not constitute a contract for employment and may be changed at the discretion of the employer.

  A common error in writing job descriptions and job specifications is to base them on the person currently doing the job as opposed to what the actual requirements of the job are in terms of duties and human abilities. Incumbents often take on additional responsibilities and bring special skills to the job, neither of which is a requirement.

Future of Job Analysis

Job analysis, job specifications, and job descriptions meet the needs of organizations experiencing stable environments and stable markets. The process allows the organization to describe its jobs in relation to its mission and specify exactly what tasks must be performed to facilitate achievement of organizational goals. These processes are recognized by the court systems, which provide guidance through case law as to the characteristics of legally defensible activities. However, more and more frequently organizations are affected by a dynamic and volatile environment with rapidly changing technology, increased competition, and fluctuating customer demands. This has led to the "dejobbing of America."

Dejobbing refers to the fact that jobs often change every day and cannot be specifically described in the traditional ways. Increased competition has often resulted in a flattening of the traditional hierarchy, removing multiple layers of management. When this occurs, employees at the bottom of the organization often are required to manage themselves and are empowered to make decisions.

To be quickly adaptive to the market and customer wants, employees must be able to make instantaneous decisions and engage in a variety of new and innovative behaviours. The nature of work has often become one of teams, projects, and task forces, requiring new skills and ever-changing job responsibilities.

Many organizations engage in the practice of enriching jobs by increasing the skill variety, task identity, task significance, autonomy, and feedback. This practice makes the jobs more flexible and increases responsibilities for planning and decision-making.

High-performance work systems and employee involvement programmes provide for more employee input into their jobs and more flexibility as to how jobs are performed. To deal with these new dynamics, many organizations are beginning the transition or have already transitioned to using competencies rather than tasks, duties, and responsibilities. Rather than task-based, job analysis has become competency-based. Competencies and competency-based job analysis are discussed in the sections that follow.

Competencies

Competencies are personal or organizational capabilities that are linked to successful performance outcomes. For the individual, competencies can be defined as characteristics of the person that enable performance. Competencies also consider how the knowledge, skills, and abilities are used. No single definition of competency has emerged as the standard because this is a relatively new area of study and practice.

However, competencies include knowledge, skills, and abilities but are more than that. There is a component of behaviour, performance outcomes, motivation, and attitude included in the concept. Many organizations believe that the use of competencies is a more strategic approach and better aligns employee behaviour with the organization's mission and values than do description of tasks and functions.

Competencies can be categorized as technical, general, and leadership. Technical competencies apply to the particular job being analyzed. General (also called behavioural) competencies are required in varying amounts throughout the workforce. Leadership competencies are required by supervisors, managers, and others that have leadership responsibilities. Table below provides some commonly used competencies.

Table: Competencies

Developing Subordinates	Resolving Conflicts
Focusing on customer satisfaction	Working creatively
Communicating effectively	Leading decisively
Working with others	Thinking
Listening	Understanding technology

Competency-based analysis follows essentially the same process as described previously, but its purpose is to determine competencies needed to successfully perform the job rather than the functions performed in the job. There is a difference in emphasis between the two processes: Traditional or task-based job analysis focuses on the job and what is actually being done, whereas competency-based analysis focuses on the person and how the job outcomes are to be accomplished.

Focusing on the "how" and the person is problematical. Discrimination law and associated case law is based on "what" is being done and the job itself. As discussed previously, one of the basic concepts is that of job-relatedness. There is very little case law on competencies at this point in time.

A transition to competency-based job analysis has implications for many other programmes. If the jobs descriptions describe the work in terms of competencies it means that associated training plans, performance management systems, compensation strategies, and so forth must be aligned.

RECRUITMENT

The outcome of the workforce strategic-planning process provides the organization with information as to how many employees and what types will be needed in the future. One of the possibilities is that fewer employees will be needed. That process is often referred to as decruitment. It is also possible, and frequently likely, that the organization might need additional employees but that the current workforce does not have and is not likely to be able to develop the skills needed. In that case, the organization might be involved in both recruitment and decruitment at the same time. Decruitment strategies and actions are discussed later, in the "Organizational Exit" section.

Recruitment is the process of attracting qualified applicants for the organization to consider when filling its positions. Two strategic determinations must be made initially before the process begins. The first is whether the organizations want to do its own recruiting or to contract it out.

Organizations lacking internal expertise might want to have an outside vendor do the recruiting for them. The vendor might be used for all recruiting or only for specified jobs. Some organizations find that it is cost-effective to outsource all recruiting gaining access to expertise and efficiencies of scale. Other organizations find that using vendors to recruit for specific jobs is most effective and efficient.

There are several scenarios in which having a vendor perform the recruiting and initial screening might be advantageous to the organization. The first scenario involves hard-to-fill jobs. Recruitment firms often specialize in filling specific positions, such as CEO or research scientist. In these cases, outside vendors may be in a better position that the organization to attract qualified candidates. The second scenario deals with entry-level workers. Organizations often find it cost-effective to deal with employment and temporary agencies to find these types of workers.

The second strategic issue is "make or buy." The organization must decide whether to engage in a practice of internal promotions and transfers (make) to fill its positions or to go to the external labour market (buy) to fill them. The decision is driven by the outcome of the strategic workforce-planning process, which evaluates the availability and skill levels of internal applicants. It is the SPHR's responsibility to ensure that the recruitment strategy is in alignment with organizational goals and objectives.

For example, an emerging organization in a highly technical field might engage in predominantly external recruitment because it does not have the time or capability to develop expertise internally and because the technical skills required are constantly changing. However, an organization operating in a relatively stable environment and attempting to compete based on cost-leadership and efficiency might find that internal recruitment is more in alignment. Also, organizations are often constrained by labour agreements that require an internal process prior to looking for applicants externally. The decision, in practice, is not an either/or choice. Organizations often pursue both strategies, frequently simultaneously.

The concept of employer branding is increasingly being discussed in relation to recruitment. Branding is a marketing concept that refers to customer perceptions of an organization or its products that differentiate it from it competitors. In a recruitment context, branding is the process by which an employer becomes the employer of choice in its relevant labour markets. Employer branding is tied to the perception and popularity of the organization and its products or services. Recruitment activities can leverage that image to facilitate attracting applicants.

To be effective, the recruitment strategy must be in alignment with the brand. If the organization has innovative products and a creative culture, the recruitment strategies should be a bit innovative and "out of the box." For example, recruitment strategies for Yahoo! would be considerably different than those for Wells Fargo bank in order to align themselves with the organizational and product image. A critical issue in employee branding is the selection and training of recruiters. Recruiters must not only have the appropriate skills and attitude, but they must also reflect the culture and image of the organization. Continuing with the preceding example, a recruiter for Yahoo! should act, dress and, in general, reflect a different attitude than one from Wells Fargo.

If the organization decides to not contract out recruitment, it must determine what types of recruitment activities to engage in and it must evaluate the effectiveness of those activities. The following sections discuss the potential methods that an organization can use to recruit both internally and externally. Also discussed are recruitment metrics used to evaluate recruitment activities.

Internal Recruiting

Internal recruiting involves recruiting current or former employees for job openings in the organization along with soliciting referrals from current employees. Various methods are discussed in this section.

HRM Information System

Sophisticated HRISs and employee databases are excellent sources of applicants. Many of these systems include data on employee training, education, and skills. In addition, some systems also include information on employee career goals and employee performance ratings. The system is able to match the requirements of a job with the characteristics and career goals of an employee to instantaneously create a potential applicant list. These employees can then be contacted, often by an automated email system, regarding their interest in a job opening.

Job Posting

Job posting is the process of advertising and publicizing job openings to employees. This might be accomplished by physically posting the opening on bulletin boards or by electronically posting them on the company's intranet or Internet. It is then up to the employee to actually apply for the position.

Job Bidding

Job bidding is similar to job posting and is more common in unionized environments. Job bidding permits an employee to apply for a position even if no openings exist. The employee's application is then held for a period of time, usually for a year, and the employee receives automatic consideration should the position come open. The process is often referred to as automatic consideration. Job bidding might be more efficient when openings for a job come open quite frequently. The employer can go to the job bid list without having to post each opening separately.

Former Employees

Former employees are often a good source of applicants. Former employees include three categories:

- Employees that have temporarily dropped out of the workforce For example, individuals that have elected to stay home with their young children. Often these former employees are ready to come back to the workforce or are willing to accept part-time employment.
- Retirees that might be willing to come back to the employer on a consultant or contract basis.
- Employees that have left the organization for work in another organization.

Assuming that these employees were good performers prior to their exit from the organization, they are likely to be good performers on their return. Many organizations have alumni and retiree clubs and groups to keep in touch with former employees. This frequently provides a rich base from which to recruit. Often employees leave thinking that a new organization provides a better working environment, better pay, or more challenging work, only to be disappointed. They often can be enticed back to the organization.

Former Applicants

Applicants that previously applied for positions with the organization are to some extent known quantities, depending on how far they got in the selection process. Good applicants should be reconsidered. Many organizations keep files on excellent candidates that were not selected for prior openings and re-recruit them for current positions. This method is both efficient and effective. Much of the screening might have already been done and, if the applicants were previously interviewed, they might have already been judged as acceptable.

Keeping in touch with prior applicants and making them feel good about the recruitment and selection process is good practice and an extension of the branding process discussed earlier. Applicants should be kept informed of their status throughout the hiring process and given feedback.

Employee Referrals

Many organizations have active formal employee referral programmes, particularly in tight job markets or where the employer has difficult-to-fill or high-turnover positions. These programmes reward employees for referring applicants to the organization. Other organizations have less formal programmes and encourage employees to refer potential applicants, but do not provide an incentive for doing so.

Experience and research show considerable benefit to the employee referral type of recruitment. First, employees are not likely to refer applicants that would not be good employees. They do not want to be embarrassed by the performance or conduct of their referral. Also, candidates that are referred by employees typically already have begun the orientation process and have somewhat of a realistic job preview via their relationship with the current employee. Finally, there is a positive correlation between employee referral and employee retention of those hired as a result.

There is, however, one potential problem that can associated with employee referrals. Employees tend to refer their relative and friends, who most likely are of the same ethnicity or sex as themselves. Therefore, this type of recruitment does not normally facilitate the achievement of diversity and affirmative action plan goals and can create adverse impact. This is particularly true if the organization has a past practice of discrimination.

External Recruiting

External recruiting involves obtaining applications from individual external to the organization. A threshold strategic issue for the SPHR is the determination of the appropriate external labour market from which to recruit. For lower-level jobs, the appropriate market is most likely to be the local labour market—defined as the geographical area from which most people are willing to commute. However, a sufficient applicant pool might not be available in the local labour market for many jobs. For certain types of jobs, particularly professional jobs, the appropriate labour market is determined in terms of the profession. Recruiting is often most effective when performed inside the profession, using professional organizations and professional journals for example. For mid-level types of positions, a regional labour market might produce a better applicant pool, whereas many top-level and highly specialized jobs require recruiting nationally and even internationally.

Of course, use of the Internet, which is discussed later, facilitates a broader recruiting area. However, Internet recruiting often is not appropriate, effective, or efficient for many jobs and the critical decision affecting the success of a recruitment effort remains in the selection of the appropriate labour market from which to recruit. External recruiting can involve many methods, the most common of which are discussed in this section.

Media Advertising

Media advertising refers to recruitment using radio, television, newspapers, and so forth. This is a technical area requiring expertise not normally available within the HR function. Writing effective advertisements frequently calls for professionals in the field. Professionally done media advertising can be an extremely effective and cost-efficient recruitment method. It allows the organization to reach a large number of potential applicants, often resulting in significant savings in hiring costs. By use of appropriate outlets targeted protected groups can be reached, which facilitates diversity and affirmative action efforts. However, when poorly done media advertising can be extremely expensive.

College and School Recruiting

College and university recruiting is a good source of entry- and mid-level managers and professionals. In general, college recruiting requires a continuing relationship with the organization and its placement office, and a history of hiring the college's graduates. These together tend to put the organization at the front of the referral queue. However, this is often an expensive proposition requiring expenditure of both staff and financial resources. Sponsoring professional clubs and providing scholarships and internships can be expensive if the organization never hires individuals from the college. Many organizations have scaled down their college recruiting efforts to focus on a few schools where they can maintain a continuing presence and hire excellent candidates in a cost-effective manner.

Two-year colleges (junior and community colleges) and technical schools can be good sources for entry-level, para-technical, and para-professional positions. The strategies associated with recruiting at these institutions are the same as for higher-level institutions—only the type of positions being recruited for is different.

High schools are a good source of blue-collar, clerical, and retail entry-level positions. Many organizations do not realize the potential of recruiting at this level, often assuming that graduates will pursue higher education. Good relationships with school counselors and athletic departments often facilitate this type of recruitment.

Labour Unions

Labour union hiring halls are often a good, and sometimes the only, source of applicants. This is particularly true in the construction trades.

Employment Agencies

As mentioned earlier in the discussion of outsourced recruitment, employment agencies and job search firms often are good sources of job candidates. First, all states have unemployment offices, displaced worker units, or similar agencies performing the same function. These are often sources of applicants.

Private employment agencies can be viable sources of applicants. These firms most frequently charge the organization a fee for referral of candidates, either on a contingency or retainer basis.

Contingency-based firms receive the fee only if the applicant is hired, whereas retainer-based firms receive a fee for engaging in the search even if no one is hired. Employment agencies normally prescreen the applicants for the organization and refer only those that are qualified. The agencies often have contacts and relationships that the organization does not, and might be able to locate excellent candidates for higher-level managerial and hard-to-fill technical and professional positions.

Although using employment agencies and search firms might be cost-effective and yield results that the organization could not achieve on its own, doing so can be extremely expensive. Costs for using these types of firms often run 25–30% of the yearly salary for the position being recruited.

Temporary Employment Agencies

Many private employment agencies provide temporary, part-time, or just-in-time workers. These employees are paid by the temporary agency and are not employees of the organization. Temporary agencies screen these workers and often provide training. These agencies have traditionally provided lower-level blue-collar and clerical workers, but that is no longer the case. There are now temporary employment agencies that specialize in providing technical, professional, and managerial temporary workers. There are even agencies that specialize in temporary executives up to and including CEOs.

The advantage of these agencies is in their flexibility. The employer has no continuing obligation to the employee and can, within limits, rotate them in and out of the organization. This is especially important to firms than have frequent variations in demand or are seasonal in nature. Employers pay a fee to the temporary agency and do not have to worry about employee benefits or employment taxes. In addition, organizations often use the temporary employment as a probationary period. The temporary agency permits the organization to hire these temporary workers as permanent employees for a fee.

Customers

Loyal customers are pleased with the organization's product or services. To some extent they have made a commitment to the organization, and might be familiar with the culture, the responsibilities of some of the jobs, and the working conditions. In other words, they have a realistic job preview. Many organizations have found customers to be an excellent source of candidates. They frequently recruit actively in their retail establishments, taking job applications on the spot and providing easy access to employment information and application procedures on their websites.

Suppliers and Competitors

Employees of suppliers and competitors are often good sources of applicants. They are familiar with the industry and frequently familiar with the organization itself.

Professional and Trade Associations

Virtually all professional and trade associations provide placement services for their members and allow employers to post job openings on their website, typically for a fee. In addition, these associations normally publish newsletters or journals in which the organization can place recruiting advertisements.

Most associations also have annual meetings or conventions that provide additional opportunities for the organization to recruit in person. Organizations have found professional and trade associations to be excellent sources of applicants, particularly for specialized types of jobs such as banking, finance, human resource management, and so forth. Some associations are organized around gender or ethnicity. They are good sources of candidates for organizations engaging in diversity or affirmative action initiatives.

Walk-Ins

Many organizations accept applications from individuals that visit the organization for the express purpose of inquiring about job opportunities. Walk-ins have been found to be good sources of entry-level employees. The mere fact that they have taken the time and effort to visit the organization shows some level of interest and commitment.

Job Fairs and Special Events

Job fairs held by other organizations—for example, the local chamber of commerce—tend to attract a wide variety of applicants and might provide the organization with numerous recruiting leads and applicants. However, many organizations have found that some individuals attending these types of events are merely shopping and are not really interested in changing jobs. In addition, many of the individuals tend to have low skills and might be largely unemployable. That being said, job fairs held by organizations such as professional associations (for example, the Society for Human Resource Management) can be an excellent source of candidates.

Internally held job fairs have proven to be an effective means of recruitment, particularly for entry-level blue-collar and clerical employees. Organizations often open up their facilities during the evening or on the weekend and provide free food and prizes as an incentive for potential applicants to visit. Actually visiting the work site begins the realistic job preview process and might result in better retention of applicants who are actually hired. Organizations have also found that using special events as a recruiting tool has proven effective. A booth or kiosk at sporting and civic events could produce viable candidates.

Internet

The Internet has opened up all sorts of possibilities and associated challenges in recruiting. It provides access to a worldwide population of potential applicants. There are essentially three major sources of applicants using e-recruiting: commercial job boards, professional/trade association websites, and the employer's website.

Many organizations have successfully used commercial job boards such as Monster.com and Hotjobs.com where, for a fee, employers can post job opportunities. Job boards have been found to provide access to a large number of qualified candidates. However, because of ease of access many of the candidates often are not seriously looking for a new job but are merely testing their competitiveness in the job market or trying to determine current compensation rates.

As discussed previously, many professional and trade associations publish job openings on their website. These can provide viable candidates for specialized positions. Most larger employers now provide employment information on their websites.

They typically find this to be an effective and efficient means of generating applications. To be effective, access to job information must be easy. Most employers provide a button on the home page that leads prospective applicant to the information.

Effectiveness is increased if the web page for employment information continues the same format and theme as the home page and is consistent with the organization's image and culture. This is an important continuation of the employer branding previously discussed.

Internet recruiting can save time because the application forms and/or resumes are readily available. Applicants can be immediately contacted via email. Internet recruiting is typically much less expensive than media advertising or onsite recruiting initiatives. Internet recruiting expands the relevant job market to the globe and has the potential to generate a large number of qualified candidates.

However, the ease of application in Internet recruiting and the wide exposure of job opening information often generate applications from those that are not qualified or that are not seriously looking for work. In fact, Internet recruiting might generate too many applications that must be screened and applicants that must be contacted, thus increasing the workload on HR. Fortunately, there are now software packages that can largely automate many of these processes.

Internet recruiting poses problems for the tracking of applicant flow data. However, recent rulings by both the EEOC and OFCCP have clarified the issue somewhat. As a general overview of that guidance, employers have to consider applications received on the Internet as applicants for applicant flow data only if the organization actually considers the applicant for an open position, if the applicant maintains continued interest and follows the organization's standard application process, and if the applicant expresses interest and is basically qualified for a particular position.

A final concern about Internet recruiting is the potential for adverse impact caused by what is known as the digital divide. Although access to the Internet has increased dramatically, certain minority groups might have less access than other groups.

Outplacement Firms

Many organizations have formed alliances with outplacement firms. These firms provide placement assistance to individuals, many of whom have been involuntarily separated from their former employer through no fault of their own. These individuals are often excellent candidates.

Evaluating Recruitment Effectiveness

Efficiency evaluation is largely operational in nature, whereas effectiveness evaluation is strategic. Unfortunately, organizations tend to do a rather good job at developing efficiency metrics, but a poor job of developing effectiveness measures. The efficiency metrics provide information regarding the accomplishments of short-term objectives. However, the critical issue is the long-term strategic impact of recruitment activities on the success of the organization (effectiveness metrics).

Typical efficiency metrics are as follows:

- Quantity of applications This is a gross measure of the effect of recruitment activities with the philosophy that the more applications an organizations gets, the more likely it is to fill its openings with highly qualified individuals. Quantities can be evaluated by source, giving a gross estimate of the cost-effectiveness of television versus newspaper advertising, for example.
- Quality of applications Organizations might want to evaluate the percentage of applications that were considered qualified for the job or that were actually offered an interview. Again, this is a gross measure of the impact of the recruitment programme and can be analyzed by the source of the application.
- Time to fill Most organizations evaluate the time it takes to fill a position, typically in terms of the number of days from the date the request is received in the HR department until new employee actually reports onboard. These data are then compared against goals, historical averages, and benchmarks to evaluate recruitment efficiency.
- Yield rates Yield rates were discussed earlier. Recruitment is often evaluated in terms of yield rates from one stage of the process to another. For example, the organization needs to know what percentage of applicants were actually considered to be qualified for the job, what percentage that were qualified passed the initial screening, what percentage passing the initial screening also passed the pre-employment tests, what percentage passing the pre-employment test were offered in-person interviews, and so forth. This provides an additional measure of efficiency in that higher yield ratios reduce wasted staff effort and produce more viable candidates for the organization to consider.

- Cost per hire Many organizations track the average cost to hire employees, typically by dividing all recruitment-related expenses by the number of actual hires. The measure provides an indication of the efficiency of the recruitment programme in terms of costs, but yields little information regarding effectiveness. Also, the calculation of recruitment costs is often difficult.
- Selection rates Selection rate provide some indication of efficiency because they evaluate the number of new hires against the total number of applicants. For example, if 50 hires were made from an application pool of 100, the selection rate is 50%.

  However, one cannot really necessarily evaluate that metric in terms of effectiveness. Presumably, the higher the selection rate, the more efficient and effective recruitment process. But are selections being made using the "any warm body" philosophy because positions must be filled with any applicant that is minimally qualified? Selection rates along with other measures of efficiency do not give the organization any indication of the actual performance of an individual after being hired, nor do they tell the organization anything about employee retention.
- Acceptance rates Some organizations track selection rates, which are typically evaluated as the number of applicants that accept the position divided by the number of applicants that were offered the position. The higher the ratio, the more efficient the recruitment programme is considered to be. However, acceptance rates can be significantly affected by outside influences that have nothing to do with the quality of recruitment efforts. For example, acceptance rates could be expected to be appreciably higher during periods of high unemployment.

This metric is frequently used to evaluate both individual recruiter and recruitment sources. When evaluating individual recruiters, the interest is in how effective the recruiter is in actually convincing the applicant to accept the job. This might be a critical issue, especially with higher-level jobs where the costs of recruiting are substantial. The organization is also interested in knowing whether the acceptance rate differs among the various recruitment methods so that it can adjust its strategies.

Effectiveness measures are those that evaluate the long-term strategic impact of the recruitment programme. As discussed, "Human Resource Development," in the context of evaluation of training and development there is often an inverse relationship between the value of data and analysis and its difficulty. However, this is the value added by the SPHR. The SPHR must develop metrics that strategically evaluate recruitment efforts in terms of their impact on organizational effectiveness and strategic success.

An effectiveness measure frequently overlooked is that of customer satisfaction with the recruitment process and results. In this case, customers can be defined in a number of ways. First, management satisfaction should be evaluated. Managers should be questioned as to their overall satisfaction with the recruitment process and the timeliness of actions and the quality of recruits in particular. Because managers at different levels often have different expectations, satisfaction should be surveyed at multiple levels in the organization. The second, and probably more important, customer group is the actual recruits themselves. This includes both those who were hired and those who were rejected for employment. They should be questioned about their perspectives regarding the various stages of the recruitment and selection process. These data often provide valuable information regarding recruitment effectiveness and identify areas that might need improvement.

The effectiveness of recruitment efforts should be evaluated in terms of eventual employee performance and retention. Therefore, the SPHR should lead the HR function in engaging in longitudinal studies in these areas. In the press of current requirements historical research is often ignored. Yet these data are the ones that allow the organization to fine-tune current operations. Organizations that have effective recruitment evaluation programmes periodically (usually yearly) evaluate a sample of hires from previous years, correlating retention, promotion rates, and performance data with recruitment sources, selection tests, and other employment practices. Evaluation of individual recruiters can also be done using the same process. These data provide rich information as to the long-term effectiveness of recruitment programmes.

The potential value of these types of evaluations is, however, moderated by the nature of the organizational environment and the organizational strategies. These data have the greatest impact in planning and engaging in activities to improve the recruitment programme when the environment is relatively stable.

Contingent Workforce

The contingent workforce is composed of those individuals who work for an organization but are not permanent full-time employees. Use of a contingent workforce is increasing and it is estimated that contingent workers represent more than 20% of the total United States workforce. The dynamics of today's organizational and business environment often drive employers to use contingent workers to achieve a strategic advantage. These drivers of change are discussed and in others, but a brief summary is appropriate.

Increased competition and the need for cost-efficiency require that employers have flexibility in adjusting employment levels and employment costs to demand for its product or services and in relationship to its level of operations, both of which might be constantly changing and volatile. A permanent full-time workforce does not permit that. The changing psychological contract encourages lack of permanency of relationships, both in employee and employer expectations.

Contingent workers are in alignment with those expectations. Changing technology often requires new skills that permanent full-time employees might not have and might not be capable of developing. Downsizing and rightsizing could result in the loss of organizational capability, which can be augmented with the use of contingent workers. The increasing difficulty of compliance with the complexity of employment laws and the cost associated with them can be largely avoided by having workers that are employees of other organizations. Finally, significant cost savings can often accrue from outsourcing the organization's work to organizations located in foreign countries in which the wage rates are low.

However, the use of contingent workers does not come without some organizational concerns and disadvantages. Increased flexibility often brings about loss of control. The employer might be able to control only the outcome of work, not the means used to obtain it. Use of some types of contingent workers might, in the long run, be more expensive than permanent employees because the source of those workers must not only be reimbursed for compensation and benefit costs but must also be paid a fee in addition.

There is a concern regarding the loyalty of employees that are not employed on a full-time basis. Will the employee act in the best interest of the organization or of the actual employer? Another issue of substantial concern is the impact of this strategy on the remaining permanent full-time workforce. Does the practice lower overall morale and induce stress and concern among the remaining workers who might become worried about their own job security?

A final issue is one of ethics and social responsibility. The SPHR must lead the organization in balancing its obligations to its employees, the community or communities in which it operates, and society as a whole against the organization's legitimate desire to maximize its profits for stockholders.

A contingent workforce can be composed of many types of workers. Employers often use several sources simultaneously. Common types or sources of contingent workers include the following:

- Part-time workers Part-time workers can be obtained from a temporary employment agency, in which case flexibility is maximized and the organization avoids liability for taxes and benefits. Part-time workers can be employees of the organization. Although that arrangement might be somewhat permanent in nature and of limited flexibility, organizations often provide no or a limited range of benefits, resulting in cost savings.
- Temporary workers Traditional temporary workers are obtained from employment agencies that specialize in providing these types of workers. However, the employer can also hire temporary workers internally.

The employer that hires temporary workers must do so based on some rational basis such as temporary or seasonal increases in operations, the need to replace workers during the peak vacation period, and so forth. The temporary workers should be terminated when the temporary demand for additional workforce ceases. Continued employment of temporary workers for extended amounts of time might negate their temporary status and obligate the employer to provide expensive benefits. Microsoft Corporation paid a 97-million dollar settlement to workers that it had mischaracterized as temporary workers.

Hiring temporary labour from a temporary employment agency can also pose potential legal problems for the employer. If the organization exercises control over the temporary employees, provides training, negotiates compensation, or engages in other employment-related practices, the temporary employee is likely to be considered by the courts as an employee of both the organization and the temporary employment agency (referred to as dual employment).

In such cases the organization might be obligated to provide certain benefits. In addition, as a dual employer, the organization must comply with all employment laws in its relationship with the temporary workers. For example, the organization might have an obligation to provide reasonable accommodation to a temporary worker under the Americans with Disabilities Act and can be found liable for illegal discrimination or harassment under the Civil Rights Act of 1964.

Temporary employees in many situations have the right to join unions that are the certified bargaining agent either of the temporary employment agency or of the organization.

- *Consultants*: Often consultants are contracted with to provide expertise not currently available to the organization and not needed on a permanent and continuing basis.
- *Contract workers*: Contract workers are often hired on a project basis. After the project is complete, the organization has no further obligation to the individual.
- *Outsourcing*: Outsourcing is the process of contracting for services or products with external vendors rather than producing them internally. Frequently outsourcing results in substantial compensation savings because of the economies of scale that are created when an organization specializes in a particular type of work and/or employs specialized software. Outsourcing often permits access to specialize expertise not available internally to the organization.
- *Offshoring*: Offshoring refers to hiring workers in foreign countries to perform tasks previously done in the United States. Oftentimes, substantial cost savings can be realized because of the lower compensation rates in those countries.
- *Leasing*: Leasing typically involves a contract with a professional employer organization (PEO). A PEO is an organization that assumes

the employer rights and responsibilities for employees that it provides to its clients. An employer wanting to lease its currently employees signs a contract with a PEO and the PEO hires the employees. The organization then leases them back, with the PEO assuming the responsibilities of an employer. Employee leasing tends to be particularly suited for small employers that do not have internal expertise to comply with the complexities of today's employment laws. Also, because the PEO has a much larger workforce, it might be able to provide the former organizational employees with much better benefit packages. Obviously these services do not come without a cost, and it is estimated that leasing raises total labour costs by about 5%. For many employers this is additional money well spent.

CONCEPT, SCOPE AND LIMITATION

Corporate financial success and a healthful organizational environment have been long viewed as juxtaposed concepts. The conventional paradigm dictates that if resources are devoted to worker well-being, fewer resources will be available to contribute to corporate profit. At the managerial level, work and health are often interpreted as a choice between productive work practices and those practices which are safe and healthy.

However, statistics reveal the cost burden that the lack of worker health imposes on the United States economy. Evanoff & Rosenstock (1994) reported that estimates of the annual direct and indirect medical costs associated with occupational stress in the United States have ranged from $80 billion to $150 billion. These estimates do not include the additional costs incurred from lost productivity.

Furthermore, research in recent years has begun to recognize the significant role of employee health in the performance of the organization as a whole. Sauter et al. (1996) acknowledged that organizational performance and worker well-being are mutually reinforcing and introduced a model developed by the National Institute of Occupational Safety and Health (NIOSH) for use in their investigation of "healthy" work organizations. Zink (2002) asserted that human resources are the most relevant enabler of success of a company.

Rapid changes in the organization of work due to the indoctrination of work improvement efforts in corporate cultures (e.g., lean manufacturing, six sigma), together with the new demographics of the American work population (e.g., increasing numbers of women, minorities, and aging workers) have far outpaced the knowledge regarding the implications of these changes on the quality of working life.

As such, this area has been established as one of the 21 priority research items under the National Occupational Research Agenda (NORA). While the physical and mental demands form the job content of the overall work-system model, the organizational environment together with the physical environment form the context in which work tasks are executed. However, an organizational environment model which aims to optimize work outcomes (i.e., productivity, quality) while seeking to optimize the quality of life of the work-system participants has received little attention in the scientific research arena. Furthermore, the set of parameters, which constitute the organizational environment as well as the concepts underlying a model's development, have been the subject of vigorous debate and terminological confusion.

The objective of this article was to develop a model for organizational health assessment to address the subsystems of factors, which interact to form the culture (the shared meanings and values) and climate (the work practices) within the totality of the work environment. Preliminary evidence suggests both positive and negative effects of changing organizational practices on the safety and health of workers. As a result of these conflicting findings, NIOSH suggests that an important focus of research should be the clarification of circumstances (for whom and under what conditions) in which these practices protect or increase the risk of harm to workers.

To address this need, a model of the organizational work system, these factors and their interrelationships must be developed. Although several recent efforts have documented correlations between various work factors and individual/organizational well-being measures, a comprehensive organizational-systems model from which to empirically define pathways to promote health is required. This article aims to fill this need. However, prior to describing the Organizational Health Model, the evolution of the organizational health concept will be reviewed.

Evolution of the Organizational Health Construct

In the many years American businesses enjoyed in the absence of global competition, a healthy corporation was simply a by-product of an environment with a lack of obvious physical or chemical hazards. The Occupational Health and Safety Act, effective in 1971, was enacted to ensure safe and healthful working conditions. As a result, the Occupational Safety and Health Administration (OSHA) establishes and monitors compliance to safety and health standards. In the occupational-health perspective at this time, a healthful organization constituted one that did not violate the enacted standards.

The roots of the organizational health concept in the United States began in the 1960s, presented through the humanistic researchers' concerns regarding how employees were treated in the work organization. Their work linked job content to individual well-being in the context of the effective organization. Argyris (1958, 1964) questioned the ability of an organization to meet the needs of its employees while remaining competitive. McGregor's (1960) descriptions of Theory X (authoritarian management) and Theory Y (democratic management) asserted that the role of the organizational environment is critical in determining effectiveness as well as utilizing worker potential. Herzberg et al. (1959), Maslow (1965), Porter and Lawler (1968), and Vroom (1964) explored the interactions between individual motivation and performance. These theories formed the basis for numerous intervention efforts aimed at improving various aspects of organizational health.

What is organizational health? In the aftermath of several popular corporate improvement programmes such as the total quality management (TQM) and downsizing, the term "organizational health" has emerged in both the occupational health and mainstream business literature, heralding a blending of the traditionally paradoxical values of productivity versus health and safety. Effectiveness, a universal organizational goal, can be regarded as a composite of the following factors: product quality, customer service, flexibility, initiative taken by employees, and capacity to meet deadlines. Jaffe (1995) characterized organizational health as implying an expanded notion of organizational effectiveness.

He offered a contextual definition of organizational health stating that a company can be healthy for:

a. Its own livelihood by growing and being efficient, adaptable, and coherent;
b. Stockholders by increasing the value of stock;
c. Employees, offering a healthy work environment as well as meeting their highest growth needs for meaning and participation;
d. Suppliers and customers by offering good products and services; and
e. The community by assuming concern for its viability as well as for the environment.

Jaffe added that the needs of all the benefactors of organizational health must be balanced to ensure success. Rosen (1991) described a healthy company as one that holds a core set of humanistic values: commitment to self-knowledge and development, firm belief in decency, respect for individual differences, spirit of partnership, high priority for health and well-being, appreciation for flexibility and resilience, and passion for products and process.

Although these descriptions provide an ideology for and list of benefactors of organizational health, they fail to define the components of an organization that interact to create its level of well-being. Williams (1994) cited the four elements of organizational health as environmental factors, physical health, mental (psychological) health, and social health; the details of interventions describe a holistic approach to employee health. Yet, he myopically equated the health of the employee to the health of the organization. To effectively assess organizational conditions for healthy work, other aspects of the work system—physical job demands, mental job demands, and physical environment demands as well as individual characteristics—must be considered simultaneously.

However, little research has been devoted directly to the concept of organizational health, especially in the United States. In the strictest sense, most work-improvement efforts are only tangentially related to the organizational health construct in that the majority of these approaches are aimed primarily at optimizing performance (improving effectiveness) rather than the quality of work life for all participants. Conversely, job-stress research has considered individual and job characteristics as they relate to individual measures of health (e.g., physical symptoms).

Overall, previous efforts to address human effectiveness in conjunction with consideration for worker well-being can be classified into three categories according to the variable identified for intervention: the individual, the job, and the organizational framework. Notably absent from this classification is the process-based orientation. Numerous contemporary work-improvement efforts, such as statistical process control, lean manufacturing, reengineering, and six sigma, regard the optimization of the process as paramount. However, these methods, focused on the pursuit of effectiveness, have failed to consider the effects of process improvements on the quality of working life for work participants.

Work improvement strategies can be classified according to these three orientations. Although no organizational health interventions can be classified as process-based, this category is included in the model for completeness. In this model, strategy boundaries are diffuse due to the likely overlap between classifications. The large circle (organization) circumscribes the smaller circles (individual, job, and process), as the intervention in the larger circle is broader in scope and therefore affects the intervention in the smaller circle. For example, organizational interventions such as restructuring a manufacturing area into an autonomous work group can alter both the scope of a job as well as the individual's role.

The orientation of the United States' research on workplace health has been overwhelmingly individual-focused, not surprisingly congruent to its cultural ideology. This orientation implicitly assumes that the aggregation of individual physically and psychologically healthy workers equals a healthy company. The majority of empirical research advancing the development of organizational health concepts in the United States has primarily resulted as an outgrowth of job stress studies. Overall, these studies have focused on individual health as affected by workplace demands.

Historically, in the occupational stress research tradition, wellness strategies were exclusively aimed at the individual's physical and mental health. Consequently, the most common interventions recommend development of individual coping strategies such as stress-management training and employee- assistance programmes. Common elements of workplace health promotion include smoking cessation, hypertension screening and control, stress management, nutrition and weight control, exercise and fitness, and drug and alcohol programmes. However, wellness promoting strategies also must refer to the improvement of intrinsic job factors and therefore serve a dual purpose of attempting to better work life on both the individual as well as organizational planes.

Wellness-promotion strategies seek to bolster individual and organizational resilience by increasing inherent capability. On the individual level, capability may be developed through the practice of conflict-resolution skills or support networks.

On the organizational level, work may be designed such that self-determination, social interaction, and professional responsibility are central concepts cited job characteristic criteria as well as strategies for good work organization, such as mastery of work, management of change processes, support of employees by occupational health services, and emphasis on career stage and future perspectives.

Inclusion of wellness- promoting strategies must emphasize the prerequisite for active job content and work-setting design in creating a robust organization. In this manner, the traditional paradigm of healthy work as that in which stress and harm are absent is expanded. Another individual-based orientation emphasizes the leader's importance in the formation of a healthy company.

This perspective largely attributes the creation and existence of an organization to its founders or leaders. Thus, the leader's personal characteristics and management style are viewed as the primary catalysts for organizational well-being. Gardell (1987) cautioned against focusing preventative strategies primarily on the individual as this emphasis translates a larger organizational problem into a private one.

Job redesign also has been used as a means for improving health. Job characteristics that support healthful work conditions are defined, and then the job is modified to possess these characteristics. Generally, the job is considered as an independent entity, in isolation from the organizational context. In this perspective, the job is used as the medium thorough which to affect individual motivation. For example, Hackman and Lawler (1971) defined five job characteristics for meaningful work: skill variety, task identity, task significance, autonomy, and feedback. The Job Diagnostic Survey was developed to assess jobs based on the five aforementioned job characteristics.

The job characteristics defined by Hackman and Lawler (1971) provided a set of variables that could be manipulated to increase job meaning and therefore worker motivation. Job enrichment adds complexity often by allowing greater worker autonomy. Techniques such as job enlargement (expanding the scope of the job by adding more task variety) and job rotation (alternating task assignments) are additional examples of job-based interventions. Job-based approaches use task redesign as the means to affect individual worker satisfaction. Critics of this orientation argue that these efforts may not succeed as psychological differences between individuals are not addressed.

Efforts focused primarily on the improvement of work life through organizational variables began in Scandinavia around the mid-1960s, and soon thereafter social science research and health research united in the investigation to improve quality of work life. The orientation in Scandinavian countries as well as Finland has tended to focus more on the resources and structure of the work environment itself rather than the individual worker or job process.

In the organizational orientation, interventions such as the establishment of autonomous production groups are used to incorporate considerations of job demands, individuals' self-determination, resources (technical, organizational, social, personal), and autonomy. Collective control allows groups to create their own distinctive adaptive strategies.

The importance of these efforts to improve quality of work life has been further emphasized in the Swedish Work Environment Act, effective since 1977, which states that "jobs shall be designed so that the employees themselves can influence their work situation" and "working conditions shall be adapted to the mental and physical capacity of human beings."

Organization-based interventions redesign the "job" by changing its overall structure within the context of the work organization. In their terminology, "job redesign" has been enlarged to "work reform." Conceptually, this approach emerged from socio-technical design theory, which advocates that work should be organized in groups that have control over decision making and are responsible for a complete work cycle.

To encourage autonomy and social support, interdependent autonomous work groups were implemented, therefore magnifying the individual's role within the context of the work environment. Several advantages of autonomous work groups are cited in Gardell (1981):

- Within a group setting, the individual can expand his or her possibilities for attaining some amount of freedom and competence at work;
- The possibilities for learning, variation, and all-around use of human resources will be improved;
- The individual and the group will be able to achieve wider control over the work system and work methods; and
- Human contact and solidarity between people will be more likely.

Karasek and Theorell (1990) later formulated a model using three factors to characterize work: job demands, job control, and social support. They concluded that high-demand– low-control jobs resulted in higher incidence of health problems than jobs that are high demand–high control, thus validating Gardell's (1982) previous experiments on work- place autonomy and participation on which his interventions were based. Critics of the socio-technical approach argue that this orientation does not go far enough to affect organizational change in that it does not address the employees' beliefs regarding organizational goals, priorities, and behaviours, except in regard to job content and social relationships. Recent efforts to describe the environment for organizational health suggest debate among research communities over the emphasis of worker or process, and individual level factors versus structural, organizational level factors.

Lindstrom (1994), of the Finnish Institute of Occupational Health, cites job characteristics such as optimal quantitative and qualitative workload, opportunities for control at work, clarified work balanced by other roles, and supportive social interactions as the psychosocial criteria for good work organization, and also cites organizational strategies to support these criteria. Sauter et al. (1996), of NIOSH, presented a model which wholly ignores job-level factors (e.g., work- load, autonomy, role stress) and shifted all emphasis to "macro-organizational" characteristics (e.g., climate, values).

Lack of attention to all four variables (individual, job, process, and organization) in intervention strategies can result in a failure to improve the level of work performance as well as quality of work life. Cox and Cox (1993) explained that health problems may arise because jobs, technology, and work environments have not been systematically de- signed with workers in mind due to management practices, organizational culture, or failure to develop workers' knowledge skills and attitudes.

For example, extended work hours due to staff reductions may increase the risk of physical injury. Frankenhauser (1991) recommended that individual-oriented programmes need to be supplemented by organization-wide changes that may involve altering the conditions under which people work, the tasks they perform, and the rewards they obtain. Gardell (1987) concluded that "preventative psychosocial work" must proceed on both the individual as well as the organizational planes. This strategy, calling for the collaboration of orientations, marks the starting point for the organizational model's development.

Organizational Health Model Development

With the recent emergence of the concept of organizational health, researchers have acknowledged the significance of the role of worker well-being in the establishment of a healthy as well as effective workplace. Several areas of study have fed the idea's germination, notably the humanistic organizational research and the job-stress research traditions. However, the concept suffers from the lack of a holistic approach on two levels. First, current descriptions of organizational health must be enlarged to include all components of the work system (e.g., physical, mental, organizational, environmental) as well as their interactions.

Second, although some researchers identified criteria for good work organization, this work has not yet been integrated within a systemic framework that lends itself to practical industrial application. Analogous to biological health, the determination of healthy work is based on a system of interrelated components functioning together, seeking balance. To assess organizational health, the resulting work-system equilibrium must be quantified. The company's values and organizational goals drive the establishment of work practices and policies. Processes dictate the job content, that is, the mental, physical, and environmental demands on the worker. Resources act to encourage worker well-being (e.g., meaningful job characteristics, mentoring, training, advancement opportunities) act to offset the negative effects of the demands on workers (e.g., fatigue, boredom) and consequently, simultaneously encourage successful achievement of organizational goals.

The interrelationships between work-system components ultimately determine the state of the organization's health. Culture is the premise upon which the climate, the everyday operations, is based. These daily practices (climate), in turn, affect the culture. The model is predicated upon the occurrence of two outcomes: effectiveness in achieving the desired goal and the wellness as described by the quality of work life of the members. Therefore, the definition of organizational health blends the historically paradoxical objectives of optimizing performance and overall well-being. This section details the model's components and explains their interrelationships.

References to organizational culture abound in both scholarly and mainstream literature. Culture can be casually defined as "how things are done around here". Organizational culture is a relatively new area of study that has experienced recent popularity through business self-help books, which target work culture as a variable for manipulation in the pursuit of effectiveness.

Much academic work has been devoted to the definition and description of the concept; however, little effort has focused on the empirical study of culture in the contemporary work organization. Although comprehensive book-length explications of the concept have been accomplished, there has been little research on methodology for practical application or reported experience substantiating the theoretical views in industry. The concept of organizational culture has suffered from the lack of a focus, causing theoretical efforts to remain inaccessible to the industrial work environment.

The problem of defining organizational culture is based on the fact that the concept of the organization is itself ambiguous. The many definitions of culture are divergent in scope, overlap with other concepts (notably, climate), and sometimes contradict other definitions; however, most include reference to both beliefs (values) and actions (behaviour).

However, to evaluate the complex interrelationships of the work system, the interactions that form the context through which individuals interpret their experiences must be evaluated. Culture constitutes a significant variable in the model of organizational life. For the purposes of this study, culture will be defined as the shared values (what is important) and beliefs (the why behind what happens) which guide the behaviour of its members. Values are common to nearly all of the varied definitions in the culture literature. Values central to an organization's being can be revealed in two ways. First, they may be enacted as ideologies represented in the way business is conducted. Second, central values may be espoused through formal means of communication (i.e., written company literature, speeches). If values are enacted without being stated, they must be deciphered by organization's members.

Therefore, espoused values provide a clearer declaration. When well defined and continually expressed, central values serve as the precepts which structure behaviour. Many researchers have fallen victim to the trap of advocating a prescribed set of values as a recipe for corporate success.

Many mainstream business books, although written from the perspective of the corporate environment, tend to offer generic "quick fixes," often proposing that their exists a model culture for effectiveness and suggesting that any organization's current culture is malleable enough to achieve the prescribed ideal. Furthermore, these mainstream writings generally lack scientific credibility in that they are based on anecdotal evidence, use a relatively small sample size, and ignore psychometric issues such as data reliability and validity.

However, while convenient to assume, central values, like personal values, cannot be dictated or imposed. Central values result from the genesis of a company's history, emerging from the organization's leaders and members. As the company grows, articulation of the central values is essential for reinforcement in incumbent members and instilling in new members. Collins and Porras (1994) reported that visionary companies usually possess between three and six central values. Some examples of well-known, visionary companies and their central values are: Wal-Mart–customer service, Procter and Gamble– product quality and honest business, and Hewlett-Packard– respect and concern for the individual.

The work culture is further shaped by an organization's goals. Organizational goals are the specific actions the company strives to accomplish. Consequently, they function as the impetus for the company's strategic plans. To be authentic and deserving of full commitment from the organization's members, organizational goals should reinforce the central values held.

For example, General Electric's goal of training every employee in six sigma methodology and basing promotional consideration on the completion of training reflects their espoused high regard for quality. Goals that conflict with an organization's central values are likely to result in dissent among its members, therefore hindering the potential for achievement.

Organizational goals in conjunction with central values constitute the organization's strategic intent. The attainment of the strategic intent, while influenced by many factors (i.e., resources, market, competition), is initially fueled by its clear communication and strength of the bond between the central values and organizational goals. These elements describe the medium of culture that influences the constitution of the climate. For organizational goals to be realized, effective work processes must be designed and maintained. Processes, in turn, must be enacted by individuals who perform various jobs in support of the process goals. Organizational climate, colloquially defined as "the way things are done around here", is a multidimensional concept which has experienced a long, prolific history in the research literature.

Although more advanced a concept than organizational culture in terms of practical application and empirical inquiry, organizational climate also has been subject to controversy regarding its definition and has assumed varying levels of focus in terms of the content it includes. Organizational climate, a concept indigenous to the field of organizational psychology, has functioned as an instrument for quantifying environmental influences on individual motivation, satisfaction, and workplace behaviour through the summary of perceptions.

From the beginning of the concept's explication, data collection and empirical analysis have been key components of the majority of studies. The breadth of the organizational climate topic results in a limitless set of elements that constitute the work environment. Thus, organizational climate as a general concept for study can include a myriad of potential dimensions for assessment. As a result, content critical for assessment may be ignored or the list of dimensions may grow so large that assessment is impossible. Schneider (1990) noted that the representation of climate as an abstract construct lacks a strategic focus.

Climate without reference to a specific outcome (i.e., safety, quality, creativity) Organizational health across four orientations has no content boundaries as well as no definitive purpose for assessment and therefore lacks practical utility. Thus, it is essential to assess climate within the context of organizational, process, individual, and job goals.

In recent years, numerous researchers have directed their efforts toward developing assessments to measure climates for a specific type of environment. Several studies have demonstrated the utility of this focus through industrial application. Zohar (1980) tested an assessment measure of a safety climate. Other measures available for the assessment of a specific climate or work outcome include conflict resolution, motivation and leadership, job satisfaction, and organizational performance.

As the purpose of this article was to develop a model for the assessment of organizational health, a practical and clear definition is needed which recognizes all variables in the determination of organizational climate. Therefore, the definition presented by Schneider and Gunnarson (1991) stating that organizational climate refers to "the themes that employees believe describe their organization based on the practices, procedures and rewarded behaviours that employees see happening to them as well as around them" will be used in this article.

For the purpose of work-system assessment, climate is more fully characterized by inclusion of job demands and resources. Job demands encompass the physical and mental task requirements as well as environmental conditions the worker may be exposed to (e.g., noise, vibration). Resources are factors in the work climate that act to encourage the worker to achieve job goals and job satisfaction. In the work system, resources may be individual based (e.g., smoking-cessation programmes), job based (e.g., expansion of task content), process based (e.g., improved work techniques), or organization based (restructuring of departments).

The relationship between culture and climate has caused much confusion and has been the subject of a multitude of debates in the research literature. While some researchers have described one concept in terms of that it is not the other, many culture researchers have wholly ignored organizational climate in their work. These two concepts, which obviously interlock in practical application, have been developed academically in parallel.

However, several researchers have acknowledged that culture and climate are distinct. Some have attempted to describe the relationship between culture and climate by stating that culture includes climate. However, this explanation fails to establish an area of demarcation between the two concepts. With greater clarity, Schneider (1985, 1987) described culture and climate as complimentary topics, and explained that climate research focuses on the what and how organizational activities and behaviours are rewarded while culture focuses on the underlying reasons why the activities and behaviours happen. In this way, culture "informs" climate by helping individuals define what is important and structure their experiences. Hence, climate can be viewed as a manifestation of culture.

Organizational climate, although subject to some debate regarding definition and details of operationalization issues, has proved a viable instrument for characterization of the work environment, especially for those work settings with a specific theme. However, the full potential of the climate concept can be realized best through its coupling with the organizational culture concept. While progress has been made in clarifying the relationship between the two, work to integrate the concepts has not progressed beyond theoretical discussions.

As these two concepts when paired are capable of wholly describing the context for behaviour in the work setting, it is essential that both be considered in the characterization of the organizational environment. This study will utilize the concepts of culture and climate in a model to describe the organizational environment to develop an analysis framework and methodology for the promotion of organizational health in the industrial work environment.

In the Organizational Health Model, culture explicitly drives the climatic conditions. Therefore, the climate represents how the culture is operationalized on a surface level. In this model, the factors selected to describe climate are those relevant to the two outcomes of interest: effectiveness as related to specific performance goals and organizational wellness as related to the quality of working life. Culture, as the essential values upon which an organization is based, provides a deep-rooted structure from which everyday policies, practices, and goals can be grounded. When this progression occurs, the organization's values are enacted, reinforced, and clarified through its practices.

In a study at a U.S. manufacturing company, values and organizational climate were found to influence organizational effectiveness while work practices were found to influence worker satisfaction and stress. Although the distinction between "climate" and "practices" was not clarified in this research, this effort provides evidence of the significance of these work-system components in the determination of organizational health.

Furthermore, numerous researchers have noted the positive effects of the congruence between cultural values, organizational goals, and daily practices. Morgan (1986) argued that a healthy organization requires its culture to be consistent with its structure, policies, and procedures. Schneider et al. (1996) proposed that what people believe is the culture and experience is the climate ultimately determines whether sustained change is accomplished.

Collins and Porras (1994), in their study of the distinguishing characteristics of visionary, high-performing companies, found that organizational alignment so that members receive a consistent set of signals to reinforce the desired behaviour and achieve de- sired progress was perhaps the key finding of their 5-year research. In evaluating a proposed practice, Collins and Porras asserted that the key question is not "Is the practice good?" but "Is this appropriate for us—does it fit with our ideology and ambitions?"

Recently, rapid changes in the organization of work precipitated by work process improvement initiatives, coupled with changes in worker demographics, have necessitated the need to assess the impact of these changes on long-term work performance.

Contemporary work-improvement strategies such as lean manufacturing and six sigma have focused their efforts to optimize process performance while largely ignoring the effects of these new work practices on workers. However, human performance plays an integral role in the determination of organizational effectiveness. The organizational health assessment model introduced in this article proposes a new paradigm for optimizing work in which the individual's health, safety, and satisfaction is viewed as the precursor of process and organizational effectiveness.

Work system interventions can be crafted only from data-driven evidence of the safety, performance, and health consequences currently faced by workers in the contemporary work environment. The Organizational Health Model introduced here provides a frame- work for health surveillance in industries with contemporary organizational practices (e.g., lean manufacturing, six sigma) and changing worker demographics (e.g., increasing numbers of women, ethnic minorities, and aging workers).

In the Organizational Health Model, culture—represented by an organization's values and goals—constitutes a company's strategic intent. Climate driven and reaffirmed by the culture establishes the context for behaviour (performance) and state of being (wellness) in the work setting. Further development of this model will serve to structure the gathering of empirical data, thus fostering the process of designing both healthy and competitive enterprises.

4

Developing the Travel Career Approach to Tourist Motivation

THEORIES OF MOTIVATION

To retain good staff and to encourage them to give of their best while at work requires attention to the financial and psychological and even physiological rewards offered by the organization as a continuous exercise. Basic financial rewards and conditions of service (e.g. working hours per week) are determined externally (by national bargaining or government minimum wage legislation) in many occupations but as much as 50 per cent of the gross pay of manual workers is often the result of local negotiations and details (e.g. which particular hours shall be worked) of conditions of service are often more important than the basics. Hence there is scope for financial and other motivations to be used at local levels.

As staffing needs will vary with the productivity of the workforce (and the industrial peace achieved) so good personnel policies are desirable. The latter can depend upon other factors (like environment, welfare, employee benefits, etc.) but unless the wage packet is accepted as 'fair and just' there will be no motivation. Hence while the technicalities of payment and other systems may be the concern of others, the outcome of them is a matter of great concern to human resource management. Increasingly the influence of behavioural science discoveries are becoming important not merely because of the widely-acknowledged limitations of money as a motivator, but because of the changing mix and nature of tasks (e.g. more service and professional jobs and far fewer unskilled and repetitive production jobs).

The former demand better-educated, mobile and multi-skilled employees much more likely to be influenced by things like job satisfaction, involvement, participation, etc. than the economically dependent employees of yesteryear. Hence human resource management must act as a source of information about and a source of inspiration for the application of the findings of behavioural science. It may be a matter of drawing the attention of senior managers to what is being achieved elsewhere and the gradual education of middle managers to new points of view on job design, work organization and worker autonomy. The current human resources shortage in the health sector – mainly of sub-Saharan African countries – threatens the realization of plans for scaling up interventions to control the spread of diseases such as HIV/AIDS, malaria and tuberculosis.

The World development report 2004 states it clearly: Without improvements to the human resources situation, the health-related Millennium Development Goals cannot be achieved. The problems are multiple, the most serious being staff shortages, particularly in rural and remote areas. In many countries, the effects of insufficient capacity development in the health system are aggravated by migration and a mounting burden of disease. The World health report 2006 gathers ample evidence of the human resource challenges, but also provides ways forward to address the problems.

With respect to existing human resources, the low level of health worker motivation has often been identified as a central problem in health service delivery. For example, the results from a survey undertaken by the Gesellschaft für Technische Zusammenarbeit (German Technical Cooperation, GTZ) among representatives of ministries of health and GTZ staff from 29 countries showed that low motivation is seen as the second most important health workforce problem after staff shortages.

From the perspective of health professionals, the challenges include lack of equipment, frequent shortages of supplies and a mounting workload – all these exacerbated in small and rural facilities. Furthermore, despite decentralization efforts, key functions of human resource management (recruitment, overall staff distribution, remuneration, promotion and transfers) remain highly centralized.

Despite interest in the issue of human resources for health, human resource management and the question of what can be done to strengthen health worker motivation in developing countries has so far not received as much attention as the subject merits.

There is a small but growing body of qualitative studies looking at motivation of health workers in developing countries that indicate the limitations of financial incentives on motivation and that reveal the importance of non-financial incentives. A study in South Africa on the effects of a newly introduced, so-called "rural allowance" showed the limited impact on retention and motivation.

Similarly, analysing the role of wages in health worker migration, Vujicic et al. conclude that what they call non-wage instruments may be more effective in reducing migration flows, as portrayed in a WHO report. The study of Kingma, while undertaken in developed countries, also provides important insights on the limited effect of financial incentives on nurses and instead points at the relevance of non-financial incentives for nurses' job satisfaction and self-esteem.

In their study on health workers' motivation and performance in Benin, Alihonou et al. suggest introducing non-financial incentives while also improving structural conditions. Stilwell shows, by reference to Zimbabwe, that health workers based in remote areas, despite lack of financial incentives and hard working conditions, frequently exhibited a high level of motivation to perform well. She traces this motivation to good leadership and supportive management, among other factors. Her analysis suggests that certain non-financial incentives can have a beneficial effect on motivation, even under adverse conditions of insufficient pay and equipment, understaffing, etc. In a review of theories and empirical evidence of health workers motivation, Dolea and Adams equally stress the importance of non-financial incentives.

Low motivation has a negative impact on the performance of individual health workers, facilities and the health system as a whole. Moreover, it adds to the push factors for migration of health workers, both from rural areas to the cities and out of the country. It is therefore an important goal of human resources management in the health sector to strengthen the motivation of health workers, from heads of health facilities to auxiliary staff.

Financial incentives are important, and the problem of low salaries must be addressed, especially in situations where income is insufficient to meet even the most basic needs of health professionals and their families. But the evidence suggests that increased salaries are by no means sufficient to solve the problem of low motivation. More money does not automatically imply higher motivation. We therefore suggest that any comprehensive strategy to maximize health worker motivation in a developing country context has to involve a mix of financial and non-financial incentives.

To support the development of effective strategies for human resources management and the improvement of health worker motivation, the German Technical Cooperation (GTZ) has assessed motivation and motivational determinants in rural districts of Benin, Kenya, El Salvador and Nicaragua. The study aims at determining the role of non-financial incentives for motivation. This chapter here presents the findings from the Benin and Kenya case studies.

The next section outlines the conceptual framework used, followed by a description of the methodology. The fourth section focuses on health workers' feelings, views and perceptions and opens the black box of the motivational process. The paper then analyses the current problems and potentials of selected HRM tools with respect to their motivational effect on health workers. The final section offers conclusions and recommendations for the way forward.

This chapter will show that health workers overall are strongly guided by their professional conscience and similar aspects related to professional ethos that keep them going. Many health workers are demotivated and frustrated precisely because they are unable to satisfy their professional conscience and impeded in the pursuit of their vocation due to lack of means and supplies at work and due to inadequate or inappropriately applied human resources management (HRM) tools. The paper also indicates that the way HRM tools are applied is characterized by severe pitfalls affecting the motivation of health workers. Motivation can be defined as "the willingness to exert and maintain an effort towards organizational goals". Motivation develops in each individual as a result of the interaction between individual, organizational and cultural determinants. Some of these factors are of more distal nature, such as cultural norms and values and individual personality, hence they lie outside the scope of human resources management.

Kanfer identifies two aspects of the internal motivation process: The "will-do" aspect concerns the establishment of congruence between personal goals and the goals of the organization (goal setting). Questions that characterize this psychological process are: "What is the personal value of devoting more of my resources to the job?" or "What is the personal value of achieving higher job performance?"

The "can-do" aspect concerns motivational effectiveness, the extent of individual resources that are mobilized to accomplish adopted goals (goal achievement). The related question is: "How likely is it to achieve the desired level of job performance?".

The "will-do" and the "can-do" component can be distinguished for analytic purposes but the line between the two is blurred, as the findings of this study will show. Efforts to strengthen the motivation of doctors and nurses have to influence one or both of these components. Kanfer and Franco et al. do not explicitly mention a cross-impact between the "will-do" and "can-do" components, but the empirical findings of this study strongly suggest that there may be such an effect, which is indicated by the two crossing arrows. The result of this psychological process can be observed as motivational consequences with impact on the behaviour (job performance), affection (job satisfaction) and cognitive aspects (work attachment) of health workers.

Kanfer's model offers a framework for the assessment of motivational determinants and the motivational process in greater detail, thereby going beyond the common and simpler distinction between motivators and satisfiers, as presented by Herzberg et al.

In this study, we assess the impact of organizational determinants on the motivational process, specifically of HRM tools and non-financial incentives as part thereof. We define an incentive as an available means applied with the intention to influence the willingness of physicians and nurses to exert and maintain an effort towards attaining organizational goals. This is borrowed from Buchan et al., who define an incentive as "one particular form of payment that is intended to achieve some specific change in behaviour".

The most common understanding of financial incentives is a transfer of monetary values or equivalents, such as wage increases, allowances, performance-related bonuses or housing. Adams/Hicks also include the basic salary, allowance schemes, health insurance premiums, housing or housing allowances in this category. Obviously, in practice it may be difficult to differentiate between the basic salary package and additional financial incentives. Non-financial incentives are by contrast those incentives that involve no direct transfers of monetary values or equivalents to an individual or group. This includes, for example, granting unpaid holidays, token awards or recreational facilities, as well as recognition and supervision.

Human resources management (HRM) is the management of people in an organization. HRM tools comprise the policies, practices and activities at the disposal of managers to obtain, develop, use, evaluate, maintain and retain the appropriate number, skill mix and motivation of employees to accomplish the organisation's objectives. There is a huge body of literature on HRM and tools, which cannot be captured here.

But as the commentary on "what difference does ("good") HRM make?" by Buchan shows, good HRM determines performance and motivation. In other words, tools and techniques applied as part of HRM also function as non-financial incentives to strengthen motivation in line with the above definition. The following list, derived from EFQM (European Foundation of Quality Management) criteria, contains some of the core HRM tools that may affect motivation.

These aspects are similarly assessed in the World health report 2006:

- Supervision schemes
- Recognition schemes
- Performance management
- Training and professional development
- Leadership
- Participation mechanisms
- Intra-organizational communication processes.

The organizational culture influences all these aspects, but changes in these aspects may also modify the organizational culture. Furthermore, work conditions constitute an important motivational determinant. Comprehensive HRM therefore also needs to look at and optimize the work conditions.

The in-depth study design entailed (semi-) structured qualitative interviews with doctors and nurses from public, private and NGO facilities in rural areas. The questionnaire contained mainly open-ended questions. The interviews took about 60 to 90 minutes. Results from individual interviews were backed up with information from focus group discussions. For further contextual information, interviews with civil servants in the Ministry of Health and at the district level were held.

The qualitative interviews with health workers covered the following topics: prevailing practice; experience and views of health workers on core HRM/QM tools, such as training, supervision, performance assessments, participation, leadership, working environment, personal and career plans; and implicitly their effect on motivation. Some of the questions were not applicable for health workers who own a private clinic; these questions were therefore left out.

The last part of the interview focused explicitly on motivation and motivational determinants, yet the word "motivation" was avoided, except for two direct questions – "How do health workers define motivation?" and later "How do they assess their level of motivation?" – based on a given definition.

The study assesses motivational determinants and is concerned only indirectly with motivational consequences, to the extent that health workers report about these. An action research setting would have been required to assess motivational changes over time, triggered by the introduction or change of specific HRM/QM tools and (non-) financial incentives.

Before prospective respondents agreed to participate in the study, the interviewer informed them about the overall subject of the questions: their experiences and views of certain HRM tools and needs around their work environment.

The actual research question on the role and relevance of non-financial incentives was not unveiled in order to avoid "socially desired behaviour" responses. The questionnaires were translated into French in a one-round decentring process and then pretested.

In each country, interviews were carried out by a consultant taking notes, rather than tape-recording. Qualitative data were coded centrally, thus avoiding inter-rater reliability concerns. The SPSS (Statistical Product and Service Solutions (formerly Statistical Package for the Social Sciences)) software package was used for the analysis of the quantitative and the coded qualitative data.

The sampling for the study was layered: The selection of districts was purposive in that it focused on GTZ-supported project areas, giving easy access to regional and district authorities. Facilities within a district were randomly selected on the basis of the district's facility list, except for the district hospital, which was always included. As the selection of facilities was based on the district's facility list, informal, non-registered private clinics were not part of the sampling process.

Random sampling on the basis of a staff list proved difficult. It was hard to arrange appointments prior to the interview, due to insufficient means of communication as well as staff absences. Ultimately, staff for the interviews were selected on the spot in cooperation with those in charge. Given the low numbers of doctors in rural facilities, every available doctor was interviewed.

A target of 50 interviews per country was set. Due to resource constraints, only 37 interviews could be held in Kenya. The Benin counterparts were interested in a larger sample and 62 interviews were realized. Except for the percentage of doctors (33% of the total sample should have been doctors), the sampling cornerstones were met: two thirds of interviews from the public sector, one sixth each from the private and NGO sector; at least one third of respondents to be female or male. No requirement was defined for the age of respondents.

The study questions touched potentially delicate and personal issues relating to health workers' behaviour and attitude. Particular attention was therefore paid to triangulation. One means used was the knowledge of national and international GTZ staff involved in this study, who have detailed knowledge and long experience in the field that enables them to provide "external" assessments of certain problems and situations. Likewise, the focus group discussions reflected individual responses or drew out some delicate topics even more explicitly. Construct validity was enhanced by the consecutive use of similar questions and the reliance on several indicators to measure the same phenomena.

Ultimately, in order to find out what can be considered "true", it is also necessary to take into account what people can be expected to say on the basis of their interest and motives. Respondents may have stressed in particular the difficulties and challenges they are confronted with at their workplace. One may also expect individuals who feel very demotivated to be reluctant to admit so to the interviewer.

Certain questions by their type or content pose larger reliability and validity concerns than others, namely those asking respondents to rank themselves on a Likert scale. Such findings must be taken with some caution. They were included to provide a general impression.

Whether health workers really tell the "truth" cannot always be fully clarified. When this is the case, we clearly point it out in the text. On the whole, health workers appreciated the interest of "outsiders" in their personal concerns and opinions. There was no indication that they held back their views and judgements.

Given the sampling procedures as well as the small sample size, quantitative statements are not claimed to be representative for the entire health workforce of a country. Despite these limitations, the strength of this study lies in its exploratory and qualitative character. It sheds much light on what is considered important by health workers. By giving them a voice, we find out what really matters to them and which instruments have the potential to increase their motivation and job satisfaction and thus, ultimately, performance.

OUTLINE RESULTS AND DISCUSSION

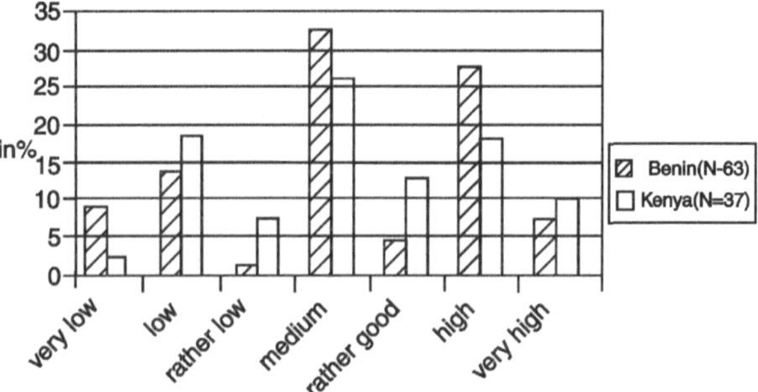

Fig; Self-assessment of motivation level

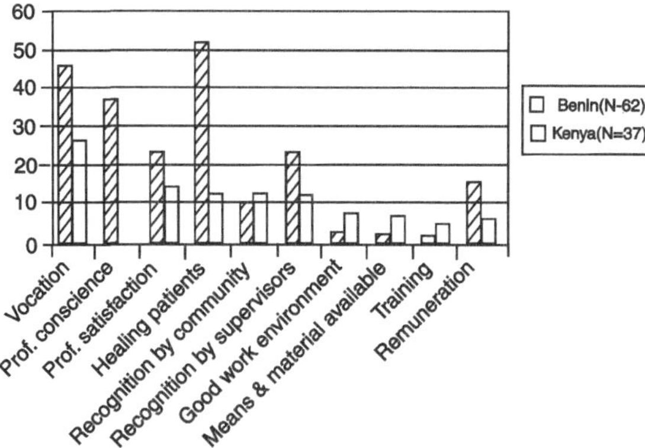

Aspects that encourage to do one's work well, in %, in Benin (N = 62), Kenya (N = 37)

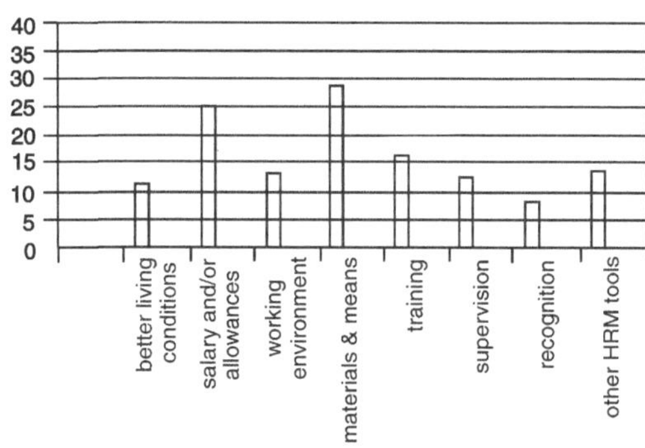

Fig: Benin: "How to boost your spirit and willingness to perform" (in %, multiple responses, N = 62)

Fig: Preferred source of appreciation

Country information

In both Benin and Kenya, the public sector is the greatest health service provider and employer of health workers. Both countries suffer from shortages in staff resources, inadequate skills and very low salaries, particularly for nurses and other lower cadres. For example, depending on the job group, Kenyan nurses earn today between KES 5757 (about USD 72) and KES 12 450 (about USD 155) per month.

In order to retain doctors in the public service and improve the situation in under-supplied areas, the Kenyan Government has introduced additional "extraneous" and "non-practising" allowances for medical doctors, dentists and pharmacists.

For doctors who enter the public service with a basic wage of KES 11 690 (about USD 145) per month, the allowances in this job group amount to KES 25 000 (about USD 311) per month. This means that wages of doctors have de facto tripled. According to a key informant in the Ministry of Health of Kenya, this measure has so far attracted 500 doctors to seek employment in the Kenyan public service. While wages have therefore improved for this job category, the working conditions in government health facilities remain largely unchanged.

In Benin, a nurse earns around 40 000 XOF (USD 75). Although a variety of allowances are paid for various kinds of tasks or functions (responsibility allowance, risk allowance, remoteness allowances), it remains difficult to survive on just this income. Most health professionals therefore engage in other income-generating activities. Especially for doctors, it is much more attractive and profitable to stay in urban areas, which is why it is difficult to attract them to rural areas.

Hotel Health Workers' Understanding of Motivation

As mentioned above, motivation can be defined as the willingness to exert and maintain an effort towards attaining organizational goals. Yet, when health workers are asked about their definition of motivation ("What does being motivated mean to you?"), a different understanding emerges.

Out of these, one fourth explicitly mention financial encouragement. Another 40% consider "being motivated" as having the means and material to work, to get recognition, or other HRM tools, such as awards, supervision and good leadership. Hence, the majority understands motivation as a "motivator", i.e. an incentive, and not as a state of mind. Only 5% refer to motivation as the "willingness" or the "pleasure" to do one's work, similar to the above definition, from the literature, of motivation as an intrinsic process and state of mind. Not surprisingly, the latter groups are mainly doctors and health workers in the private sector.

In Kenya, one fifth understands motivation as encouragement. However, there is a larger share of health workers who refer to that intrinsic state of willingness and pleasure to do one's work. This difference in the connotation between Kenyan and Benin respondents may be due to the fact that so-called "motivation allowances" ("primes de motivation") have been introduced in Benin, that may have changed the meaning of motivation from a state of mind to that of an incentive.

This understanding of motivation matches health workers' perceptions of motivational consequences: For the majority of Benin respondents (70%), motivating someone serves to improve work performance, while only 30%

perceive motivation as a means to increase job satisfaction and job attachment. Again, for Kenyans, there is a stronger focus on the satisfaction element (48%). Especially in Benin, this view of motivational consequences may represent a legacy from previous decades, when job satisfaction and pleasure were not part of the prevailing organizational cultures. As one key informant put it, individual health workers were merely seen as a part of the production chain.

The introduction of a quality management system, which is currently under way in Kenya and partly in Benin, may provide the opportunity to gradually change this mindset and to give the word motivation a new meaning. Alternatively, it may seem necessary to avoid the word motivation altogether and use a different terminology, such as for example "boosting one's work spirit or work morale". In contrast to their own definition of motivation, health workers were asked to assess their level of motivation, by considering the following definition: "Willingness to do a good job, according to organizational objectives".

The health workers' replies suggest that they may not have responded in line with the given definition, but also referred to their own understanding of motivation. With the caveat that the validity of the answers may be somewhat limited, more so as the Likert scales for Benin and Kenya were not internally validated, the figure still provides an overall idea of how health workers see their own level of motivation: In both countries, more than 55% do not place themselves in the categories "rather good", "high" or "very high".

In Benin, health workers from the private sector/NGO facilities appear more motivated than those in public health facilities. Two thirds assess their level of motivation as "very high", "high" or "rather good" (14/21), compared to around a quarter from the public services (11/41). Nurses from the public sector appear to be the least motivated group and therefore a likely focus for efforts to increase motivation by means of human resources management and incentives. In Kenya, such clear tendencies cannot be derived, but then the sample size is also much smaller.

Motivational determinants: professional values and goals versus endangered self-efficacy. To identify the motivational determinants that account for perceived level of health worker motivation, respondents were asked: "Which aspects currently encourage you to undertake efforts to do your work well?".

Health workers in Benin strongly referred to vocation and professional conscience, i.e. their personal professional values. Likewise, the wish to help patients and professional satisfaction were frequently mentioned. Pangu carried out a study in Benin on the reasons why health workers stay in function despite decreasing motivation and identifies exactly those four aspects. Among Kenyan respondents, vocation was equally very dominant. Also, healing patients, professional satisfaction and recognition were considered important. These aspects nurture health workers' goals. Both dimensions – values and goals – indicate a strong professional ethos and commitment and strongly appear to translate into the "will-do" component of the motivation process. Other factors, such as work environment and HRM tools that relate more to the "can-do" component are also mentioned, but particularly in Benin they do not feature as prominently as values and goals.

About 6% of respondents in Benin and Kenya mention regular salaries and allowances. Finally, half of the health workers in the private sector in Benin, that is 10% overall, consider that earning revenue is an important encouragement to do one's work well. When health workers were asked, with respect to the future, what would have to happen so as to boost their spirit and increase their willingness to perform (this was asked only of Benin respondents), they emphasize to be able to perform one's work, namely having the materials and means available as well as further training and supervision.

This corresponds with the findings of Alihonou et al. as well as with a staff survey from Zimbabwe cited in USAID, which revealed that the number one reason provided by health workers for resigning their government job was the lack of equipment and supplies. Also, a more conducive working environment and atmosphere, recognition and feedback, and other HRM tools such as better leadership, management and participation, are reported to contribute to increasing health workers' self-efficacy, i.e. their self-perception of being able to do a good job and fulfill their duties ("can-do" component of motivation).

It also emerged from the interviews that health workers appreciate small benefits as relevant to their motivation. For example, in public health facilities, unpaid holidays or small amenities such as free tea for staff on night duty were perceived as motivating. Their absence, temporary or permanent, was considered demotivating.

The two questions on current versus future motivational determinants accordingly revealed different answers: Several aspects that featured low under the question on current motivational factors – precisely due to their (perceived) non-existence or poor state, such as organizational factors – then emerged in the second question as potential motivating factors.

These aspects do not dominate, however. Instead, very prominent were health workers' request and need for available means and materials to carry out their work in a professional way. Subsequent questions, e.g. how health workers could improve their performance, persistently revealed the frustrations that health workers experience because of the lack of means and materials and the inadequate work environments as well as deficits in HRM.

It appears that these frustrations are so strong precisely because of the high professional commitment of health workers. In fact, there is a danger that perceived self-efficacy, constrained by inadequate HRM and work environment, becomes so weak that it may ultimately negatively affect health workers' commitment and professional ethos. Health workers' commitment and professional ethos is, moreover, endangered by the existence of HIV/AIDS, which, as for example Aitken and Kemp have shown for Southern Africa, has a severe impact on health workers' behaviour and above all attitude to work. In fact, throughout the interviews, health workers refer to HIV/AIDS issues. Asked about their feelings and reactions with respect to HIV/AIDS at the workplace, few health workers feel sufficiently protected. Most health workers fear becoming infected and report reacting in general more reserved towards patients. Some respondents said that every patient is seen as a potential source.

The next section assesses some core HRM tools and derives their effect on the "will-do" and "can-do" component of motivation. Respondents were asked about their experience with and perceptions of certain non-financial incentives and HRM tools. The findings reveal present shortcomings, but also reveal further potentials in the application of such tools, which is supported by the vast evidence and examples collected by the WHR 2006.

Supervision as Control Versus Support Supervision and Recognition

Ideally, supervision is a formalized HRM instrument to correct shortcomings and to support good practice, on the basis of which recommendations are provided to help improve individual and facility performance. Supervision can contribute considerably to health workers' self-efficacy and relates therefore to the "can-do" component of Kanfer's model of motivation. To the extent that supervision is used to communicate a facility's goals and that it takes account of health workers' personal goals and needs, it also strengthens goal coherence and affects the "will-do" component of motivation.

The interviews revealed that 40% of respondents from Benin and more than 50% from Kenya perceive supervision as an exercise of control. As the following quotes reveal, existing schemes for supervision are sometimes perceived as unhelpful and distant, rather than personal and supportive:

- "Supervision is not very useful. The supervisors remind nurses of the procedures they should apply. Right now, under given circumstances, you cannot implement them. They remind you of the rules and control you."
- "While individual efforts go unnoticed, mistakes or shortcomings are noticed immediately."
- "The supervision went without difficulties, but the supervisors did not give me any feedback afterwards."

Health workers criticize the low frequency and irregularity of supervision as well as the top-down approach used by supervisors. Supervision that involves discussions of health workers' conduct in the presence of patients is seen as particularly demotivating. Responses revealed that not knowing whether or when the next supervision takes place can also have a negative effect on health workers' commitment to improve their work.

In Kenya, almost half the respondents and one in ten of the respondents in Benin claimed that they do not receive any personal feedback from their superior. Judging from the answers provided, the feedback that health workers receive from their supervisors in rural facilities usually centres on specific shortcomings or technical aspects of service provision. It rarely appears to focus on the personal perspective of the health worker herself or himself. Feeling neglected by the superiors or the health administration has a strongly demotivating effect. There are indications that supportive supervision, recognition and personal feedback tend to be more common in religious and private health centres in Kenya than in public facilities.

Despite these shortcomings, health workers consider supervision useful and desirable to the extent that it helps improve personal performance, to avoid mistakes and to update knowledge. When personal needs and concerns are taken seriously, supervision provides the feeling of being cared for and of appreciation. This aspect appears particularly important for health workers posted to remote facilities with little contact with other professionals.

There is a large potential for improvement in the supervision process, according to the respondents' suggestions: Apart from a more frequent, regular and reliable supervision, many respondents ask for a different approach, in that supervision should be more supportive, instructive, needs-oriented, participatory and should provide a direct and timely feedback on their problems. There was also a call for more meetings to discuss problems and solutions. Direct observation of health worker activities is considered helpful to identify the bottlenecks in service delivery, provided that health workers are not criticized in front of the patients.

In conclusion, support supervision that exists appears to contribute significantly to health workers' self-efficacy. There are potentials to strengthen the "can-do" component of motivation through a more regular supervision routine and follow-up. Moreover, supportive supervision that takes account of the supervisee's personal and professional goals of recognition and learning and that communicates organizational goals clearly offers a potential for a positive motivational effect both in the "will-do" and "can-do" component that is so far not sufficiently used.

Lack of recognition versus institutionalized recognition and appreciation by superiors and communities. Through an encouraging and supportive attitude, superiors can strengthen their subordinates' self-efficacy and thus foster personal efforts for the achievement of organizational goals: the "can-do" component of motivation. Community recognition and appreciation can have the same effect.

While most felt that their leaders are accessible, critique focused on lack of encouragement and insufficient consideration of staff views, as health workers did not feel adequately supported and recognized by their superiors. In other words, the leaders seemed to fail to contribute as much as possible to strengthening health workers' self-efficacy. In general, health workers criticized their leaders' inadequate communication and bad treatment of staff. When leaders fail to be role models by not adhering to organizational goals, health workers may wonder why they should adopt them, thereby reducing the drive for the "will-do" component. In fact, a good number of respondents wished for supervisors to receive training on management and leadership issues. Clearly, health workers highly value recognition and appreciation from superiors and colleagues as well as patients. The role of good working relationships with superiors and colleagues similarly emerged as one important motivational determinant in a study in Georgia by Bennett et al.

However, asked whose appreciation health workers find most relevant, 80% of Benin and 50% of Kenya respondents referred to the patients' appreciation. There is no correlation by type of institutions, hence client appreciation is not of greater importance to health workers from the NGO and private sector than from the public sector. This is not to say that in practice, health workers are indifferent to their supervisors' appreciation. After all it is important for career promotion and adequate postings, but as Buchan also notes, the "avowed first loyalty [of doctors and nurses] tends to be to their profession and their patients ..."

Appreciation from clients is seen as an indicator for successful professional conduct and the achievement of the health workers' goal to cure patients. The importance of patient appreciation stems primarily from health workers' search for professional satisfaction and their professional goals of helping patients, as revealed throughout the interviews, for example:

"Appreciation from the patients is most important, because it is sincere and heartfelt." The above finding strongly supports ideas and efforts for strengthening community participation in health service provision. Client satisfaction surveys, community dialogue and interaction with health unit management committees should be managed in such a way as to not only ensure client orientation and accountability towards the community but also to convey appreciation and strengthen staff motivation.

Such improved mechanisms may also help to reduce health workers' perceptions of too much interference by the community, lack of patient compliance or lack of cooperation by patients and their relatives. These issues formed frequent complaints by health workers and appeared to affect the "can-do" component of their motivation.

Inadequate training versus needs- and problem-adapted training.

Training and professional progress are important motivational determinants, as they nurture health workers' personal objectives and their value system. In fact, training as a tool of human resources management can serve several purposes. It can help health workers to cope better with the requirements of their job. It can also enable them to take on more demanding duties and positions and to achieve personal goals of professional advancement. Training can have strong motivating effects.

When asked about the effect of training courses they had taken over the past two years, nearly all health workers in Kenya and Benin mentioned that they felt more comfortable and confident with their work afterwards. Some

20% also mentioned increased interest and work commitment. These answers suggest a considerable effect of training courses on both the "can-do" and the "will-do" component of motivation. Overall, respondents were very interested to receive more continued medical education/continued professional development. This is similar to other study findings.

Contents of courses and seminars that were out of touch with the reality of the rural health facilities of developing countries were considered the most important problem by health workers. After a training course, those confronted with treatment guidelines based on standards of equipment and supplies that do not exist at their workplace experience their daily work environment as an insurmountable obstacle to the provision of "adequate" health care. Improvisation to make up for shortcomings in equipment and supplies was considered inferior practice.

Overall, training can have a strong effect not only on the "can-do" component, but also on the "will-do" component of motivation. Yet, to have this effect, i.e. to exploit this motivational potential, training courses must be adapted to the local context: the actual working conditions in rural facilities.

Non-transparent allocation versus equal opportunities for training and professional progress. Further education and professional progress rank highest among the professional objectives of the nurses and doctors interviewed in Kenya and Benin. These objectives were mentioned by about two thirds of respondents. The answers reveal that the interest in further education is motivated by the chance to rise within the hierarchy of the health system, to reach a higher status and to increase earnings.

In Kenya, the prospect of sponsorship for further qualifications in the public health system appears to make public sector jobs more attractive for health workers working in private and mission facilities, although working conditions were acknowledged to be better in some of the private facilities.

Health workers in the public sector, by contrast, often feel demotivated by the limited realistic prospects of professional progress and personal advancement and the rather slow and cumbersome promotion process. Where access to training and further qualifications is limited or granted in line with reasons that are not equitably available or merit-based, this can likewise have detrimental consequences for the motivation effect of training as a tool of human resources management.

Opportunities for training must be allocated in a transparent and fair way, since a sense of unequal treatment demotivates and leads to frustration. As such, it affects both the "will-do" and "can-do" component of motivation.

The use of training and further qualification as a human resources management tool is limited by financial resource constraints, of course. However, as individual examples show, there may be options for gradual improvement and needs-adapted training even in resource-poor rural settings. In Kenya, whereas the management of one facility ruled out Continued Medical Education for lack of funds to invite teachers, in another facility, the medical superintendent provided short information leaflets to update staff on basic guidelines and procedures. Given that 10% of health donor funds are spent on training activities, there is a great need – but also opportunity – in policies that address these deficits.

Passive Staff Involvement Versus Active Staff Participation

Staff participation and staff involvement is an important HRM tool. It permits making the best use of health workers' knowledge, hands-on experience and ideas for improvements. In addition, staff participation involves recognition and appreciation of health workers and their competences. It appeals to their need to be taken seriously. This has important implications for motivation, both for the "will-do" component (e.g., self-realization, professional satisfaction) and the "can-do" component (e.g., self-confidence, improvements around the workplace by taking account of health workers' knowledge and ideas).

Most respondents in Kenya and Benin felt they could contribute ideas and efforts, particularly with respect to daily activities. While Kenyan respondents seem to see this happen primarily through staff meetings, Benin respondents rather refer to their efforts on the job.

By contrast, 57% of Kenyan respondents felt they couldn't participate in decision-making at their facility, a perception shared by nearly 80% of Benin respondents. There was no difference between the different provider types. Still, nearly everybody considers participation as important and, with a few exceptions, the vast majority would like to be involved much more actively. The respondents indicate that the relevance of participation consists in sharing one's views and knowledge of a situation or of a problem-oriented solution, to be involved in decisions that concern oneself or to react where necessary in order to avoid frustrations.

Interestingly, under current conditions hardly any feeling of professional satisfaction or self-realisation among respondents appeared to result from participation. Staff involvement appeared to be a passive undertaking. It serves to collect ideas and proposals. It allows staff to get informed rather than to take part in actual decision-making.

Given that health workers are socialized in a rather top-down, hierarchical organizational culture within the public sector, which ultimately reflects cultural values and characteristics of the wider society, the idea of participation as a means of self-realization and particularly of recognition appears now to be hardly present.

The findings suggest that increased participation could have an effect on both the "can-do" component (ideas of staff are taken into account to improve the work process) and the "will-do" component (influence on decisions to the benefit of health workers – satisfaction with respect to personal goals, appreciation of health workers' skills and competences – satisfaction with respect to professional goals). Hence, there is a great need to institutionalize participation, e.g. by holding regular meetings, in which health workers not only share ideas and suggestions for improvements, but in which health workers ultimately participate in decision-making on issues that concern their work and immediate work environment.

Infrequent performance appraisals versus culturally adapted performance management. Performance management tools serve to improve performance of health workers. Performance management assists in setting, communicating and internalizing organizational goals, thereby nurturing the "will-do" component.

At the same time, this provides feedback to health workers as regards their capabilities and skills to achieve these goals, hereby addressing the "can-do" component. One specific tool is performance assessment, which this section looks at specifically. Other tools include the communication of the organizational mission, vision and objectives, self-assessments, quality improvement teams, performance related payments, benchmarking and awards. Performance assessment constitutes a review of a health worker's skills and achievements.

In Kenya, government health workers must pass an annual performance review. The interviews revealed that not everybody appears to know what this is about and which indicators are applied. Attitudes regarding the relevance of the annual performance assessments seem to be mixed. Some health workers – especially those with a very good report – say it is motivating. Also, several think the performance assessment leads to a change in practice and behaviour. Yet, some few say that it has no effect on one's practice and behaviour. Moreover, less than 30% (27%) state that the performance assessment can potentially have an impact on one's promotion. A good assessment is required for a promotion, and even though bad assessments appear to be rare, promotions are not forthcoming, as they are contingent upon vacancies and the availability of financial resources. Also, as one respondent says,

"It is a slow and painful process; you have to follow up on the promotion you are meant to receive in Nairobi." (female nurse, government facility, Kenya, in focus group discussion)

Furthermore, individual award schemes at the district level ("best unit" of district health facilities), although carried out on the basis of a detailed performance assessment, were considered unfair and thus demotivating by the staff, probably because the method and criteria of the selection process had not been sufficiently communicated.

In contrast to Kenya, there are no such performance assessments in Benin. Instead, Benin respondents from the public sector referred to the biannual supervision process that serves to monitor key indicators. After the exercise, all facility managers in a district get together to receive feedback, advice and recommendations from the district health authorities, as well as congratulations in some cases. Health facilities are ranked, which allows health workers to find out about their relative facility performance. The majority of respondents report that that they know the procedures as well as the indicators by which facilities are monitored. However, according to some respondents, the responsible facility managers do not always share the results with the rest of the team, which is considered frustrating or annoying. In practice, the facility-based supervision process seems to be translated to the level of individual health workers and can hence be understood as a form of performance assessment.

Several health workers mentioned that good performance may be rewarded through participation in training or by means of a scholarship. However, on the whole, respondents appear to see no direct impact of good performance on career development. One positive effect are the so-called "primes de performance" (performance allowances), which are paid for good indicator results. The public ranking and public congratulations appear to have a strong effect on health workers.

By providing feedback on health workers' work, performance assessments have some effect on the "can-do" component overall, since they help improve knowledge and skills. Yet this effect is currently small, as is the effect on the "will-do" component.

Although the responses suggest that health workers are performance-oriented, the potential of performance management as a motivating instrument has not been not fully realized yet. Given the fertile ground for performance orientation, there appears to be scope for the gradual introduction of a performance culture, the search for excellence. The responses also suggest that health workers are receptive to performance assessments. Any initiative to promote a performance culture must take into account cultural values, norms and characteristics, as shown by the following section.

Individual Success and Team-based Performance Promotion

The findings reveal certain cultural factors that may impinge upon motivation and performance. Respondents were asked whether there are barriers that impede personal efforts and act as barriers to better performance. They were prompted specifically on envy among colleagues.

In Kenya, nearly half the respondents stated that individual efforts are appreciated, while 30% confirm that envy indeed impedes individual efforts. In contrast, only a sixth of Benin respondents, among them all the private-sector doctors, feel it is possible and worthwhile to engage in individual efforts. Yet, nearly two thirds clearly expressed that individual efforts are futile and that team efforts are necessary to reach further. Half of the respondents mentioned envy as a barrier to individual efforts.

With respect to performance management, such feelings and views are problematic, because they may lead individuals to discount outstanding performance and the acceptance of responsibilities beyond theirs duties. The development of a performance culture, based on individual efforts, appears to be closely circumscribed by the social context. The findings indicate that it may be necessary to build performance management schemes upon group identities. This requires a focus on building teams and creating team spirit. Likewise, this suggests designing awards for groups rather than for individuals, more so as the latter creates conflicts within facility teams.

Supporting health workers and making them feel cared for: a call for quality management. The previous section has shown that health workers are strongly guided by their professional conscience and similar aspects related to professional ethos overall, relating to the "will-do" component of motivation.

Many health workers appear to be demotivated and frustrated precisely because they are unable to satisfy their professional conscience and impeded in pursuing their vocation due to lack of means and supplies and due to inadequate or inappropriately applied HRM tools. These appeared to negatively affect the "can-do" component of motivation. Due to the extent of the problems at hand, they also affect the "will-do" component of motivation.

In conclusion, efforts to strengthen health worker motivation must protect, promote and build upon the professional ethos of medical doctors and nurses. This entails appreciating their professionalism and addressing health workers' professional goals such as recognition, career development and further qualification.

It must be the aim of HRM and quality management to develop the work environment so that health workers are enabled to meet personal and organizational goals. This requires strengthening health workers' self-efficacy by offering training and supervision, but also by ensuring the availability of essential means, materials and supplies as well as equipment and the provision of adequate working conditions that enable them to carry out their work appropriately and effectively.

The findings confirm our starting point that non-financial incentives and HRM tools do play an important role when it comes to increasing motivation of health staff. The findings suggest that HRM tools have the dual task to promote health workers' professional ethos and commitment, and to strengthen their perception of self-efficacy.

The discussion of HRM tools above showed that there are serious deficits in their application, resulting in and reinforcing health workers' low motivation, primarily within the "can-do" component, but also affecting the "will-do" component.

On the other hand, the analysis of health workers' responses and suggestions indicates that the HRM tools analysed above clearly constitute motivational determinants. In fact, the "toolbox" of HRM appears to have a great potential for improving health worker motivation. Also, only a small range of the available HRM tools have so far been applied in the countries that have been assessed. The key message obtained from the interview data is the need to make health workers feel they are cared-for. Health workers require support in a variety of ways, ranging from technical aspects to personal and psychological needs. It is necessary to move to a culture of support supervision, to institutionalize recognition of health workers, to allocate training opportunities in an equal and transparent way, to fulfil health workers' drive for learning and acquiring new knowledge, to increase participation opportunities and to strengthen leadership. Ultimately, this requires changes in the organizational culture and individual attitudes, which can improve only by means of a gradual process in an enabling environment.

Therefore, greater awareness among superiors is needed in relation to their role as leaders. Leadership must become clear part of a superior's function and skills. It is important to note that good leadership is more than one single tool of human resources management; it is a fundamental and cross-cutting element interrelated with the style of participation, supervision and feedback, performance management and quality improvement activities.

The analysis also showed the applicability and usefulness of Kanfer's and Franco et al's differentiation into the "will-do" and "can-do" component, thereby shedding some light into the black box of the motivational process. Policy implications and recommendations therefore can become more specific and targeted. There is a different angle to it when we take high professional commitment as the starting point for a strategy of improving motivation. Furthermore, when contextualizing these findings into a quality management approach, there is additional impetus and additional implications as well as clearer guidance for action.

There is substantial overlap between HRM and quality management in terms of contents. Staff is considered and valued as a key resource in all major QM frameworks. QM is about leadership and HRM. It aims at improved management capacity of health workers and strengthens the capacity for participatory problem-solving.

A QM perspective and approach offers numerous benefits when it comes to optimizing human resources management. The QM framework permits developing, applying and evaluating HRM tools comprehensively, coherently and systematically. It offers a comprehensive set of tools that can be adjusted to fit specific circumstances and requirements – whether of a district, a hospital or a health centre. Furthermore, QM introduces the perspective of a continuous improvement process that looks at both outcomes and process. The process orientation ideally provides for continuous efforts to improve HRM under given circumstances.

Moreover, QM aims not only at changing and improving HRM tools and working conditions, it may also affect (or address) organizational values and hence organizational culture. QM is concerned with both organizational as well as individual determinants of motivation, while recognizing the importance of cultural values. The most widely used QM methods include self-evaluation and quality improvement projects, in which a team sets realistic objectives for process (and outcome) improvement and monitors the realization of the plan. Equally important are staff and client satisfaction surveys, as well as training. While we do not aim to promote a specific quality management model, the following process requirements are considered essential for a contribution of QM to HRM:

- Search for excellence: contribution of the whole staff body to quality improvement efforts;
- Orientation on quality as an outcome as much as on quality of the process;
- Strong emphasis on self-evaluation of individuals and organizations;
- More autonomy and responsibility for health workers;
- Focus on participation and self-realization, empowerment and to a certain extent emancipation of health workers.

The findings indicate that the values on which QM is based are equally shared and referred to by health workers in the two countries under investigation. While certain HRM tools have become increasingly popular, also in African countries, the potential of QM seems far from exhausted.

Recommendations and the Way Forward

Each country has a unique human resource situation, reflecting its stage in the health sector reform process. Accordingly, there is no overall blueprint on how to best improve health worker motivation. Each region, and even each facility, may require a specific mix of financial and non-financial incentives as part of a larger HRM or QM framework.

Findings from a survey on HRM experiences among health projects and programmes supported by GTZ in 29 countries (18 in Africa) suggest putting together a mix of incentives and HRM tools, aiming at both individuals' aspirations and organizational changes. These entry points can be realized incrementally even in resource-poor settings and make a difference when it comes to service delivery. This goes well hand-in-hand with the bundle of measures suggested by the World health report 2006 to enhance health worker performance.

Specifically with respect to performance management, there is a need to inform health workers about the process and indicators and to provide thorough feedback on the results. Also, consistently good performance should be the basis for promotional schemes by including elements of merit rather than length of service. This also necessitates streamlining the promotion process and making it more transparent. In Benin, the competition among facilities seems promising.

However, within this ranking process, it is important to consider not only absolute scores, but also to take into account efforts and improvements over time. This is particularly relevant, as some facilities may suffer from much more serious drawbacks than others. Recognition and awards, which do not always have to be financial, appear to be highly appreciated. They should be applied in a systematic and transparent way.

Experience from the health projects supported by GTZ, which have relied on applying a mix of financial and non-financial incentives, shows that positive impacts can be achieved. For example, in Zambia, the introduction of refresher training for medical staff seems to have led to a higher retention rate. In Ethiopia a mix of continued medical education, the provision of housing, the establishment of a clear career structure and a defined number of services in hospitals has led to improved staff satisfaction and retention. An awards scheme, closer supervision and team-building efforts have improved both some service output indicators and the motivation to stay in rural districts of Ghana. As a result, higher antenatal care and EPI coverage as well as fewer applications for transfers have been reported.

These experiences call for a more systematic assessment. In fact, most countries, whether in the public or the private sector, in donor-supported programmes or NGO-run projects, apply a range of non-financial incentives. However, often this is not done systematically or specifically in relation to motivation and performance increases. As such, the impacts and effects of non-financial incentives are rarely monitored or evaluated. Hence there is great need to develop simple and practical methods to monitor the impact of incentives on staff motivation.

There are many challenges concerning the effective and sustainable implementation of incentive schemes and HRM tools, let alone comprehensive QM frameworks. With respect to allowances and financial incentives, the effect on staff motivation is often temporary in nature because such benefits become part of the general benefit package. Likewise, although training is seen as a good motivating instrument, high staff turnover may limit the sustainability of staff training.

Furthermore, there is a particular challenge with respect to introducing performance-related payment: It is difficult to define objective and commonly accepted performance criteria and even more difficult to implement and apply those performance criteria, given political interference and lack of good governance and transparency and the existence of corruption as well as nepotism.

In addition, it is very difficult to change old habits and long-term institutionalized norms and rules, such as promotion schemes that are based on age rather than merit. Another problem is caused by cultural norms that may negatively sanction an individual who is willing to show initiative beyond his or her duty, thus outperforming colleagues.

Hence, ultimately, HRM and QM measures must be imbedded in a good governance agenda in order to be effective and successful in the long run. Fostering transparency and accountability is necessary, since many of the factors that have a detrimental effect on health worker motivation are rooted in systemic or structural deficits. The role of donors and development partners is to strengthen institutional capacities at headquarters levels and at the district level to make a meaningful decentralization process, also in the field of human resources management, possible. Likewise, we must be aware that the introduction and institutionalization of non-financial incentives and the various HRM tools or their improvement has its costs. It requires training, supervision from higher levels and follow-up. Change in organizational culture takes time. It is therefore important to develop realistic HRM plans and to provide for the financing to implement such measures.

Moreover, united action is needed from the donor community. The use and motivational effect of non-financial and financial incentive schemes in public health systems and private practice may remain limited as long as other development partners provide high top-up allowances as a financial incentive. Thus, donors should seek agreement on a code of conduct that establishes guidelines for orienting the development partners' activities – ranging from remuneration for health staff to sitting allowances, i.e. allowances paid for attending a training or a workshop.

Finally, we must be realistic: improved human resources management cannot compensate for many other factors, at both the macro and micro level, that seriously impinge upon work performance and staff retention, such as staff and supply shortages, heavy workload and difficult working conditions, migration pull factors originating from developed countries, as well as the threatening HIV/AIDS pandemic.

Non-financial incentives and HRM/QM tools are not a magic bullet that solves the pressing HRH problem and compensates for the lack of investment and the structural deficits that characterize health systems in many low-income countries – there is no such magic bullet. However, as the discussion above indicates, these tools can make a difference and may be effective even in a resource-constrained context.

USE OF REWARD TO MOTIVATE EMPLOYEES

Since motivation influences productivity, supervisors need to understand what motivates employees to reach peak performance. It is not an easy task to increase employee motivation because employees respond in different ways to their jobs and their organization's practices. Motivation is the set of processes that moves a person toward a goal. Thus, motivated behaviours are voluntary choices controlled by the individual employee. The supervisor (motivator) wants to influence the factors that motivate employees to higher levels of productivity.

Factors that affect work motivation include individual differences, job characteristics, and organizational practices. Individual differences are the personal needs, values, and attitudes, interests and abilities that people bring to their jobs. Job characteristics are the aspects of the position that determine its limitations and challenges. Organizational practices are the rules, human resources policies, managerial practices, and rewards systems of an organization. Supervisors must consider how these factors interact to affect employee job performance.

Simple Model of Motivation

The purpose of behaviour is to satisfy needs. A need is anything that is required, desired, or useful. A want is a conscious recognition of a need. A need arises when there is a difference in self-concept (the way I see myself) and perception (the way I see the world around me). The presence of an active need is expressed as an inner state of tension from which the individual seeks relief.

Other Theories of Motivation

Many methods of employee motivation have been developed. The study of work motivation has focused on the motivator (supervisor) as well as the motivatee (employee). Motivation theories are important to supervisors attempting to be effective leaders. Two primary approaches to motivation are content and process. The content approach to motivation focuses on the assumption that individuals are motivated by the desire to fulfill inner needs. Content theories focus on the needs that motivate people.

Maslow's Hierarchy of Needs identifies five levels of needs, which are best seen as a hierarchy with the most basic need emerging first and the most sophisticated need last. People move up the hierarchy one level at a time. Gratified needs lose their strength and the next level of needs is activated. As basic or lower-level needs are satisfied, higher-level needs become operative. A satisfied need is not a motivator. The most powerful employee need is the one that has not been satisfied. Abraham Maslow first presented the five-tier hierarchy in 1942 to a psychoanalytic society and published it in 1954 in Motivation and Personality.

- *Level I* - Physiological needs are the most basic human needs. They include food, water, and comfort. The organization helps to satisfy employees' physiological needs by a paycheck.
- *Level II* - Safety needs are the desires for security and stability, to feel safe from harm. The organization helps to satisfy employees' safety needs by benefits.
- *Level III* - Social needs are the desires for affiliation. They include friendship and belonging. The organization helps to satisfy employees' social needs through sports teams, parties, and celebrations. The supervisor can help fulfill social needs by showing direct care and concern for employees.
- *Level IV* - Esteem needs are the desires for self-respect and respect or recognition from others. The organization helps to satisfy employees' esteem needs by matching the skills and abilities of the employee to the job. The supervisor can help fulfill esteem needs by showing workers that their work is appreciated.
- *Level V* - Self-actualization needs are the desires for self-fulfillment and the realization of the individual's full potential. The supervisor

can help fulfill self-actualization needs by assigning tasks that challenge employees' minds while drawing on their aptitude and training.

Alderfer's ERG identified three categories of needs. The most important contribution of the ERG model is the addition of the frustration-regression hypothesis, which holds that when individuals are frustrated in meeting higher level needs, the next lower level needs reemerge.

Existence needs are the desires for material and physical well being. These needs are satisfied with food, water, air, shelter, working conditions, pay, and fringe benefits. Relatedness needs are the desires to establish and maintain interpersonal relationships. These needs are satisfied with relationships with family, friends, supervisors, subordinates, and co-workers. Growth needs are the desires to be creative, to make useful and productive contributions and to have opportunities for personal development. McClelland's Learned Needs divides motivation into needs for power, affiliation, and achievement.

Achievement motivated people thrive on pursuing and attaining goals. They like to be able to control the situations in which they are involved. They take moderate risks. They like to get immediate feedback on how they have done. They tend to be preoccupied with a task-orientation towards the job to be done. Power motivated individuals see almost every situation as an opportunity to seize control or dominate others. They love to influence others. They like to change situations whether or not it is needed. They are willing to assert themselves when a decision needs to be made.

Affiliation motivated people are usually friendly and like to socialize with others. This may distract them from their performance requirements. They will usually respond to an appeal for cooperation. Herzberg's Two-Factor Theory describes needs in terms of satisfaction and dissatisfaction. Frederick Herzberg examined motivation in the light of job content and contest. Motivating employees is a two-step process. First provide hygienes and then motivators. One continuum ranges from no satisfaction to satisfaction. The other continuum ranges from dissatisfaction to no dissatisfaction.

Satisfaction comes from motivators that are intrinsic or job content, such as achievement, recognition, advancement, responsibility, the work itself, and growth possibilities. Herzberg uses the term motivators for job satisfiers since they involve job content and the satisfaction that results from them. Motivators are considered job turn-ons. They are necessary for substantial improvements in work performance and move the employee beyond satisfaction to superior performance. Motivators correspond to Maslow's higher-level needs of esteem and self-actualization.

Dissatisfaction occurs when the following hygiene factors, extrinsic or job context, are not present on the job: pay, status, job security, working conditions, company policy, peer relations, and supervision. Herzberg uses the term hygiene for these factors because they are preventive in nature. They will not produce motivation, but they can prevent motivation from occurring. Hygiene factors can be considered job stay-ons because they encourage an employee to stay on a job. Once these factors are provided, they do not necessarily promote motivation; but their absence can create employee dissatisfaction. Hygiene factors correspond to Maslow's physiological, safety, and social needs in that they are extrinsic, or peripheral, to the job. They are present in the work environment of job context.

Motivation comes from the employee's feelings of accomplishment or job content rather than from the environmental factors or job context. Motivators encourage an employee to strive to do his or her best. Job enrichment can be used to meet higher-level needs. To enrich a job, a supervisor can introduce new or more difficult tasks, assign individuals specialized tasks that enable them to become experts, or grant additional authority to employees.

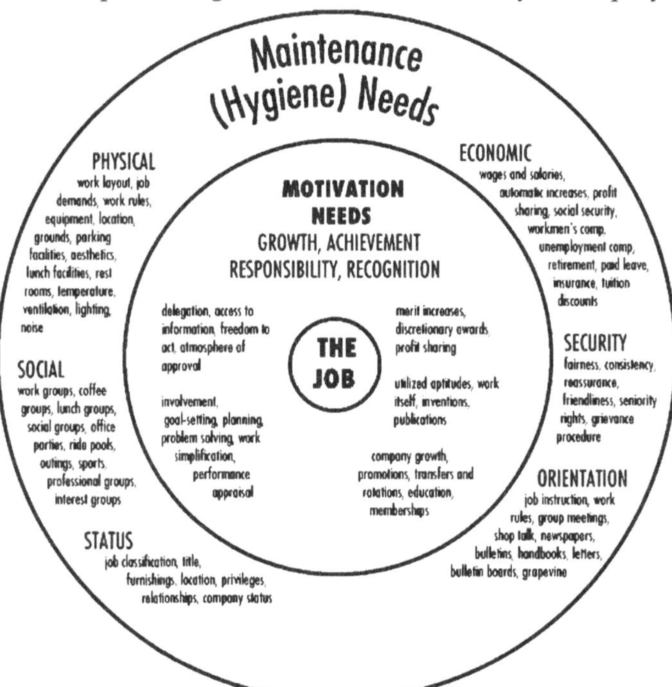

The process approach emphasizes how and why people choose certain behaviours in order to meet their personal goals. Process theories focus on external influences or behaviours that people choose to meet their needs. External influences are often readily accessible to supervisors. Vroom's Expectancy Model suggests that people choose among alternative behaviours because they anticipate that particular behaviours will lead to one or more desired outcomes and that other behaviours will lead to undesirable outcomes. Expectancy is the belief that effort will lead to first-order outcomes, any work-related behaviour that is the direct result of the effort an employee expends on a job.

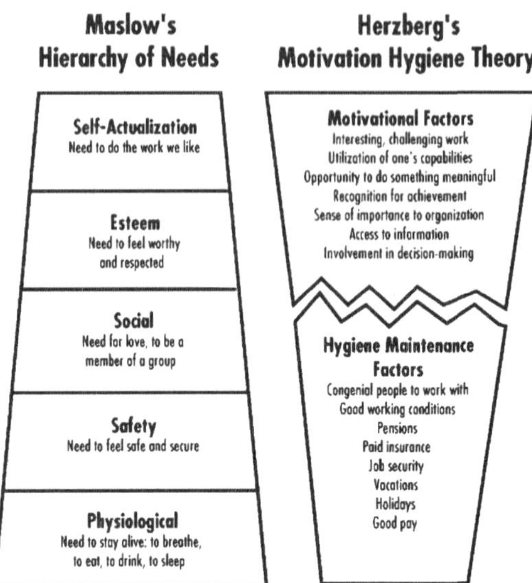

Equity is the perception of fairness involved in rewards given. A fair or equitable situation is one in which people with similar inputs experience similar outcomes. Employees will compare their rewards with the rewards received by others for their efforts. If employees perceive that an inequity exists, they are likely to withhold some of their contributions, either consciously or unconsciously, to bring a situation into better balance.

For example, if someone thinks he or she is not getting enough pay (output) for his or her work (input), he or she will try to get that pay increased or reduce the amount of work he or she is doing. On the other hand, when a worker thinks he or she is being paid too much for the work he or she is doing, he or she tends to increase the amount of work. Not only do workers compare their own inputs and outputs; they compare their input/output ratio with the input/output ratio of other workers. If one work team believes they are doing more work than a similar team for the same pay, their sense of fairness will be violated and they will tend to reduce the amount of work they are doing. It is a normal human inclination to want things to be fair.

Bowditch and Buono note that while equity theory was originally concerned with differences in pay, it may be applied to other forms of tangible and intangible rewards in the workplace. That is, if any input is not balanced with some fair output, the motivation process will be difficult. Supervisors must manage the perception of fairness in the mind of each employee. If subordinates think they are not being treated fairly, it is difficult to motivate them.

Reinforcement involves four types of consequence. Positive reinforcement creates a pleasant consequence by using rewards to increase the likelihood that a behaviour will be repeated. Negative reinforcement occurs when a person engages in behaviour to avoid unpleasant consequences or to escape from existing unpleasant consequences. Punishment is an attempt to discourage a target behaviour by the application of negative outcomes whenever it is possible. Extinction is the absence of any reinforcement, either positive or negative, following the occurrence of a target behaviour. Employees have questions about their jobs.

Equity Theory

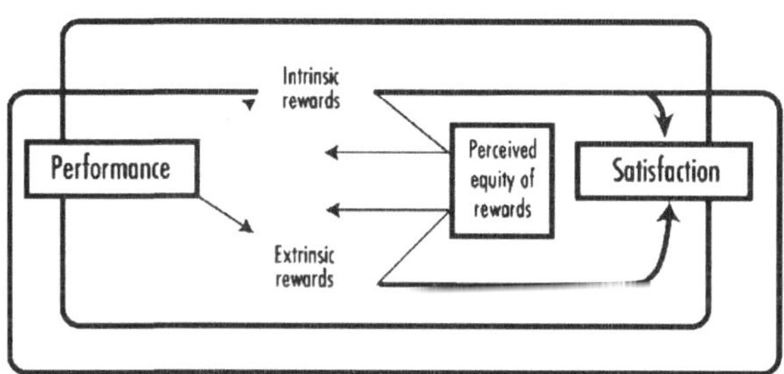

Reinforcement is based primarily on the work of B.F. Skinner, a psychologist, who experimented with the theories of operant conditioning. Skinner's work shows that many behaviours can be controlled through the use of rewards. In fact, a person might be influenced to change his or her behaviour by giving him or her rewards.

Employees who do an exceptionally good job on a particular project should be rewarded for that performance. It will motivate them to try to do an exceptional job on their next project. Employees must associate the reward with the behaviour. In other words, the employee must know for what specifically he or she is being rewarded! The reward should come as quickly as possible after the behaviour. The reward can be almost anything, but it must be something desired by the employee. Some of the most powerful rewards are symbolic; things that cost very little but mean a lot to the people who get them. Examples of symbolic rewards are things like plaques or certificates.

The Reinforcement Process

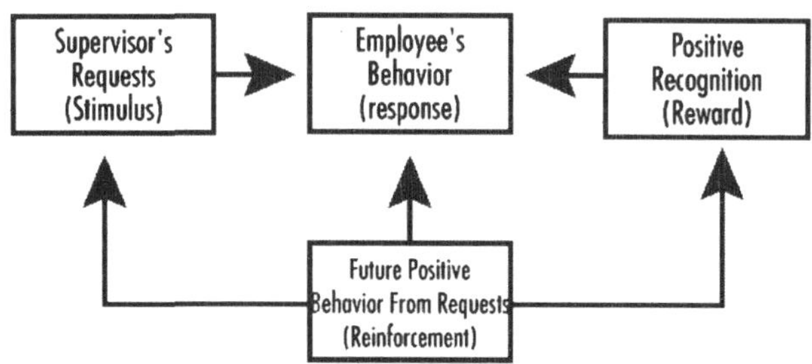

5

Employee Education, Training and Development

In general, education is 'mind preparation' and is carried out remote from the actual work area, training is the systematic development of the attitude, knowledge, skill pattern required by a person to perform a given task or job adequately and development is 'the growth of the individual in terms of ability, understanding and awareness'.

Within an organization all three are necessary in order to:

- Develop workers to undertake higher-grade tasks;
- Provide the conventional training of new and young workers (e.g. as apprentices, clerks, etc.);
- Raise efficiency and standards of performance;
- Meet legislative requirements (e.g. health and safety);
- Inform people (induction training, pre-retirement courses, etc.);

From time to time meet special needs arising from technical, legislative, and knowledge need changes. Meeting these needs is achieved via the 'training loop'. (Schematic available in PDF version.)

The diagnosis of other than conventional needs is complex and often depends upon the intuition or personal experience of managers and needs revealed by deficiencies. Sources of inspiration include:

- Common sense - it is often obvious that new machines, work systems, task requirements and changes in job content will require workers to be prepared;
- Shortcomings revealed by statistics of output per head, performance indices, unit costs, etc. and behavioural failures revealed by absentee figures, lateness, sickness etc. records;
- Recommendations of government and industry training organizations;
- Inspiration and innovations of individual managers and supervisors;
- Forecasts and predictions about staffing needs;
- Inspirations prompted by the technical press, training journals, reports of the experience of others;

- The suggestions made by specialist (e.g. education and training officers, safety engineers, work-study staff and management services personnel).

Designing training is far more than devising courses; it can include activities such as:

- Learning from observation of trained workers;
- Receiving coaching from seniors;
- Discovery as the result of working party, project team membership or attendance at meetings;
- Job swaps within and without the organization;
- Undertaking planned reading, or follow from the use of self–teaching texts and video tapes;
- Learning via involvement in research, report writing and visiting other works or organizations.

So far as group training is concerned in addition to formal courses there are:

- Lectures and talks by senior or specialist managers;
- Discussion group (conference and meeting) activities;
- Briefing by senior staffs;
- Role-playing exercises and simulation of actual conditions;
- Video and computer teaching activities;
- Case studies (and discussion) tests, quizzes, panel 'games', group forums, observation exercises and inspection and reporting techniques.

Evaluation of the effectiveness of training is done to ensure that it is cost effective, to identify needs to modify or extend what is being provided, to reveal new needs and redefine priorities and most of all to ensure that the objectives of the training are being met.

The latter may not be easy to ascertain where results cannot be measured mathematically. In the case of attitude and behavioural changes sought, leadership abilities, drive and ambition fostered, etc., achievement is a matter of the judgment of senior staffs. Exact validation might be impossible but unless on the whole the judgments are favourable the cooperation of managers in identifying needs, releasing personnel and assisting in training ventures will cease.

In making their judgments senior managers will question whether the efforts expended have produced:

- More effective, efficient, flexible employees;
- Faster results in making newcomers knowledgeable and effective than would follow from experience;
- More effective or efficient use of machinery, equipment and work procedures;
- Fewer requirements to implement redundancy (by retraining);
- Fewer accidents both personal and to property;
- Improvements in the qualifications of staff and their ability to take on tougher roles;

- Better employee loyalty to the organization with more willingness to innovate and accept change.

DIFFERENCE BETWEEN ORIENTATION AND TRAINING

Training constitutes a third set of practice modifications for effective team implementation. There is often a mistaken belief that people who are highly educated have the basic skills to work effectively in team settings. In fact, highly specialized individuals are often used to working alone and may lack some of the basic interpersonal skills necessary for collaboration.

Training programmes designed for interpersonal skills in teams take one of two approaches: traditional classroom instruction in which a lecturer delivers material about techniques or strategies for working in teams and creative off-site team-building sessions in which teams participate in athletic, artistic, or competitive activities unrelated to their actual day-to-day responsibilities.

What is generally missing is the development of hands-on team capabilities, which is best accomplished by treating the team as a whole and applying the training as the team performs its actual tasks. In this way, the value of the training is established in the context of the work that the team does. In addition to teaching interpersonal skills, training must focus on establishing the skills necessary for self-management. First, considerable attention must be given to determining an optimal degree of autonomy. Self-managing teams are an appropriate response to situations where performance can be enhanced by taking decisions closer to the organization's environment.

In contrast, self-management is not appropriate when the team is particularly large, when there is a high degree of functional diversity, or when the team is newly formed. In these situations, the team is faced with a high level of complexity, information-processing requirements are extensive, and managerial tasks are particularly challenging.

Having an external leader provide direction in these instances can improve team effectiveness. Perhaps the most substantial costs associated with increasing self-direction in teams are associated with the level of training and development needed to ensure that all or most of the members have the KSAs required to perform what were previously managerial responsibilities. In addition, on some teams employees are asked actually to carry out the training and development of their fellow members. Another training focus pertains to learning. In a team-based system, multidirectional learning is required across functions, levels, and organizations. This requires norms that are far different from those that prevailed in the traditional organization.

For example, learning requires the willingness to surface bad news and act on it. But that will not happen unless the traditional reaction— negatively evaluating the messengers of bad news—changes. Organizations that encourage experimentation and innovation and set up mechanisms for shared reflection can capitalize on this learning potential. Lateral learning must occur through dialogue and collaboration, and vertical learning must occur between teams at different levels in the organization. Local learning and innovation occurs through trial and error, but broader learning depends on whether organizations establish mechanisms for reflecting on and capturing learning from a variety of experiences.

If organizations wish to motivate teamwork, they must incorporate teamwork KSAs into their appraisal systems. It is important that the appraisal system not only reward good team players but also discourage behaviours that are not conducive to team effectiveness. An organization-specific job analysis should be conducted to determine the precise nature of the behavioural and performance measures to be included in the appraisal form for each individual team member.

Categories of teamwork KSAs such as conflict resolution, collaborative problem solving, communication, goal setting, performance management, planning, and task coordination could be translated into critical work behaviours or performance dimensions and incorporated into such an appraisal form. Equally important, however, is that team behaviours then be assessed. Imagine four teams, each performing the same task.

In the first team, each team member is given an individual goal. In the second, a goal is set for the team as a whole only. The third team is given both individual and team goals. The fourth is given no specific goal at all. Which team will do the poorest work? In an experiment that replicated this situation, the team with individual goals only was the poorest performer among all four teams. The team with both individual and team goals performed the best.

Most organizations might claim they have both individual and team goals if they have profit sharing or gain sharing. However, psychologically, these types of "team goals" are often overshadowed by individual goals, because the personal sense of control over performance lessens as one focuses on larger and larger groups, such as the entire organization. Each team should identify a set of critical measures representing a combination of results and process-oriented outcomes.

Focusing only on results (for example, return on sales, revenue growth, and so on) does not help inform the team about which behaviours should be adjusted. Process measures (time spent per call, days before call returned, and so on) identify key behaviours that the team can change in order to improve results. Teams should avoid developing too many measures. If a measure is not critical in guiding the team's behaviour, then discard it. Most experts recommend that teams track six to ten performance areas.

Finally, in team-based organizations, people are responsible for collective performance at multiple levels. Individual, team, and business unit performance must be evaluated. Optimizing performance at any one level may hurt performance at other levels. The link between behaviour at one level and performance at another may be uncertain. People are often concerned that they will not get adequate feedback on how they are performing when the focus is on collective performance. Therefore, appraisal systems should assess behaviours that contribute to performance of other units or other levels within the organization. Team members should receive feedback from multiple sources, not just a manager. In small teams, each person can receive peer feedback, that is, feedback from all other team members and, where appropriate, feedback from customers.

Customers may be external to the organization (for example, a person who purchases a product or service) or internal (a person downstream in the process who receives the work of the team). It is also critical that feedback be given on multiple levels. It should be provided on individual performance, individual contributions to the team, team performance, and the team's contribution to the organization as a whole. Especially for the latter, feedback from customers and about competitors is critical. Whenever possible, it is best for teams themselves to document their own performance. This documentation should be developed and then discussed regularly at team meetings.

A final set of HR practices that should be examined when implementing teams pertains to compensation. Good practices for rewarding team performance require good processes for defining what the performance should be and for measuring and evaluating the performance. Some researchers have advocated that rewards should be the last component put in place in the transition to teams. This argument is made because team rewards are difficult to develop and have to be tailored to the organization.

Individual compensation should then be based on the accomplishment of these objectives. This is an intermediary step on the path toward team-based rewards; it allows recognition for teamwork and allows time for the organization to adjust other systems. Next, HR professionals can work to change the organizational compensation and reward practices. For example, team awards and team bonuses help team members focus on the performance of their own team. Profit sharing and gain sharing help team members focus on unit wide performance and orient employees to the larger performing unit by making it in everyone's interest to improve the performance of the enterprise as a whole.

This combination ensures that performance at each level is recognized and encouraged, in turn ensuring that individual behaviour is in the best interest of the team and that team behaviour is in the best interest of the organization. HR professionals may face several additional impediments. We see four challenges in particular: the inability of work teams to make a dramatic improvement in organizational performance quickly; the inevitable inter team conflict inherent in team-based organizations; resistance to work teams in foreign affiliates; and North American cultural barriers to working in teams. An unwillingness to communicate between teams destroys one of the reasons that organizations implement teams in the first place: to create a higher level of integration in a complex organizational environment. Inwardly focused teams that fail to collaborate with others or communicate with external customers perform more poorly than externally focused teams. Several strategies are available to the HR professional for overcoming problematic inwardly focused teams.

First, managers should keep teams focused on a higher level, or super ordinate, goal. Such a goal can be organization-, plant, or unitwide. A super ordinate goal keeps teams focused on the big picture, lowers competition between teams, and ties everything that all do more closely to overall organizational success.

A second strategy is to implement rewards (possibly based on goals) that are tied to the success of a set of teams as whole (a work unit, for example). Unit-level rewards are tricky in that all team members have to know how their contribution affects their rewards (also known as line of sight). A final strategy is to create linking or integrating teams composed of members from each of the competitive teams. Integrating teams tend to dilute original team member loyalties and ensure that each team's concerns are heard. Regardless of the strategy chosen, ignoring the problem of combative teams will inevitably erode any potential gains to be realized from the implementation of work teams.

HR professionals should take a proactive stand by designing strategies to reduce competition before the teams are allowed to become inwardly focused. A third impediment may arise when multinational organizations use work teams in their foreign affiliates. Organizations often wish to "export" their management practices because having similar HR practices in each country streamlines operations and reduces costs. For example, the Goodyear Tire and Rubber Company has begun using work teams in Europe, Latin America, and Asia; Sara Lee Corporation currently uses teams in Puerto Rico and Mexico; and Texas Instruments Malaysia has organized its entire workforce into teams.

Organizational scholars have pointed to national culture as a determinant of the success or failure of management initiatives that are developed in one culture and implemented in another. Some employees may resist management initiatives or react angrily when those initiatives clash with their deeply held cultural values.

HR professionals should learn about the cultures in which the company's work teams will operate. Through better understanding of cultural differences comes the knowledge of potential stumbling blocks to successful implementation before attempts are made to export work teams. Success stories about work teams in foreign affiliates exist, but that success depends on an understanding of the cultural forces that shape employee reaction to teams.

Just as some cultures are more individualistic or more collectivistic than others, individuals within cultures also vary on this dimension—even though there is, on average, more variation across cultures than within cultures. For example, when faced with the prospect of moving to a team-based work environment, some employees in a study conducted in the United States expressed concerns that reflected their individualistic values. Their comments included these: "Why should someone else's performance affect my pay?" "Will the team get credit for what I do?" "Individual achievement won't count anymore." "My achievement will be diluted by overall team success." These comments suggest that some employees may resist work teams because they are not compatible with their own work-related values.

Tests exist for measuring individualistic and collectivistic values at the individual level. Other measures such as preference for teams could be used as selection tools to evaluate prospective team members before they are placed on a team.

If the teams are self-managing or autonomous, measures such as need for growth or need for achievement could be used to assess prospective member preferences for increased autonomy and responsibility. Whatever the measures used, HR professionals need to be aware of the role of individual differences in a team's success or failure in order to select more carefully individuals who are suited to working in a team. Barring the availability of such individuals, training must attempt to enhance employee receptivity to work teams.

Facilitators

First, in the years during which Total Quality Management enjoyed its heyday (the 1980s), many companies began a practice that had previously seemed contradictory to maintaining competitive advantage: benchmarking HR practices in other organizations. In years past companies viewed their internal operations as sources of extreme value.

But with the growth in international competition—especially in automobiles, electronics, and textiles—some businesses in the United States have realized the benefits of sharing information more openly to increase the global competitiveness of entire industries. This realization coupled with the work team success stories in the popular press have fueled an unprecedented exchange of both ideas and visits between companies and even competitors interested in adopting or improving work teams. For example, companies such as General Electric have looked to other seemingly unrelated businesses, such as Southwest Airlines, in order to adapt team-based practices. The benchmarking of HR practices also occurs within industries.

Several major semiconductor manufacturers (for example, Intel, DEC, Texas Instruments) have benchmarking agreements that allow for information exchange around HR best practices. Second, in many industries, organizational environments are becoming exceedingly dynamic and complex. Scholars and practitioners alike have long realized the importance of aligning organizational structures with environmental characteristics. For example, the rapid changes witnessed in the computer industry forced companies such as IBM to restructure to achieve a better organizational structure-environment fit. There is general consensus that increasing environmental complexity will continue for the foreseeable future for organizations in many industries.

As these changes continue, the use of work teams will continue to serve as an integrated and flexible means of responding to organizational environments. Finally, regarding cultural change, researchers have suggested that there may be a substantial amount of cross-national convergence of management practices, values, and beliefs as a result of the interactions between organizations across cultures.

As cultural convergence continues, a common set of values and assumptions may develop across national boundaries. This implies that eventually it may be possible to develop a universal set of best practices that will be appropriate no matter the cultural setting. In other words, less cultural adaptation may be necessary. Thus, HR practitioners in multinational corporations may gradually have an easier time dealing with cultural impediments.

We caution, however, that although some convergence is likely to take place, there are fundamental cultural values within nations that will remain stable. Researchers have referred to this phenomenon as the distinction between peripheral and core values. Therefore, it will always be necessary to adapt HR practices to some degree to fit the cultural context if the effectiveness of those practices across national boundaries is to be enhanced.

The Prospect of Teams Work

First, as the environment grows increasingly complex, temporary team structures will supplant more permanent work teams. As the forces outside organizations continue to change, the structures inside organizations will become more fluid. Rather than permanently assigning people to work teams, team composition will shift as projects, problems, or customers demand. Ad hoc teams or project teams will be more prevalent, placing extraordinary demands on employees to be flexible and demonstrate their value to organizations consistently through their team efforts.

The challenge for HR managers will certainly involve compensation and evaluation for employees who may be constantly moving from one project team to another without a regular supervisor or team members with whom they have any long-term contact.

Second, the use of multicultural teams and globalized teams is likely to rise as trade barriers continue to fall. National culture plays a strong role in determining employee attitudes and behaviour. If a significant rise in these more culturally diverse teams occurs—and we feel strongly that it will—then HR managers must familiarize themselves with the cultures in which their organization operates. For example, if peer evaluations are part of the performance appraisal process on a multicultural team, HR managers must identify the key cultural characteristics that may serve as stumbling blocks to these evaluations. If globalized teams are used, it is likely that entirely different compensation systems will be needed depending on the dominant cultural values of the areas in which an organization has business.

Finally, with more telecommuting and flextime there will be less face-to-face time in work teams. We predict that traditional work teams will be replaced by virtual teams, whose members may seldom or never meet in person. Also referred to as "mobile, " these teams have no geographic centre. The members work out of their homes, automobiles, and clients' facilities and communicate via e-mail, fax, telephone, and videoconference. Team meetings may take place only once each quarter. The challenge for HR professionals is to assist managers in integrating team members, building cohesive teams, and facilitating communication and information exchange without having team members together in one place.

Teams are a powerful design option for organizations that hope to meet the challenges of increased global competition, improve output quality, and address the social needs of the ever-changing global workforce. However, the success or failure of work teams in multinational organizations will depend largely on the HR professional. Effective implementation of teams requires that HR practitioners adapt key assumptions about motivation, structure, and accountability.

Adapted assumptions must support lateral thinking, collaboration, interdependence, a focus on process, permeable boundaries, and mutual responsibility. At the same time, HR practices must evolve to support teambased systems. Modifications in recruitment and selection, task design, training, evaluation, and compensation are all key to the effective use of teams in multinational organizations. Key to effective selection and recruitment for teams is the identification of teamwork KSAs.

Critical for task design is the development of teams around task processes and the integration of functional areas. Developing interpersonal, managerial, and learning skills are important training needs in team-based organizations. Finally, effective evaluation and compensation for teams requires a multilevel perspective and a balance between individual and team-based systems. Numerous impediments will challenge the effective implementation of teams across national contexts, including the inherent time lag between implementation and results, the often tenuous relationships between teams, cultural differences that require adaptations in practices to fit the context, and increasing domestic demographic diversity within nations.

To address these potential impediments, HR practitioners can encourage sharing practices within and between organizations, observe and adapt to organizational environmental trends, and maintain awareness of cultural convergence. HR professionals who can change their assumptions and are adept at modifying basic HR practices will be better poised to face future trends in the use of teams that are just on the horizon. As temporary team structures, multicultural teams, and virtual teams proliferate, these team-savvy practitioners will be able to lead their organizations through successful implementation and use of teams in multinational contexts.

DEVELOPING A HRM STRATEGY

Faced with rapid change organizations need to develop a more focused and coherent approach to managing people. In just the same way a business requires a marketing or information technology strategy it also requires a human resource or people strategy.

In developing such a strategy two critical questions must be addressed:

- What kinds of people do you need to manage and run your business to meet your strategic business objectives?
- What people programmes and initiatives must be designed and implemented to attract, develop and retain staff to compete effectively?

In order to answer these questions four key dimensions of an organization must be addressed.

These are:

- Culture: the beliefs, values, norms and management style of the organization
- Organization: the structure, job roles and reporting lines of the organization
- People: the skill levels, staff potential and management capability
- Human resources systems: the people focused mechanisms which deliver the strategy - employee selection, communications, training, rewards, career development, etc.

Frequently in managing the people element of their business senior managers will only focus on one or two dimensions and neglect to deal with the others. Typically, companies reorganize their structures to free managers from bureaucracy and drive for more entrepreneurial flair but then fail to adjust their training or reward systems.

When the desired entrepreneurial behaviour does not emerge managers frequently look confused at the apparent failure of the changes to deliver results. The fact is that seldom can you focus on only one area. What is required is a strategic perspective aimed at identifying the relationship between all four dimensions.

If you require an organization which really values quality and service you not only have to retrain staff, you must also review the organization, reward, appraisal and communications systems.

The pay and reward system is a classic problem in this area. Frequently organizations have payment systems which are designed around the volume of output produced. If you then seek to develop a company which emphasizes the product's quality you must change the pay systems. Otherwise you have a contradiction between what the chief executive is saying about quality and what your payment system is encouraging staff to do. There are seven steps to developing a human resource strategy and the active involvement of senior line managers should be sought throughout the approach.

Steps in Developing HRM Strategy

Get the 'Big Picture'

Understand your business strategy:

- Highlight the key driving forces of your business. What are they? e.g. technology, distribution, competition, the markets.
- What are the implications of the driving forces for the people side of your business?
- What is the fundamental people contribution to bottom line business performance?

Develop a Mission Statement or Statement of Intent

That relates to the people side of the business. Do not be put off by negative reactions to the words or references to idealistic statements - it is the actual process of thinking through the issues in a formal and explicit manner that is important.

- What do your people contribute?

Conduct a SWOT Analysis of the Organization

Focus on the internal strengths and weaknesses of the people side of the business:

- Consider the current skill and capability issues.
  Vigorously research the external business and market environment. High light the opportunities and threats relating to the people side of the business.
- What impact will/ might they have on business performance?
- Consider skill shortages?
- The impact of new technology on staffing levels?

From this analysis you then need to review the capability of your personnel department. Complete a SWOT analysis of the department - consider in detail the department's current areas of operation, the service levels and competences of your personnel staff.

Conduct a Detailed Human Resources Analysis

Concentrate on the organization's COPS (culture, organization, people, HR systems)

- Consider: Where you are now? Where do you want to be?
- What gaps exists between the reality of where you are now and where you want to be?

Exhaust your analysis of the four dimensions.

Determine Critical People Issues

Go back to the business strategy and examine it against your SWOT and COPS Analysis:

- Identify the critical people issues namely those people issues that you must address. Those which have a key impact on the delivery of your business strategy.
- Prioritize the critical people issues. What will happen if you fail to address them?

Remember you are trying to identify where you should be focusing your efforts and resources.

Develop Consequences and Solutions

For each critical issue highlight the options for managerial action generate, elaborate and create - don't go for the obvious. This is an important step as frequently people jump for the known rather than challenge existing assumptions about the way things have been done in the past. Think about the consequences of taking various courses of action.

Consider the mix of HR systems needed to address the issues. Do you need to improve communications, training or pay? What are the implications for the business and the personnel function? Once you have worked through the process it should then be possible to translate the action plan into broad objectives.

These will need to be broken down into the specialist HR Systems areas of:

- Employee training and development
- Management development
- Organization development
- Performance appraisal
- Employee reward
- Employee selection and recruitment
- Manpower planning
- Communication

Develop your action plan around the critical issues. Set targets and dates for the accomplishment of the key objectives.

Implementation and Evaluation of the Action Plans

The ultimate purpose of developing a human resource strategy is to ensure that the objectives set are mutually supportive so that the reward and payment systems are integrated with employee training and career development plans.

There is very little value or benefit in training people only to then frustrate them through a failure to provide ample career and development opportunities.

DEVELOPING AND DESIGNING A TRAINING PROGRAMME

Attracting the most qualified employees and matching them to the jobs for which they are best suited is significant for the success of any organization. However, many enterprises are too large to permit close contact between top management and employees. Human resources, training, and labour relations managers and specialists provide this connection.

In the past, these workers have been associated with performing the administrative function of an organization, such as handling employee benefits questions or recruiting, interviewing, and hiring new staff in accordance with policies and requirements that have been established in conjunction with top management.

Today's human resources workers manage these tasks and, increasingly, consult top executives regarding strategic planning. They have moved from behind-the-scenes staff work to leading the company in suggesting and changing policies. Senior management is recognizing the significance of the human resources department to their financial success.

In an effort to enhance morale and productivity, limit job turnover, and help organizations increase performance and improve business results, they also help their firms effectively use employee skills, provide training and development opportunities to improve those skills, and increase employees' satisfaction with their jobs and working conditions. Although some jobs in the human resources field require only limited contact with people outside the office, dealing with people is an important part of the job.

In a small organization, a human resources generalist may handle all aspects of human resources work, and thus require an extensive range of knowledge. The responsibilities of human resources generalists can vary widely, depending on their employer's needs. In a large corporation, the top human resources executive usually develops and manages human resources programmes and policies. (Executives are included in the Handbook statement on top executives.) These policies usually are implemented by a director or manager of human resources and, in some cases, a director of industrial relations.

The director of human resources may supervise several departments, each headed by an experienced manager who most likely specializes in one human resources activity, such as employment, compensation, benefits, training and development, or employee relations.

Employment and placement managers supervise the hiring and separation of employees and supervise various workers, including equal employment opportunity specialists and recruitment specialists. Employment, recruitment, and placement specialists recruit and place workers.

Recruiters maintain contacts within the community and may travel considerably, often to college campuses, to search for promising job applicants. Recruiters screen, interview, and occasionally test applicants. They also may check references and extend job offers. These workers must be thoroughly familiar with the organization and its human resources policies in order to discuss wages, working conditions, and promotional opportunities with prospective employees. They also must keep informed about equal employment opportunity (EEO) and affirmative action guidelines and laws, such as the Americans with Disabilities Act.

EEO officers, representatives, or affirmative action coordinators handle EEO matters in large organizations. They investigate and resolve EEO grievances, examine corporate practices for possible violations, and compile and submit EEO statistical reports.

Employer relations representatives, who usually work in government agencies, maintain working relationships with local employers and promote the use of public employment programmes and services. Similarly, employment interviewers—whose many job titles include human resources consultants, human resources development specialists, and human resources coordinators—help to match employers with qualified jobseekers.

Compensation, benefits, and job analysis specialists conduct programmes for employers and may specialize in specific areas such as position classifications or pensions. Job analysts, occasionally called position classifiers, collect and examine detailed information about job duties in order to prepare job descriptions. These descriptions explain the duties, training, and skills that each job requires. Whenever a large organization introduces a new job or reviews existing jobs, it calls upon the expert knowledge of the job analyst.

Occupational analysts conduct research, usually in large firms. They are concerned with occupational classification systems and study the effects of industry and occupational trends upon worker relationships. They may serve as technical liaison between the firm and other firms, government, and labour unions.

Establishing and maintaining a firm's pay system is the principal job of the compensation manager. Assisted by staff specialists, compensation managers devise ways to ensure fair and equitable pay rates. They may conduct surveys to see how their firm's rates compare with others and to see that the firm's pay scale complies with changing laws and regulations. In addition, compensation managers often manage their firm's performance evaluation system, and they may design reward systems such as pay-for-performance plans.

Employee benefits managers and specialists manage the company's employee benefits programme, notably its health insurance and pension plans. Expertise in designing and administering benefits programmes continues to take on importance as employer-provided benefits account for a growing proportion of overall compensation costs, and as benefit plans increase in number and complexity. For example, pension benefits might include savings and thrift, profit-sharing, and stock ownership plans; health benefits might include long-term catastrophic illness insurance and dental insurance.

Familiarity with health benefits is a top priority for employee benefits managers and specialists, as more firms struggle to cope with the rising cost of health care for employees and retirees.

In addition to health insurance and pension coverage, some firms offer employees life and accidental death and dismemberment insurance, disability insurance, and relatively new benefits designed to meet the needs of a changing workforce, such as parental leave, child and elder care, long-term nursing home care insurance, employee assistance and wellness programmes, and flexible benefits plans. Benefits managers must keep abreast of changing Federal and State regulations and legislation that may affect employee benefits.

Employee assistance plan managers, also called employee welfare managers, are responsible for a wide array of programmes covering occupational safety and health standards and practices; health promotion and physical fitness, medical examinations, and minor health treatment, such as first aid; plant security; publications; food service and recreation activities; carpooling and transportation programmes, such as transit subsidies; employee suggestion systems; child care and elder care; and counseling services.

Child care and elder care are increasingly significant because of growth in the number of dual-income households and the elderly population. Counseling may help employees deal with emotional disorders, alcoholism, or marital, family, consumer, legal, and financial problems. Some employers offer career counseling as well. In large firms, certain programmes, such as those dealing with security and safety, may be in separate departments headed by other managers.

Training and development managers and specialists conduct and supervise training and development programmes for employees. Increasingly, management recognizes that training offers a way of developing skills, enhancing productivity and quality of work, and building worker loyalty to the firm, and most importantly, increasing individual and organizational performance to achieve business results. While training is widely accepted as an employee benefit and a method of improving employee morale, enhancing employee skills has become a business imperative. Increasingly, managers and leaders realize that the key to business growth and success is through developing the skills and knowledge of its workforce.

Other factors involved in determining whether training is needed include the complexity of the work environment, the rapid pace of organizational and technological change, and the growing number of jobs in fields that constantly generate new knowledge, and thus, require new skills. In addition, advances in learning theory have provided insights into how adults learn, and how training can be organized most effectively for them.

Training managers provide worker training either in the classroom or onsite. This includes setting up teaching materials prior to the class, involving the class, and issuing completion certificates at the end of the class. They have the responsibility for the entire learning process, and its environment, to ensure that the course meets its objectives and is measured and evaluated to understand how learning impacts business results.

Training specialists plan, organize, and direct a wide range of training activities. Trainers respond to corporate and worker service requests. They consult with onsite supervisors regarding available performance improvement services and conduct orientation sessions and arrange on-the-job training for new employees. They help all employees maintain and improve their job skills, and possibly prepare for jobs requiring greater skill. They help supervisors improve their interpersonal skills in order to deal effectively with employees. They may set up individualized training plans to strengthen an employee's existing skills or teach new ones.

Training specialists in some companies set up leadership or executive development programmes among employees in lower level positions. These programmes are designed to develop leaders to replace those leaving the organization and as part of a succession plan. Trainers also lead programmes to assist employees with job transitions as a result of mergers and acquisitions, as well as technological changes. In government-supported training programmes, training specialists function as case managers. They first assess the training needs of clients and then guide them through the most appropriate training method. After training, clients may either be referred to employer relations representatives or receive job placement assistance.

Planning and programme development is an essential part of the training specialist's job. In order to identify and assess training needs within the firm, trainers may confer with managers and supervisors or conduct surveys. They also evaluate training effectiveness to ensure that the training employees receive, helps the organization meet its strategic business goals and achieve results.

Depending on the size, goals, and nature of the organization, trainers may differ considerably in their responsibilities and in the methods they use. Training methods include on-the-job training; operating schools that duplicate shop conditions for trainees prior to putting them on the shop floor; apprenticeship training; classroom training; and electronic learning, which may involve interactive Internet-based training, multimedia programmes, distance learning, satellite training, other computer-aided instructional technologies, videos, simulators, conferences, and workshops.

An organization's director of industrial relations forms labour policy, oversees industrial labour relations, negotiates collective bargaining agreements, and coordinates grievance procedures to handle complaints resulting from management disputes with unionized employees. The director of industrial relations also advises and collaborates with the director of human resources, other managers, and members of their staff, because all aspects of human resources policy—such as wages, benefits, pensions, and work practices—may be involved in drawing up a new or revised union contract.

Labour relations managers and their staffs implement industrial labour relations programmes. Labour relations specialists prepare information for management to use during collective bargaining agreement negotiations, a process that requires the specialist to be familiar with economic and wage data and to have extensive knowledge of labour law and collective bargaining trends. The labour relations staff interprets and administers the contract with respect to grievances, wages and salaries, employee welfare, health care, pensions, union and management practices, and other contractual stipulations. As union membership continues to decline in most industries, industrial relations personnel are working more often with employees who are not members of a labour union.

Dispute resolution—attaining tacit or contractual agreements—has become increasingly significant as parties to a dispute attempt to avoid costly litigation, strikes, or other disruptions. Dispute resolution also has become more complex, involving employees, management, unions, other firms, and government agencies. Specialists involved in dispute resolution must be highly knowledgeable and experienced, and often report to the director of industrial relations.

Conciliators, or mediators, advise and counsel labour and management to prevent and, when necessary, resolve disputes over labour agreements or other labour relations issues. Arbitrators, occasionally called umpires or referees, decide disputes that bind both labour and management to specific terms and conditions of labour contracts. Labour relations specialists who work for unions perform many of the same functions on behalf of the union and its members.

Other emerging specialties include international human resources managers, who handle human resources issues related to a company's foreign operations; and human resources information system specialists, who develop and apply computer programmes to process human resources information, match job seekers with job openings, and handle other human resources matters.

CREATING TRAINING SESSIONS

Human resources play a critical role in developing and implementing organizational strategies and structures. Successful HR professionals will be those who can align their organizational HR practices with the unique demands of team-based organizational structures.

First, we provide HR professionals with a brief history of the use of teams in the United States, reviewing definitions and types of teams, evidence regarding the impact of teams, and the factors that led to their proliferation. Second, we aim to provide the HR professional with tools to increase the effectiveness of teams, discussing the key assumptions underlying supportive conditions for teams. Third, we review modifications in HR practices that are necessary to implement teams effectively. Finally, we discuss potential challenges that HR practitioners may face in implementing teams in multinational organizations; looking to the future, we present guidelines for meeting these challenges. We conclude with some predictions about the use of teams that will likely develop as our team-based organizations continue to evolve.

What Teams Are

In general, a work team can be defined as a group of individuals working interdependently to solve problems or accomplish tasks. However, a single definition is not sufficient to capture the key differences that exist between the various types of teams being used in organizations. A number of key differences between these types of teams will determine the efficacy of HR practices designed to enhance their effectiveness.

For example, compensation structures are normally altered for self-managing work teams to include team-based rewards to encourage cooperation between members and motivate them to reach team goals. Because self-managing members are working on permanent teams, the effort and expense involved in changing compensation structures is often justified. However, in more temporary teams, such as cross-functional or problem solving teams, other types of HR policy changes (for example, altering an evaluation system to include team behaviours) may be more appropriate to encourage positive behaviours.

Our point here is not to review all of the appropriate HR policies for each type of team but rather to acknowledge that our use of the term work team includes several different types of teams.

Contrary to popular belief, teams are not a new phenomenon. The origins of teams can be traced to the Tavistock studies of post–World War II and the Swedish socio technical movement generally associated with the Volvo Corporation. The first work teams in the United States were found in the Procter & Gamble Company in the early 1960s, the Topeka work system at a General Foods pet food plant in the late 1960s, and the Rushton Quality of Work Project in Pennsylvania in the mid–1970s. Given that teams were identified as a mechanism for improving employee performance as early as the 1960s, why has it taken over thirty years to implement work teams on a large scale in the United States?

We attribute the recent rise in the interest in and use of teams over the last ten years to three factors: a higher concern for the social component of work; the globalization of the U.S. economy and resulting downsizing; and the early adoption of work teams by highly visible companies such as General Motors, AT&T, General Electric, Xerox, and Motorola. Although many believe that organizations have adopted work teams to improve employee morale or productivity, the forces behind their adoption have been much larger in scale and much more connected to global patterns of international business. Organizations have adopted work teams because many had no choice.

Dramatically reduced numbers of managers could not keep up with employee activities on a day-today basis. Furthermore, the increased use of teams can be attributed, in part, to evidence of their success.

Work teams have been associated with higher levels of productivity. It should be noted, however, that most of these studies have been conducted with self-managing work teams that have considerable control over their own structure and process. For traditional work teams, much of the evidence of impact has been collected on a case-by-case basis. Wellins, Byham, and Dixon (1994), for example, chronicle the pervasive positive impact teams have had in twenty companies. These companies claim that implementing teams resulted in improvements in bottom-line indicators such as cost savings, quality and service improvement, speed, absenteeism, and turnover.

This is not to say that teams are a panacea. Several studies on the impact of teams have failed to find effects for performance on more quantitative measures, such as productivity; others report only modest findings for productivity. Smaller effect sizes for productivity may be the result of using work teams in contexts where they are not appropriate. Clearly, work teams are not ideal for every task (even if you have a hammer, not every problem is a nail). Work teams are more effective under the right circumstances and situations.

For example, work teams are most effective when there is high task interdependence or a high degree of coordination and collaboration required between team members to accomplish tasks. Thus, a group of insurance sales agents who are geographically dispersed and have little interaction with one another to carry out their tasks would most likely be an inappropriate context in which to implement teams. The agents would probably see such an effort as an empty, poorly developed strategy designed to capitalize on a management fad.

Work teams are also more appropriate when the tasks that their members carry out are complex and well designed. If a group's work is routine and unchallenging, of dubious importance, and wholly preprogrammed with no opportunity for feedback, teams will probably not make much difference in productivity.

As Johns (1996) has stated, "Taking a bunch of olive stuffers on a food processing assembly line, putting them in distinctive jumpsuits, calling them the Olive Squad, and telling them to self-manage will be unlikely to yield dividends in terms of effort expended or brainpower employed". Work teams, especially those that increase autonomy and responsibility, are most effective when members are given complex tasks that capitalize on their diverse knowledge and skills.

Thus, teams should view their tasks as significant, the tasks should require the use of a variety of skills, and members should, where possible, assemble an entire product or deliver a complete service. The effectiveness of work teams also depends on whether an organization has high integration needs as a result of operating in a complex environment. Complex environments usually force organizations to serve a wide variety of customers, deal with rapidly changing technology, and satisfy large numbers of different stakeholders.

IBM, for example, faces a much more complex environment than McDonald's (compare the rate of change in PCs with that of Big Macs over the last fifteen years). Organizations must simultaneously deal with all of these issues—in other words, differentiate into smaller, more responsive units—and then integrate these widely dispersed efforts and units back into one cohesive organization. Teams will be most effective when a team structure is the best solution to obtaining the integration required to accomplish goals in a complex organizational environment. Without effective integration, the benefits attributed to work teams (increased productivity, higher quality, better job satisfaction) will not be realized.

Thus, companies implementing teams from a "bandwagon" perspective will not realize the benefits to be had from an appropriate fit between teams and context. In fact, many organizations are currently struggling with team effectiveness. We argue that this is the result, in part, of traditional assumptions about work that still prevail. In order to implement teams effectively, assumptions must change. We next discuss these adaptations.

Adapt Our Assumptions

We discuss the assumptions that shaped the decisions made by HR professionals in traditional hierarchical organizations in three areas: motivation; structure of work; and accountability. Traditional assumptions must be adapted in order to support effective implementation of teams.

Motivation

The first set of assumptions that must be examined pertain to motivation. National culture helps determine what motivates people. For example, some cultures can be classified as individualistic, where people tend to value their own self-interest and welfare over the interests of groups or societies; other cultures are known as collectivistic, where people tend to value the welfare of groups more than their own. Individualists are motivated by the opportunity to gain personal recognition.

They resist working in teams more than people from collectivistic cultures. Such resistance lowers team effectiveness on outcomes such as productivity, job satisfaction, cooperativeness, and organizational commitment. It takes time and experience for people to adjust their notions of fairness and equity to include collective accountability. Taking a longer-term focus and understanding the eventual payoffs for early investments in team-based systems is essential for harnessing the motivational power of teams. In understanding motivational assumptions, it is also important to consider expectations. Research attests to the importance of collective expectations in determining our level of motivation and subsequently our performance. When we believe we can accomplish objectives as a team, we are motivated to stick with our work tasks and prevail. But sometimes these high expectations get out of hand, to the point that teams hold unrealistic expectations. Cohesive teams often fall prey to this phenomenon, which is referred to as groupthink. Coinciding with extremely high expectations, teams suffering from groupthink also hold illusions of invulnerability.

They ignore important external information sources that might help them adjust their performance to fit the needs of customers better. Teams in individualistic cultures appear to be particularly susceptible to overconfidence. This may be because individualists view their team as an entity in and of itself rather than one that is connected to the external context and are therefore even less apt to use external sources of information to make corrections in their behaviour and improve their performance. Particularly in individualistic cultures, team-based organizations need to have systems that help teams set realistic expectations. This allows them to stay motivated while at the same time remaining open to learning from feedback and mistakes.

Work Structure

A second domain of assumptions concerns the structure of work. Traditional work groups were generally formed around common technical or functional skills and areas of expertise (for example, accounting, finance, or production). In recent years, it has become apparent that organizing work around a process (for example, new product development) rather than around a specific task or function is more effective.

Doing so often requires extending team members' task skills. Multi skilled teamwork involves teams made up of individuals with multiple and overlapping skills that are deployed around the performance of a whole task, which represents a significant part of a larger work flow. Members are multi skilled so that work can be flexibly allocated among them.

In organizing work around processes, organizational boundaries must often be renegotiated. Increasingly, work teams include external customers and suppliers. For example, General Electric Medical Systems invites representatives from leading health maintenance organizations (HMOs) to serve on its sales and service teams.

The American Red Cross has members of communities serving on key committees that set organizational objectives. Eastman Kodak allies itself with key competitors to form market segment task forces. These types of work structures require a whole new notion of collaboration—collaboration with external constituencies. Those who were previously viewed as "them" are now viewed as "us."

The reorganization of work around processes and across boundaries has numerous benefits. For example, multi skilling (the learning of new skills in addition to functional expertise) can result in reduced staffing as fewer workers can perform the same range of tasks. It can create efficiencies through more flexible task assignment. Multi skilling also often leads to lower inventories because there is more effective work flow coordination. It also makes the team more flexible in meeting fluctuating market demand through operational flexibility.

Finally, it can lead to a more differentiated response to the needs of particular customer segments and so contribute to strategic flexibility. Multi skilling leads to greater awareness of the whole task and enables the team member to take part in problem solving, innovation, and strategic thinking. These same benefits do not accrue when tasks and organizations are structured under traditional assumptions of static, independent jobs.

Accountability

A third domain of assumptions that shape team effectiveness pertain to accountability. The focus of most HR departments has been on the individual. Individual accountability and responsibility have been the foundation on which all of the business practices in the United States have been built. Furthermore, accountability in traditional work organizations was vested in those with formal positions—the managers and supervisors. Individual employees showed deference to people in these positions. Reporting structures were vertical and a command-and-control philosophy reigned. Skills such as planning, coordination, personnel functions, quality management, health and safety, and boundary management were the domain of managers. But increasingly, these duties are becoming the domain of teams.

Managerial responsibility is shifting from individual accountability to collective, mutual accountability. As this has occurred, the notion of self-management has gained acceptance. Self-management grows as the team's operational tasks are delegated to the team itself. Many different terms have evolved to describe and distinguish varying degrees of autonomy, including self-directed work teams, empowered teams, and superior work teams. The common distinguishing characteristic of such teams is that they operate with some degree of autonomy.

As nonmanagers become collectively responsible for managerial duties, basic assumptions about the legitimacy of authority are challenged. Team members may begin to question what gives peers the right to set rules for others. They may have difficulty dealing with authority that does not stem from position. Rather than depending on a job description and direction from the manager, people work jointly with coworkers to determine what they do. Because personal success depends on collective success, an individual's fate is tied to coworkers. Feelings of mutual trust and partnership must develop. The organization must help people learn to deal with greater ambiguity, uncertainty, continual change, and collaborative relationships. Both managers and employees in the team-based organization need to adjust to this shift in accountability and responsibility. We discuss the HR systems that increase team effectiveness in the next section.

Modify HR Practices to Support Teams

In addition to recognizing and adapting the assumptions on which they base their practices, HR professionals must also modify those practices to support teams. The practices to be modified cluster in five areas: recruitment and selection; task design; training; evaluation; and compensation. In the following sections, we summarize the modifications and provide references for practitioners interested in exploring them in greater depth.

Recruitment and Selection

Working effectively in a team requires a particular set of knowledge, skills, and abilities (KSAs) that were not as critical in traditional organizations. Proficiency is needed in at least five areas: conflict resolution, collaborative problem solving, communication, goal setting and performance management, and planning and task coordination. During recruitment, organizations aspiring to create a workforce of effective team members should clearly communicate the importance of these proficiencies. Doing so provides a realistic job preview and can therefore help to reduce turnover. Recruiting individuals who prefer these activities also makes sense because team members' preferences for teamwork are related to team effectiveness.

It is also important to consider teamwork KSAs in the selection process. It might seem easy to include measures of KSAs in most selection systems, but most selection instruments focus on basic learning abilities (for example, math, language, perceptual skills) or specific technical abilities (for example, mechanical, electrical, and so on). In the last few years, employment tests designed to measure teamwork KSAs have been under development.

Early results suggest that the tests can predict subsequent performance beyond the level of prediction from a large battery of traditional employment aptitude tests. These initial findings offer encouraging support for such instruments. Interviews might also be a viable method of assessing social and interpersonal attributes that contribute to teamwork. There is evidence that a structured interview designed to measure social KSAs can predict future team effectiveness. Finally, selection techniques that involve collecting biographical information may be another way to assess teamwork KSAs.

Task Design

The second set of practices that must be modified relate to task design. Effective teams are designed around the tasks they perform. Two key considerations are that teams should be relatively self contained and handle many aspects of their own functioning. First, teams should be collectively responsible for an identifiable and substantial part of the work of the organization. To the extent possible, support services should be included in the team so that it has the resources necessary to accomplish its goals. Members should be multi skilled and dedicated to the team so that they do not have to split priorities. Finally, the team should report as a unit so that members do not have conflicting directions from different managers. Second, the team should be responsible for many aspects of its own functioning. For example, it should be able to determine how to apply the team's resources, strategies for completion of work, and quality monitoring. It should also be responsible for working with internal and external customers. Finally, part of the team's task should be performance evaluation. Whenever appropriate skill levels and task conditions exist, team members should be involved in reviewing their own performance and determining their own rewards.

Beyond these two fundamental design principles, a third issue is whether teams should be functional or cross-functional. Functional organizations group people by common specialties and break work down into functional packets that translate into individual assignment. Project organizations combine different specialties required to perform the entire project but then break the work down for members of functional groups within the project. Team-based organizations require a shift away from a hierarchical breakdown to focus instead on the lateral distribution and integration of work.

Whether teams should be functional or cross-functional is a choice to be based on an analysis of the work to be accomplished. Process analysis can be used to determine the sets of activities that have to be carried out and integrated to deliver value to customers. If within an identifiable set of activities coordination must occur across different functional areas, then teams should be cross-functional. In the cross-functional teams members can integrate work across disciplines and make trade-offs that require a multidisciplinary perspective. But if the process analysis indicates that an identifiable set of activities occurs within a functional area, then teams should be functional.

HR PROFESSIONALS IN MANAGING PERFORMANCE

Given the substantial issues of diversity that all organizations are confronting today, the successful human resource (HR) practitioner needs a conceptual framework to deal with them in both global and single-country business environments. Diversity should be viewed not as a confounding factor but rather as a source of energy that drives change and growth.

Rhinesmith (1993) points out that globalization has arrived and that "diversity—both domestic and international—will be the engine that drives the creative energy of the corporation of the twenty-first century. Successful HR managers will be those who are able to manage this diversity for the innovative and competitive edge of their corporation."

We believe that diversity can no longer be discussed only from a single-country perspective. Workforces in all countries are be- coming more diverse, not just in gender, age, and race but also in culture. The workforce of any industrialized or developing nation will increasingly be a mix of domestic and international ethnicities. To deal with this challenge, the HR practitioner of tomorrow will have to understand the impact of cultural or global diversity, as well as of country-specific diversity, on the effectiveness of the organization and the workforce.

Hospitality and Loadging

Organizing, the process of structuring human and physical resources in order to accomplish organizational objectives, involves dividing tasks into jobs, specifying the appropriate department for each job, determining the optimum number of jobs in each department, and delegating authority within and among departments. One of the most critical challenges facing lodging managers today is the development of a responsive organizational structure that is committed to quality.

The framework of jobs and departments that make up any organization must be directed toward achieving the organization's objectives. In other words, the structure of a lodging business must be consistent with its strategy. Managers give structure to a hotel and lodging through job specialization, organization, and establishment of patterns of authority and span of control.

Job Specialization

There are as many degrees of job specialization within the lodging industry as there are types of organizations—and there are many types of organizations. One extreme is the case of a hotel where the owner/operator is responsible for checking in the guests, servicing their needs, taking care of the housekeeping for the guest rooms, maintaining the building and grounds, and checking out the guests. There is, to be sure, much to recommend this method of work. It is rewarding to have total control over a project from beginning to end, and many people find it motivating to see the results of their efforts.

However, as the demand for additional products or services increases (i.e., if additional rooms are added or another hotel is purchased), it becomes more and more difficult for an individual to do his or her job well. One benefit of the increased workload is increased revenue, which would enable the individual hotel operator to add housekeeping staff, one or more front desk agents to check in and check out the additional guests, and engineering and maintenance personnel to care for the building and grounds.

As a general rule, specialization increases worker productivity and efficiency. On the other hand, delegating jobs increases the need for managerial control and coordination. Someone has to make sure that housekeeping staff come in after the painters have repainted a room (and that the paint is dry), not before! A crucial element of hotel and lodging management is coordinating the many specialized functions within hotels so that the organization runs smoothly.

Specialization has its own set of problems; it can result in workers performing the same tasks over and over again. A point can be reached where the degree of specialization so narrows a job's scope that the worker finds little joy or satisfaction in it. Signs of overspecialization include workers' loss of interest, lowered morale, increasing error rate, and reduction in service and product quality.

One solution to this problem is to modify jobs so that teams can perform them. Instead of a single guest room attendant being assigned to a group of rooms, a work team in a hotel housekeeping department might clean all of the rooms on a particular floor. Some establishments use teams regularly throughout the organization; others use teams more selectively. Teams can be directed by a manager or can be self managed. The idea behind self-managed work teams is for workers to become their own managers, which increases their self reliance as well as develops a talent pool.

A concept called the quality circle is based on the belief that the people who actually do the work, rather than their managers, are the ones who are best able to identify, analyze, and correct problems they encounter. The idea originated in Japan in 1962. The quality circle is a group of employees, usually fewer than ten, who perform similar jobs and meet once per week to discuss their work, identify problems, and present possible solutions to those problems.

For example, a quality circle might be formed among front desk agents. The group forwards its findings and proposals to management for evaluation and action. Quality circles are most successful when they are part of an organization- wide improvement effort. American business picked up on the quality circle concept in the mid-1970s.

EVALUATING THE TRAINING PROGRAMME

Long-term employment security is no longer promised or implied, and this has changed the degree of mutual commitment that employees and organizations feel toward one another. The consequences are paradoxical for many companies. On the one hand, they want to be freer to shed employees who are not needed; on the other hand, they want to encourage needed employees to stay as long as possible. But employees who know they have no long term security are often busy looking for better opportunities. Instead of a long-term relationship or even a "marriage, " both employees and companies can wind up in a "dating game" as they look for short-term selfish advantage.

As an HRM strategy in tight labour markets or when employees with rare skills are involved, some firms have committed themselves for specific contracted periods or offered stock options and incentive-based schemes to hang on to desired individuals. Nevertheless, at least one organizational survey consortium reports that employee attitudes on job security have become much less favourable in all companies over the last decade, even as other attitudes have remained relatively constant Corporation, private communication with the authors, January 1998). As several commentators have noted and as the chapters by Noer and others in this volume note, the psychological contract has changed. One noticeable effect of this change is in college recruiting, where companies no longer promise long-term careers and actually use "signing bonuses" to get the most talented graduates to join them. In other words, short-term payoffs are being used to make up for long-term inducements.

Nonwork Obligations

Most companies now see family responsibilities as a more acceptable counterpoint to work obligations. Many employees desire flexible work schedules and supervisor support for emergencies and use these criteria to select employers when there is a choice. Some books have become best-sellers because they rate and describe "the best places to work". Underlying realities that have helped give voice to such concerns include changes in marriage patterns. Divorce rates have gone up substantially during recent decades, leaving many women dependent on their own efforts for economic well-being and creating many more single parents than in the past. For single parents, work is an economic necessity but it also competes with family for time and energy. In a related phenomenon, age at first marriage has increased by almost a year per decade for the last half century, so that it is now about twenty-four for women and twenty-six for men.

With this shift, many couples now live together without benefit of the clergy's blessing. Their concerns include many mutual career decisions, which may affect accepting a job or relocating. In recent years, this concern has sometimes emerged as a desire for company benefits to be extended to domestic partners. This has been especially noted when homosexual partners, who do not have the option of legal marriage, want such coverage. The open expression of such living arrangements and sexual orientations by workers represents another major shift in attitudes and values.

Assumptions

This review of the environmental forces affecting industry and HRM indicates that many of the assumptions made in the past about people in the work setting are no longer valid. If the assumptions are no longer valid, then the concepts and practices based on them may also be invalid. As we indicated in our opening discussion, many of these assumptions arose in the 1950s, and it is these beliefs that need to be reexamined and reevaluated.

Current Assumptions

The changes in the environment we have noted, which most companies operate in today, have required a new set of assumptions that are more appropriate for the times and that generate new HRM concepts and practices. These new assumptions may be subdivided according to their application to organizations and to individuals. Organizations today contrast in several respects with those of the past.

The shifts are evident in corporate forms and dynamics:

- More than ever, organizations are likely to be fluid, continually changing, and have many new relationships, from joint ventures, alliances, and partnerships to use of vendors and subcontractors.
- Embattled organizations are continually under pressure to increase outputs, improve cycle time, enhance competitiveness.
- A focus on short-term achievements is an imperative. Corporate acquisitions may often be seen as a better bet than undertaking long-term product development.
- Important skills and talent are to be hired as needed rather than developed internally over a long period. Conversely, unneeded employees should be quickly converted or disposed of.

HRM concepts and practices arise from a complex set of forces that form the operating environment for the organizations HRM serves. When the environment is stable, many of the changes are determined by the organization itself, often in a desire to give itself a competitive advantage in attracting, retaining, and motivating employees. Sometimes the concepts and practices arise out of the company founder's personal philosophy and preferences. But the environment has not been very stable during the last two decades.

Many of the operating assumptions on which HRM operates have been severely but gradually challenged in the last two decades in a series of inexorable changes. As a story popular in some management circles puts it, a frog dropped into a pot of boiling water will instantly jump out. But if the frog is placed in a pot of cool water that is gradually brought to a boil, the frog will simply grow warmer and doze off until it is too late. It is the suddenness of change that makes it vivid for people as well.

Many of the shifts noted have taken place gradually and in different spheres, and they may not have been given sufficient notice at the time of their occurrence. But when we look back over the last twenty-five years, it is obvious that many principles that were simply taken for granted are no longer true. This is as dangerous for us as the slowly warming pot is for the frog. To be effective, it is necessary for HRM concepts and practices to be lined up with assumptions that are based on the reality of our environments.

For organizations to assess their environments accurately it is useful periodically to go through a disciplined scan of their current and expected environments. In fact, many large firms and some consortia conduct environmental scans on a regular basis.

This certainly seems like a healthy practice. We believe that a useful framework for doing environmental scans is one that looks at the DELTA forces around us, that is, the demographics, economics, legal and regulatory issues, technology, and attitudes and values. These are the forces that have greatly affected us in the past and seem the right places to look to for future change.

Employers and Employees

Most knowledgeable observers in the field of human resource management (HRM) would agree that its major development as a profession came during the half century or so between the end of World War II and the early 1990s. As organizations employing as many as hundreds of thousands became dominant influences in the world of work and as questions about selection, training, work motivation, and compensation practices became more challenging in a growing, dynamic society, the need for professionally trained, skilled personnel became great. Also, despite occasional downturns in the economy, the professional growth of HRM took place against a general culture of prosperity, a belief that such good patterns would continue and even improve, and an assumption that work organizations should and would share in such growth.

Important too as HRM developed during this era was that the policies and practices developed and implemented were based in large part on the assumption that a desire for personal growth was the most important motivational characteristic of the workforce, along with the belief that more of everything (particularly economic outcomes) is better. Korman (forthcoming) has referred to this pattern as self-enhancing motivation and has cited as illustrative of this type of motivation such actions as making choices that match and fulfill one's personal needs, engaging in activities that foster self-growth, attempting to attain high levels of work performance, and working for goals that legitimately enhance oneself in one's own eyes and those of others. Given the cultural context and the assumption of the dominance of this type of motivational pattern, it was a relatively short step for HRM professionals during this era to develop a perspective that reflected them.

Characteristic programmes of this type included job enrichment, career management and career development, self-appraisals and peer performance appraisals, and income incentives of various kinds. Less significant as an influence on HRM during this era but still of some importance were programmes based on what Korman (forthcoming) has called self-protective motivation, defined as the desire to defend oneself from perceived threatening environmental and personal forces that might affect one's sense of identity. Korman suggests that it is this motivational force that underlies the need for personal and job security. Despite its importance, however, this need was generally viewed as less important than employee needs for growth, development, and achievement during the years of prosperity.

There were several reasons for this difference in emphasis. One factor, certainly, was the prosperity and the continued expectations of same. It was not a climate that generated a sense of anxiety, whether warranted or not. Second, the strength and membership of labour unions—organizations that have traditionally made job security a keystone of their efforts—were declining. With the assumption of continued prosperity and the weakness of labour unions, human resource (HR) managers and their allied professionals, such as industrial-organizational psychologists, worried less about providing job security than about providing the opportunity for growth, development, and achievement. Third, theorists on motivation in work organizations generally had a low level of interest in such concepts as anxiety, even though important research findings were beginning to be reported on the significance of such related variables as fear of failure in performance settings. Instead, theories were popular if they saw people as growth-oriented, desiring meaningful work achievement, and interested in attaining both intrinsic and extrinsic goals.

Nevertheless, despite these influences, there was some concern even during these years about providing a greater sense of security for employees. Prominent among those expressing such interest was Frederick Herzberg, an important management writer who saw in the reduction of anxiety that came with job security a significant approach to reducing job dissatisfaction. In addition, although their membership continued to decrease, labour unions and their emphasis on job security did not totally disappear from the work scene. Unions remained strong in some areas, particularly the federal, state, and local civil services, and their presence did much to ensure that job security remained on the table as an employee concern, at least in some instances.

There were, then, these two patterns of HR practice. One, the more influential, assumed that the more important motivational patterns were desires for growth, development, achievement, and self-enhancement. The second, less significant as an influence, assumed desires for job security and self-protection. Both were recognized, and both influenced HRM practices. Less recognized was that the disparity in influence of these patterns of practice encouraged another important underlying assumption. This assumption was that HRM policies and practices could be developed in a manner that would enable the attainment of two goals.

The first of these goals was to help organizations obtain their objectives. The second was that HRM could help employees meet their most important needs because the employees' desire to attain positive outcomes (both intrinsic and extrinsic), that is, self-enhancement, and their willingness to work for them were congruent with organizational needs for effective performance. Furthermore, this congruence could be maintained and encouraged because of the continuing expected affluence. In contrast, rarely if ever discussed was that these practices and policies and the assumed congruence between employer and employee depended on these assumptions of continued prosperity and that other approaches would become necessary if the situation changed.

The New World of Work

Now that time has come. A new and different world of work has begun to emerge, one that exists alongside the traditional work setting and that may eventually come to supplant it. It is a world characterized by at least three major trends that have implications for HRM.

- First, downsizing is now a frequent key component of managerial decision making, with all the potential short- and long-term anxiety-inducing effects on employee motivation that we would expect.
- Second, the work-family conflict is an endemic part of the lives of both employers and employees.
- Third, we live in a world marked by the extensive use of temporary workers, part-time employees, and outsourcing.

Workforce Reduction

Downsizing has become so much a part of the world of work during the past decade that it is a term familiar to almost all who work or who wish to. Table lists some of the more dramatic illustrations of downsizing that have occurred in American corporations during the past five years. Downsizing is a phenomenon that continues to this day. Downsizing is a fact of the world of work that influences the lives, attitudes, and emotions of millions. That other jobs are continually being created—and they are—may not significantly affect those concerned about their long- and short-term job prospects.

Work-Family Conflict

Also part of this new world of work is conflict with the family, an inevitable fact of life as our society is increasingly characterized by women in the workforce, dual-career couples, and single-parent families. The increasing presence of women in the workforce contributes to this conflict, a conflict that is among the most serious facing American families and work organizations as we approach the new millennium. It is a problem, both actual and potential, that is becoming increasingly widespread. It is also one of the characteristics of the new world of work that has had and continues to have a major impact on the motivational and attitudinal characteristics of people in the workforce, both men and women.

Noncore Workers

We now also have a work setting marked increasingly by outsourcing agreements between companies, relocation of companies from high- to low-wage areas, globalization, a desire for individuals to develop multiskill capability rather than job specialization, and explosive growth in the use of temporary and contingent employees.

Feelings of ambiguity and conflict have resulted from these changes. On the one hand, there are now new ways for individuals to seek self-enhancement in the world of work, paths that have important implications for the practices and policies HRM may adopt. But on the other hand, the resulting anxiety from these changes has led to a high level of self-protective motivation. The outcome has been a world of work where the two different motivations are assuming equal significance. In other words, it is a world in which the desire and need for security has become as relevant as the need for achievement, growth, and development. It is therefore a world in which both motivational patterns will need to be addressed by HRM, but in different ways than they have been previously.

The New Assumptions

HRM needs new and different assumptions on which to base policy and practice. One necessary change, I believe, is to assume no longer that there is a congruence of interests between employees and employers. Sometimes there may be, but sometimes there may not be. Second, we need to assume that the key interpersonal and intergroup relationships in a particular work setting are as likely to be among individuals from different organizations with different investments as they are to be among individuals within the same organization. The following paragraphs elaborate on these recommendations in greater detail.

Because self-enhancement was assumed to be the dominant work motivation during the years of the growth of the field, it is not surprising that HR professionals operated on the belief that it was both possible and desirable to design and implement policies and practices that could and would integrate the goals of both employees and organizations. In fact, one of the major books of this era, and one which served as a sort of conceptual guideline for many, was titled Integrating the Individual with the Organization.

In a similar vein and serving as further illustration of this assumption of congruence between employer and employee was the growth of job enrichment as a management tool, fueled by the belief that individuals would respond to the challenge of enriched jobs. According to this perspective, the enriched job provided a mechanism for self-enhancement and, in satisfying such desires, the individual would be more highly performance motivated and contribute more to the attainment of organizational goals.

Now, however, we need to change this assumption. More specifically, we need to view the individual and the organization as separate entities who will be able to integrate their efforts and cooperate with one another under certain conditions but not under others. Furthermore, determining what those conditions might be will be an important objective for HRM professionals in the coming years.

A second assumption about people and organizations during the years of growth and prosperity was that the interpersonal and inter group relationships HRM needed most to be concerned with were those that took place within the organization, that is, intra organizational relationships. In other words, the focus was on the relationships between people in different jobs, in different functions, and at different hierarchical levels, but all within the same organization. Although it was recognized that individuals often met with salespeople, suppliers, and others, such meetings with "outsiders" were generally limited to specifically designated occupational groups. Now, however, more attention will have to be paid to relationships between those with primary allegiance to a particular organization and those who may work in that organization but not have primary allegiance to it.

Today, individuals work full-time in an organization to which they have primary loyalty while next to them or with them are individuals on temporary assignments, part-time workers, and people working in joint venture settings and in outsourcing situations.

The result may therefore be individuals working together whose allegiances and concerns may involve differences that are highly important to us. Relationships, views, and expectations among those who are all part of one group—or who view themselves as part of the same company or as "insiders"—are different from the types of relationships and communication patterns that develop among those who view themselves as belonging to different groups.

For example, Korman (1988) has proposed that in situations in which we find insiders and outsiders, the former are more likely to discriminate and act in a prejudicial manner toward the latter. The result may be unnecessary conflict and sometimes even "tribalistic" patterns, where each group cares only about itself and not about the other or joint goals.

Although cases of severe conflict may be extreme—because there are usually some reasons for these different groups and individuals to at least try to work together— the potential for conflict between groups and individuals exists in this new work setting and there will be a need to take account of such possibilities in developing future HRM programmes.

These new assumptions, which I believe to be more appropriate for the emerging work setting, suggest the need for new HRM approaches, techniques, policies, and practices that will allow satisfaction of both the self-enhancing and the self-protective motivational processes.

Some Programme Suggestions

Programmes consistent with the new assumptions need to be developed for HRM as it confronts this new world of work. The remainder outlines four such programmes, with each discussed in greater detail in the following sections.

- Effective self-career management programmes based on the desire for self-enhancement.
- Labour pool associations designed to meet needs for both self enhancement and self-protection.
- Performance incentive programmes that are not based on organizational commitment, including financial rewards providing direct income as well as health, welfare, and pension benefits.
- Insider-outsider training programmes.

Self-Career Management

Self-career management programmes are designed primarily for those individuals who view themselves as relatively independent professionals or "businesses, " rather than as organizationally dependent job holders. These are individuals who can and do make their own decisions about their careers, know their capabilities, and understand where they can find the types of work opportunities where they can "sell" themselves as a business or service. Self-career management is a different way of looking at oneself and one's work capabilities.

It is a mechanism for declaring oneself independent of an organizational control system but at the same time being willing to negotiate mutual terms of acceptability concerning work contributions to that system. Self-career management—thus defined as the giving up of relatively permanent organizational relationships in favour of more self-controlled career decision making—has become increasingly recommended to and by HRM professionals as a possible approach to dealing with challenges presented by the emerging world of work, a world still dominated in great degree by the use of downsizing as a management strategy despite continuing questions about its outcomes.

Clearly, there are reasons for such positive evaluation. Self career management recognizes the tentative nature of a specific employment relationship while also emphasizing the need for employee skills and meaningful contributions and the opportunity to fulfill the desire for self-enhancement that is so important in the work setting.

In addition, for the appropriate individual and the appropriate situation, self-career management also provides an approach to meeting the need for self-protection, because this can be negotiated by the individual involved. The key, however, is in the word appropriate. Self-career management is appropriate when the individual has or can develop both meaningful self-knowledge and the types of skills and abilities that are in demand. In addition, self-career management is appropriate when the individual has knowledge of the job market and the freedom to respond to the opportunities available.

A variety of techniques reflect self-career management when it is defined in this manner. Perhaps the most important and first question that needs an answer (for which the HRM professional must provide input) is whether a specific organization should provide financial and other resources for developing and implementing self-career programmes for its employees, particularly programmes emphasizing personal growth. This is not an easy question to answer. At first glance, there are clearly reasons for companies to undertake such programmes.

They provide recognition of the frequently temporary nature of contemporary work settings while at the same time encouraging positive relationships between individuals and organizations over the long run. Both of these outcomes may serve the individual and the organization in good stead at once or at some time in the future. In addition, these programmes may serve to illuminate and develop skills in the participants not previously realized and thus eventually prove beneficial to the individual and the organization. Finally, such programmes help the organization in situations where downsizing may become inevitable. Clearly, preparing individuals to deal with the loss of employment before it happens is to be preferred over sudden notices of termination.

Still, some negative aspects also need to be recognized before a corporate decision is made to undertake a personal growth programme encouraging self-career management. One obvious problem is the cost involved. The cost may be considerable, depending on the number of individuals involved and the type of programmes chosen. Second, there is the continuing reality that all the benefits the programmes may provide to employees may never be of value to the organization that pays for them (and, indeed, may turn out to be of value to competitors).

Third, it needs to be realized right from the beginning that such programmes are not for everyone. They should not be oversold as "the answer" to the problems of the new world of work. Rather, companies need to keep in mind that other programmes will be necessary regardless of what they decide about self-career management programmes. To be blunt, self-career management is not and cannot be appropriate for those who have neither the personality nor the technical skills, educational levels, or likelihood of developing the skills to the degree needed to make the approach fruitful. For these individuals, other alternatives will be necessary.

Assuming these pros and cons have been considered and the company decides to proceed with such programmes, how might they do so? One possible procedure is to make self-career management programmes a voluntary aspect of the HRM process. Such an approach would increase the probability of successful outcomes by making it likely that the individuals participating in the programmes possess the skills, abilities, interests, or personality that would enable them to benefit from the programmes.

In addition, once the decision to proceed is made, HRM can increase the effectiveness of self-career management programmes by generating and making available as much information as possible about the nature of potential and actual career possibilities in a particular job market for those participating in the programmes. Self career management programmes are much concerned with personal growth but are not aimed at personal growth alone. They also have career and work-oriented goals.

The more work opportunities available that the participant knows about and the more the participant has the time, knowledge, and personal characteristics to carry out a job or career search, the more self-management career programmes will be useful. A further advantage of providing job knowledge to those undergoing self-career management is that doing so will help identify those for whom such programmes might not be useful, that is, those who will not have job opportunities for the skills they have or are likely to develop. For this latter group, other types of programmes will be necessary, perhaps programmes of the type we now turn to.

Labour Pool Associations

HRM also needs to begin to develop mechanisms that are appropriate in assisting the adaptation of current and potential employees for whom the concept of self-career management is inapplicable. Among these are the unskilled and semiskilled, immigrant workers, single parents whose job freedom is limited, and people with little growth potential. Two factors concerning these individuals are crucial. First, there are great numbers of such employees and they may, in fact, be increasing relative to the population at large. Second, despite their numbers, economically they are falling farther and farther behind people with higher skill levels, as evidenced by the findings of an increasing disparity in income between those at the higher and lower levels of our population.

Yet despite their numbers and this disparity, it is fair to say that little attention has been paid to how the new world of work can meet the needs of these people. For these individuals, basic educational training may have been insufficient, job training opportunities may not be available, and financial resources to keep up skill development may not be there. Also, the habit and encouragement of self-reliance in the occupational sphere may be more foreign to these individuals than those who are higher on the occupational hierarchy. Rather, these individuals may have, perhaps, more of a tendency to rely on traditional employment relationships and organizational reward systems as sources of meeting self enhancement and self-protection needs. Because the characteristics of the emerging world of work makes this pattern increasingly unlikely, it is even more important to pay attention to helping these groups adapt to the new and different setting.

Such associations can be conceived of as organizations based on cooperative relations among different companies (and perhaps government agencies) that focus on maximizing the human resources available to all of them. As cooperatively managed HR personnel from different organizations, labour pool associations would have several objectives. First, they would keep a continuing registry of individuals and their skills, thus ensuring a labour supply as needed by member organizations, large or small.

Second, they would serve as training-retraining-counseling centres for occupational entry and upgrading as desired and available. Third, and perhaps most uniquely, they would serve as "permanent employers" who, besides supplying and making available job and training opportunities, would also provide such "security type" benefits as health insurance and pension plans. These benefits would be paid into accounts maintained for each individual by the organizations. They would thus replace the security systems traditionally used by organizations, which are increasingly difficult to maintain in this era of downsizing and rapid corporate change.

One step toward this type of organization is the Talent Alliance (TA), an association of companies that has been operating since spring 1997 and includes such members as AT&T, Du Pont, GTE, Johnson & Johnson, Lucent Technologies, NCR, TRW, Unisys, and UPS. The TA, has several goals. One is to keep individuals employed in companies and settings where they are most needed when they are needed.

It is therefore an employee allocation system (or labour pool association) of the type we envision here. A second objective is to increase employee marketability; this is done in a number of ways, including through career growth counselors, training and retraining programmes for employees, and strategic planning seminars for corporate management aimed at adapting HR practices to the new world of work.

The TA is, therefore, a step toward the type of organization suggest here because it has some of the aspects recommend. However, it lacks at this time a focus on the necessity of meeting the needs underlying self-protective motivation, that is, the desire for the security of health and welfare benefits and pensions. A second possible limitation is that it is designed for the occupational spectrum of relatively big organizations employing large numbers of individuals, a considerable percentage of whom may be at a high technical level.

Such organizations are, of course, crucial as major employers and these occupational groups are of legitimate concern. However, believe that labour pool associations need also be concerned with those individuals who, though working for small, sometimes marginal organizations, nevertheless have traditionally looked to organizations as the mechanisms through which they will meet their needs for both enhancement and protection.

One Further Note

Labour pool associations may be of value to those for whom self-career management programmes are appropriate as well as for those for whom it is not. This is because systems need to be developed to bring individuals and organizations at all levels together for their mutual benefit in this emerging world of short-range assignments as well as long-range jobs and rapidly changing skill and competency demands. Labour pool associations, as we have envisioned them, would satisfy this need.

In sum, we need organizations like the TA and others like it, such as Job Link in Louisville, Kentucky, to meet self-enhancement needs but also to meet the need for self-protection. It is basically a referral and counseling centre that makes training available as a final resort.) We need organizations such as the TA and Job Link because the two major motivations in work settings—self-enhancement and self-protection—increasingly may not be met by individual companies. For some organizations, self-career management will be an appropriate alternative mechanism. However, for others, cooperative efforts like labour pool associations will be needed to help them find qualified workers and to help workers find jobs that meet both self-enhancing and self-protective needs. Key here is the need for cooperative activity among different organizations, including accepting the principle of having these associations serving as an "employer" designed to meet self-protective concerns. This is perhaps a somewhat different perspective from that we are used to, but it is an idea that reflects the new world of work and the needs it has generated.

Nonorganizationally Linked Incentive Systems

Financial incentive systems for performance have long been one of the staples of HRM and there is little reason to think they would or should lose their relevance in the new world of work. On the contrary, they may become even more relevant as other types of incentives—those that assume organizational links and commitment, such as promotion and transfer opportunities—will become less relevant to those who see their future as falling into the self-career management pattern or who are attaining employment through "labour pool associations."

Purely financial incentives, on the other hand, are not limited to any specific type of setting. Bonuses tied to individual or unit performance are innately transferable (or fungible) and do not have to be linked to any particular organization. That is, the value of financial incentives as mechanisms to self-enhancement are not limited to any particular context and will usually hold their meaning regardless of where they are offered. Financial incentives will, then, retain significance in the new world of work and may become even more significant as the ties of organizational loyalty become less common and less relevant. First, direct monetary income in this changing world of fewer commitments will gain increased significance.

Second, incentive programmes that enable individuals to meet their needs for self-protection will have increased value. Such needs might be met by developing and applying incentive payments directly into health, welfare, and pension programmes even though the employees involved may be temporary workers who frequently change employers. Consistent with the logic underlying the labour pool associations described earlier, HR professionals might well consider developing financial incentive programmes using individual "benefit" accounts into which employers (and employees) would contribute based on employment, no matter how temporary or varying that employment might be.

These would be financial incentives for performance designed to satisfy self-protection needs by paying into health, welfare, and pension accounts maintained by the labour pool association. In addition to being of value to the individuals involved, such contributions are likely to increase commitment and loyalty to an organization's needs. (One might note that the type of account we are referring to here is somewhat analogous to Social Security accounts. However, there are two major differences. First, these accounts are linked to individual work patterns and individual work behaviour in a more immediate manner. Second, these plans focus on health and welfare benefits as much as if not more than pay and pension concerns.)

Insider-Outsider Training Programmes

Training programmes designed to integrate individuals of diverse backgrounds and views into cohesive work teams are not new. They have been a standard part of HRM programmes in recent years as cultural and ethnic diversity has become a major challenge for organizations. Some of these training programmes have proved fruitful and some have not.

However, the challenge to HRM here is somewhat different in that the programmes we refer to have generally made one major assumption that we cannot make in the new context: that the individuals and groups in these programmes, diverse though they may be, all wish to maximize the effectiveness of the same organization, that is, the organization to which they are all committed by reason of employment.

In the new world of work, group members may include permanent employees committed to the same organization and work unit as well as temporarily assigned employees who rotate from assignment to assignment within the same organization and are sent to different units with not always consistent goals.

Even more difficult, however, will be dealing with people who are individual contractors or temporary workers who go to different organizations once a specific job is finished. It is not just that there will be changing memberships and changing interaction patterns in these organizational settings. Rather, there are and will also be individuals working together who have different, perhaps even conflicting loyalties. How does one get these groups to work together for some superordinate goal when some are truly insiders and some outsiders?

It is not clear how one proceeds here. Appeals to superordinate goals may not be appropriate over the long run (although they may be for the short run). In addition, the need for emotional cohesion may not be great because the groups may not be conceived of as even quasi-permanent. It is also uncertain which type of development programme might be most appropriate and which type of incentive programme might be best. One possibility may be the extensive use of financial incentives to integrate such groups into a common effort because financial benefits are not tied to any particular organization or setting. These incentives may be performance based, perhaps even providing stock options keyed to the length, level, and quality of performance in a particular setting.

We really do not have any answers to these questions at this time, but the potential for conflict between insider-outsider groups within organizations is great, as is the potential for conflict among those with different perspectives who also need to work together, such as suppliers and vendors. Hence, it is in the development of appropriate training and performance incentive programmes to meet this need that HRM may make another significant contribution in the new world of work.

A work setting is beginning to emerge that is radically different from the one that has traditionally provided the context for HRM policies and practices. In this world downsizing is a tool of managerial decision making, work-family conflict is a fact of life for millions and, increasingly, contingent workers, part-time workers, and outsourcing are used. It is a work setting where opportunities to meet self-enhancement and growth needs exist for some individuals but not for all, and where opportunities for self-protection such as job and benefit security are increasingly difficult to come by.

These changes have made it necessary for HRM as a profession to reevaluate its traditional practices and begin to develop and implement programmes that meet these needs for self-enhancement and self-protection in the new work setting. This offered illustrations of such programmes, including effective self-career management programmes based on personal growth principles; labour pool associations for those for whom self-career management is inappropriate; performance incentive programmes not based on organizational commitment, including financial rewards of both direct income and health, welfare, and pension benefits; and insider outsider training programmes.

Underlying these recommendations is my view that HRM professionals, regardless of specific training, need to take an active role in meeting the demands of the new world of work. Key to this process is recognizing that the opportunities for meeting and satisfying the primary motivational patterns of self-enhancement and self-protection are no longer what they used to be, whatever level of the occupational spectrum we are focusing on. For the benefit of both organizations and individuals, developing new mechanisms for responding to these changes is a major challenge facing HRM today.

6

Attitudes, Careers and Need for Tourism Modelling

The TPF model consists of an innovative integration of tourism and travel analysis within a computable general equilibrium (CGE) modelling framework, to assist the formation of government policies relating to tourism and travel. The current research with Tourism Satellite Accounts (TSAs) can be complemented and extended by the use for analysing tourism and travel. These models are formal economic models that extend, rather than replace, tourism satellite accounts (TSAs). Indeed, the increasing implementation of TSAs is a stimulus to the use of TPF models because they provide data that is ideal for implementing a TPF model.

These models allow the full potential of the detailed data contained within TSAs to be realised and facilitate:

- The assessment of tourism's overall economic impact,
- The analysis of tourism policy,
- Tourism forecasting, predicting long-term trends in tourist numbers and expenditures.

Tourism Satellite Accounts and TPF Models

Tourism satellite accounts are being formulated by countries across the world, in order to provide accurate measures of the size of tourism sectors, the nature of demand for tourism, the nature of supply in tourism sectors, and the direct contribution of tourism to GDP and employment. This makes an invaluable contribution to our knowledge of the tourism sector. When measuring the economic impact of tourism, input-output (IO) models have often been used in the past. While these models successfully capture some of the economic impact of tourism, they do not capture all of the economic impact, leading to estimates of the economic impact of tourism that are not only unreliable but heavily biased.

Computable general equilibrium (CGE) models have their historical origins in input-output methodology, but were developed to overcome the many shortcomings of IO models. In particular, CGE models allow prices to vary and resources to be reallocated between production sectors. Tourism Policy and Forecasting (TPF) models build upon this framework by including tourism data from TSAs to provide a consistent means of modelling tourism in the entire economy.

Computable general equilibrium modelling is one of the most flexible and innovative economic techniques developed in recent decades. It has been used extensively by such international organisations as the World Bank, the World Trade Organisation and the OECD as well as in academia. It has been used in the fields of international trade, economic development, agricultural economics and environmental economics. Tourism impact models have traditionally relied on input-output (IO) modelling.

More recently, there have been initial applications of CGE models in the tourism field. The use of CGE models uses the latest methodology and gives more accurate predictions than techniques such as IO modelling. CGE models are formulated in a way that is radically different from input-output modelling, macroeconomic modelling, partial equilibrium modelling or, indeed, any other form of numerical simulation. Whereas the other modelling techniques rely on an initial stimulus which is then traced through the economic system in a systematic and deterministic manner, CGE models are formulated by specifying how economic agents react to changes in the economy. A CGE model is then solved simultaneously for all markets, production sectors and economic agents.

This gives CGE models a significant advantage in flexibility over other forms of modelling, because other forms of modelling can only trace the effects of specific initial stimuli, and do so in a one-way deterministic system. In a CGE model, the initial stimulus can originate anywhere in the economy, and can be literally anything that can occur in an economic framework, ranging from changes in taxes and subsidies, to technological change, population growth, shifts in demand and regulatory changes. CGE models are not deterministic in the same way that other simulation approaches are.

The initial stimulus affects markets, production sectors and economic agents who react to the stimulus and provide further changes to the economy. These changes do not work in a one-way direction, so effects can feed back to where the stimulus started. Broadly speaking, the construction of a CGE model is a process of setting up a series of markets (for goods, services and factors of production), production sectors and demand groups (households). Each market, sector and household has its own set of economic rules that determine how it reacts to external changes.

Typically, markets for goods and services are market clearing, so that if demand exceeds supply, the price of the good or service will increase until the market clears. If the price of the good that a production sector produces increases, the output of the sector will increase. Consequently its use of factors of production will increase and the supply of the good will increase. Eventually these demand and supply changes will (due to the demand-supply correcting behaviour of prices in markets) increase the price of factors of production and decrease the price of the output good, until it is no longer profitable to increase output any further.

By setting up the economic conditions whereby each market, sector and household reacts to changes in the economy, a CGE model can then model a variety of possible scenarios. In other forms of numerical simulation, models are set up whereby the simulation follows a direct causal relationship from one effect to the next.

CGE models by their very nature allow interactions between markets, and between sectors, that may be very complex. IO models rely on an input-output table for data, and trace the intermediate demands for goods and services that are needed to satisfy final demands by consumers, the government, investment and exports.

Hence, they calculate the indirect effects of final demand. The earnings of income (by private consumers and the government) can also be included to calculate the induced effects, which are similar to Keynesian multipliers. CGE models include other effects through factor markets and foreign currency.

In doing so, the CGE models include not only the indirect effects but also the induced effects. Tourism Policy and Forecasting models extend the CGE framework to incorporate tourism and travel, with data on tourism demand and the supply of tourism industries, and frameworks for modelling tourism and travel.

Four basic characteristics differentiate Nottingham TPF models from IO models of tourism and travel:

- A TPF model includes flexible prices and wages. This enables factors of production, such as labour and capital, and foreign exchange markets to be modelled.
- Income-expenditure consistency must be maintained for all private households, the government, firms and any other economic agents that are modelled.
- Consumers' responses to changes in prices and income levels are taken into account by behavioural assumptions.
- Substitution between intermediate inputs and factors of production, as prices and wages change, is taken into account by production assumptions.

A TPF model contains four types of equation:

- Equilibrium conditions for each market ensure that supply is equal to demand for each good, service, factor of production and for foreign exchange.
- Income-expenditure identities ensure that the economic model is a closed system. All earnings must be accounted for through expenditure or savings. These conditions apply to all private house holds, the government, firms and any other economic agents that are modelled.

- Behavioural relationships state how economic agents react to changing prices and income levels. These then determine consumers' demand levels for each good and service.
- Production functions determine how much is produced for any given level of factor employment. With assumptions regarding market structure, these determine what levels of labour employment, capital usage and intermediate input usage are required to satisfy a given level of output for a set of prices.

One of the strengths of the TPF models is their flexibility. The TPF models usually contain certain core components of the model structure, and can be expanded by extending the scope of the model to suit the circumstances of the tourist origin/destination country or region.

Model structure components include:

- Market competition. Various forms of market competition can be included, from perfect competition to monopoly.
- Labour markets can be modelled in various forms, with the possibility of allowing for unemployment.
- Foreign trade can be treated in several different ways, to enable the modelling of small and large countries.
- Dynamics can be incorporated to show how the economy moves through time, with economic agents' expectations about future events incorporated into their decision-making processes.

In addition, extensions to the model scope can be made, such as:

- Income distribution can be modelled by incorporating many household groups. The distributional effects of tourism or tourism policies could then be examined.
- Inter-regional effects could be modelled by modelling distinct regions within a country.
- International effects can show how tourism's effects are spread between countries.
- The environment can be incorporated to show the effects of tourism and tourism policy on environmental issues.

Impact Modelling

TSAs represent a major step forward in the measurement of the economic size of tourism, but do not assess the total impact of tourism. Estimating the impact of tourism has the advantage of showing the desirability of tourism, in addition to measurement of size. It can also show what impact tourism has on different sectors, regions or on income distribution, depending on the specification of the model.

One problem with any attempt to measure the size of a sector such as tourism is that it is usually measured from the demand-side and it is difficult to compare results with sectors such as mining, agriculture or manufacturing that are usually measured from the supply- side. The direct impact of tourism is, on the surface, the most comparable with supply-side sectors, but falls into definitional problems. If an aircraft is owned by an airline, for example, a proportion (corresponding to the proportion of airline services consumed by tourists) of the aircraft will be included in the direct measurement of tourism.

If, however, the airline rents the aircraft from another company, the value of the rental service will be attributed as an intermediate input into tourism, and the corresponding returns to investment will not be included in tourism value added. In an attempt to rectify this situation, various countries have included indirect effects through input-output (IO) models as an alternative in their TSAs.

While this solves problems relating to definitions of intermediates, it goes beyond the measurement of the size of tourism in an accounting sense and loses direct comparability with supply-side sectors. IO models include some intermediate purchases (such as food and fuel, for example) that should clearly be thought of as intermediate purchases and not as being within the tourism sector itself. In short, the IO models go some way beyond measuring the size of the sector to measuring its economic impact. IO models do not, however, measure the full impact of tourism.

These models make various assumptions that evidently exclude some of the economic effects that a sector has. Therefore the measurement of indirect impacts through IO models gives only a partial picture of the full impact of tourism. In fact, the TPF results are more comprehensive and IO results more misleading because they incorporate only some of the impact of tourism.

Tourism Policy Analysis

The TPF models can be readily utilised to provide other forms of economic analysis. Policy analysis is an important way in which the potential of TPF models can be further demonstrated.

The TPF models offer the ability to perform "what-if" simulations:

- Examine the economic effects of existing policies on tourism or of proposed alternatives. For example, they can show the net effective taxation of tourism that exists or provide a quantitative assessment of policy alternatives.
- Provide a theoretical viewpoint or an applied quantitative estimate.
- Examine purely taxation issues, or other policy instruments such as investment incentives and planning regulations.
- Examine the effects of tourism policy, or the effects that other policies have on tourism.

These examples demonstrate that the scope for tourism policy analysis with the TPF models is large.

Cases of particular relevance include:

- Examination of the current levels of tourism taxation, i.e. whether tourism is taxed at too low or too high rates relative to the rest of the economy.

- Quantitative estimates of tourism policy alternatives, such as planned tax changes or tourism development plans.
- Quantitative estimates of the effects of other policies on tourism, such as trade liberalisation or general taxation changes.

Forecasting

TPF models can be used to forecast future trends in the tourism industry. Such forecasting models show how changes in the world economy will feed through to tourism.

Three main causes of change are highlighted here:

- Factor accumulation, including capital accumulation through investment, labour growth through population growth, and changes to the skills of labour through education and training.
- Technological change, through technical progress.
- Policy changes, which may be foreseeable.

These factors influence both income growth on the demand side and production costs on the supply side. As each factor may be changing at different rates in different sectors and in different countries, forecasting their total effect requires a TPF model.

Relative prices balance the demand and supply side factors to achieve equilibrium in each market. Continuing increases in overall skill and education levels will, for example, lead to high growth rates in sectors that use highly skilled and highly educated labour.

How this affects tourism depends very much on the skill and education levels in tourism characteristic sectors, and on the intermediate relationships between tourism characteristic sectors and the rest of the economy. Differential growth rates between tourist source countries will affect international tourism growth rates in different destination markets.

Tourism growth will, in general, be highly responsive to increases in income levels in source countries, and will depend on the relative prices for tourism and other goods and services.

The TPF models provide the opportunity to assess the potential long-term growth of tourism in response to changes in the economy (such as population growth and changing education levels) that are highly predictable, as well as the short-term impact of macroeconomic changes such as currency market crises and natural disasters.

TSAs and a TPF Model of the USA

Tourism satellite accounts provide detailed data on tourism activities that are not otherwise available in national accounts because national accounts provide data classified according to production activities and commodities, and tourism spans many of these standard classifications. The U.S. TSA used here specifies 18 industries and 23 commodities.

The tables that it provides are:

1. Production Account of Tourism Industries and All Other Industries. This table provides a "make" matrix showing the output of each commodity in each industry and a breakdown of costs by industry into three categories: intermediate inputs, compensation of employees, and other value added.
2. Supply and Consumption of Tourism and All Other Commodities. This table shows
   - A breakdown of total supply of each commodity into various categories - such as domestic production, imports government sales; and
   - A breakdown of demand into categories - intermediate, personal consumption, investment, exports and government expenditures.
3. Tourism Demand by Type of Visitor.
   This provides expenditures on each category by visitors, broken down into the following categories: business, government, resident and non-resident.
4. Tourism GDP of Tourism Industries and Other Industries.
   Using a tourism industry ratio derived as tourism output divided by industry output, this table provides details of how much GDP is generated by tourism in each industry.
5. Tourism Employment and Compensation of Employees.
   Using the tourism industry ratio, this table derives tourism employment and compensation of employees by industry. The ability to define different categories of tourism expenditure and trace the effects of this expenditure through the economy is an important and substantial step in tourism research. The data provided by such tables are invaluable for economists when modelling tourism.

The data requirements of tourism policy and forecasting models are that input-output tables and tourism demand data are available for a consistent classification of industries and commodities. Therefore, where published input-output tables adequately classify tourism and travel sectors, only the demand data is required from TSAs.

Where published input-output tables do not adequately define tourism industries, data from the TSAs on the structure of supply may also be necessary. The U.S. TPF model combines the tourism demand data for 1997 with the published 1997 benchmark input-output table containing data for 494 sectors and 37 categories of final demand, in addition to other sources of data.

We present illustrative results here of an aggregated version of the Tourism Policy and Forecasting Model for the USA. It has 18 sectors and commodities that correspond as closely as possible, given the necessary matching of TSA data, IO data and data from other sources, to the published TSA.

The Effect of a 10% Increase in Foreign Tourist Expenditures

In order to measure the impact of foreign tourism, we simulate a 10% increase in foreign tourist expenditures. This 10% increase is $9.6bn. Economic welfare, as measured by equivalent variation rises by $5.8bn, just under 0.1% of GDP. These comparative illustrate that just over half of the expenditure is captured as an increase in welfare, as markets adjust to reallocate resources, imports increase, and other exports are crowded out.

The impact of this expenditure is captured by GDP, in terms of:

- Direct expenditure impact,
- Input-output estimates, and
- General equilibrium estimates with the TPF model. While the direct impact of the $9.6bn extra expenditures is $4.5bn and the input-output estimate is $9.4bn, the TPF estimate is $6.0bn. This indicates that:
  - A large proportion of the expenditures leads directly to purchases of intermediate inputs, hence the low figure for the direct expenditure impact.
  - Almost all of the expenditure leads to increased GDP in the input-output estimate. The IO estimate has no crowding-out, and there is very little import leakage.
  - The TPF estimate includes significant levels of crowding-out and resource reallocation.
  - Some tourism and travel sectors have significantly higher increases in GDP in the TPF model than the IO model suggests. Here, the initial stimulus of foreign tourism expenditures is reinforced by domestic expenditures as firms benefiting from the initial expenditures increase there own expenditures on business tourism, and private households which have increases in income spend more on domestic tourism.
  - Others tourism and travel sectors, such as water and rail transport, have a lower GDP increase than the IO model suggests. These are sectors that sell products that are relatively small proportions of the foreign tourist's expenditures. Resources are reallocated to other sectors that are able to pay higher wages. These reallocation effects outweigh the induced effects that these sectors experience from higher incomes.
  - Non-tourism industries (here, 'all other commodities') have a decline in sector GDP that the IO model completely misses, because it does not include price crowding-out effects and resource allocation. Here, there is no direct stimulus from the foreign tourism expenditures. Indirect (intermediate demands, as captured through the IO model) and induced effects are positive, but are outweighed by resource allocation effects.

Indirect Taxation

The overall effect of indirect taxation exposes the levels of effective protection that the structure of taxation gives to industries, and shows how distortions that indirect taxes introduce lead to economic loses. As such, it is an important indicator as to how economically efficient taxes are in each sector. The results therefore remove arguments about the motives for taxation because the total level of taxation is maintained. The changes to the GDP contribution of labour and capital are given in the first column.

Changes to the GDP contribution of taxation are given in the second column. Changes to the total GDP contribution by sector, and in total, are given in the third column, and in the fourth column as a percentage of the 1997 GDP contribution. Overall, removing all indirect taxes and replacing them with non-distorting direct taxes leads to an improvement to GDP of $528.4bn, which is 2.1% of GDP in 1997. This therefore is the measure of the total distortionary impact of the indirect taxation system.

This improvement to GDP comes about through an increase in the GDP contribution of labour and capital ($1,033.8bn) outweighing the loss in indirect taxation revenue ($-505.4bn). With some exceptions, tourism and travel sectors have a lower GDP increase than the national average of 2.1%. Non-tourism sectors ('all other commodities' is a much larger sector than 'gasoline and oil' or the wholesale sector) have a larger GDP effect than the national average. This implies, since tourism sectors do not expand by the national average when indirect taxation is removed, that the tourism sectors have levels of effective taxation that are higher than the national average. The results of these 17 separate simulations are summarised as the welfare effect of removing the individual taxes.

Taxes in a range of sectors such as auto and truck rental, recreation and entertainment and retail margins, impose distortions on the economy that lead to a higher welfare loss than the tax revenue that they raise. Some sectors, such as water transport, air transport and hotels and lodging places, have much lower distortionary impact when compared to the tax revenue.

There are many reasons why sectors have different distortionary impacts, including:

- The distortionary impact of tax rates are often more than proportional to the tax revenue raised, so that higher tax rates lead to a higher distortion/revenue ratio.
- The distortionary impacts are related to other sectors through intermediate demands, and substitution in final demand. Sectors that have high distortions can effectively pass some of these distortions to related sectors.
- The distortionary impacts are related to how readily supply and demand change in response to price changes, in other words to the elasticities of supply and demand. Sectors with inelastic supply and

demand (i.e. low levels of supply and demand response to prices) tend to have lower distortionary impacts from taxation. In a general equilibrium framework, the responsiveness of supply and demand depends on many factors, such as who purchases the product (a product mainly purchased by firms will often have a lower demand elasticity than one purchased by households) and the structure of production (an industry that relies heavily on one type of input will tend to have a lower supply elasticity than other industries).

What-if' scenarios can simulate the effects of anything from productivity growth, changes to competition (anti-trust) legislation and environmental controls. The total general equilibrium effects of such diverse issues can be a complex product of many different changes. Here, we show the results of a productivity improvement in air transport. The $20.6bn increase in GDP that results is spread across industries, with air transport itself increasing in size to account for an extra $2bn in GDP, industries that use air transport such as 'all other commodities' also increasing.

Most sectors that have a reduced GDP contribution are other transport industries, which compete with air transport. The Nottingham Tourism, Policy and Forecasting models apply tourism within a general equilibrium setting. They are an innovative and significant means of combining tourism satellite accounts, input-output tables and economic modelling. They expand on the TSA's measurement of tourism's economic size to provide estimates of tourism's economic impact, including many effects that are not captured in input-output models.

TPF models also provide an important tool for policy analysis, enabling the complex interactions in the economy that result from policy actions to be traced through a general equilibrium framework and assessed. The ability to have quantitative estimates of the effects of policy is of vital importance to policy makers.

TPF models can also be used as a basis for forecasting the levels and expenditures of tourists, taking relatively stable and predictable long-term trends in tourism source and destination countries to provide a method of robust long-term forecasting. The results presented here for the USA Tourism, Policy and Forecasting model provide an example of the TPF model's capabilities.

The impact of tourism when including induced income effects and resource reallocation effects is dramatically different to the standard input-output results. In particular, the IO models overestimate the total GDP effect, underestimate the total effect on tourism sectors and completely miss the negative effects on non-tourism sectors. The results of the policy analysis using the TPF model are that most tourism sectors are effectively taxed at higher than the national average level.

In sectors such as hotels and transport sectors indirect taxation imposes lower welfare losses on the economy than in other sectors. This implies that the most urgent sectors for tax reductions (i.e. those where welfare distortions are disproportionately high relative to tax revenues) are auto and truck rental, retail, eating and drinking, recreation and entertainment, participant sports, and parking, automotive repair and highway tolls. We also report the results of a 'what-if' scenario that shows the effect of improved productivity in the air transport sector. The results show that increases in GDP are spread across the economy in sectors that use air transport. Competing transport sectors may contract as a result. The USA TPF model is intended to give an indication of the potential applications that TPF modelling has.

While the sector classification for this model is small to match the U.S. TSA as closely as possible, a full 494-sector model is also in operation. For the U.S., the model can be extended in various directions: tourism demand data on domestic tourism by state would enable the TPF model to include state effects.

Otherwise, the model can be expanded to include different skill categories of labour and different households groups according to geographical location, income category, or other classification. This would be able to show how these different household groups are affected by both an expansion in tourism and by policies. Other possible ways of expanding this model are to incorporate similar data from other countries: a model of North America would, for example, include Canada and Mexico.

This would incorporate cross-border effects, to assess the effects that a tax on a tourism sector in the U.S. has on the economies of Canada and Mexico. As well as these extensions the U.S. TPF model, it is of course possible to build similar models for any country where a TSA and input-output table exist, and these can also incorporate regional differences, household distributions and different types of labour as well as incorporating more than one country. The underlying methodology of TPF models is well suited to developing countries, for which computable general equilibrium modelling has long been used.

THE IMPORTANCE OF TOURISM

Tourism can also be one of the most effective drivers for the development of regional economies. These patterns apply to both developed and emerging economies. Travel & Tourism is the world's largest industry and creator of jobs across national and regional economies. WTTC/WEFA research show that in 2000, Travel & Tourism will generate, directly and indirectly, 11.7% of GDP and nearly 200 million jobs in the world-wide economy. These figures are forecasted to total 11.7% and 255 million respectively in 2010. Jobs generated by Travel & Tourism are spread across the economy - in retail, construction, manufacturing and telecommunications, as well as directly in Travel & Tourism companies. These jobs employ a large proportion of women, minorities and young people; are predominantly in small and medium sized companies; and offer good training and transferability.

Contributing to sustainable development

The 1992 United Nations Conference on Environment and Development (UNCED), the Rio Earth Summit, identified Travel & Tourism as one of the key sectors of the economy which could make a positive contribution to achieving sustainable development. The Earth Summit lead to the adoption of Agenda 21, a comprehensive programme of action adopted by 182 governments to provide a global blueprint for achieving sustainable development. Travel & Tourism is the first industry sector to have launched an industry-specific action plan based on Agenda 21.

Travel & Tourism is able to contribute to development which is economically, ecologically and socially sustainable, because it:

- Has less impact on natural resources and the environment than most other industries;
- Is based on enjoyment and appreciation of local culture, built heritage, and natural environment, as such that the industry has a direct and powerful motivation to protect these assets;
- Can play a positive part in increasing consumer commitment to sustainable development principles through its unparalleled consumer distribution channels; and
- Provides an economic incentive to conserve natural environments and habitats which might otherwise be allocated to more environmentally damaging land uses, thereby, helping to maintain bio-diversity.

There are numerous good examples of where Travel & Tourism is acting as a catalyst for conservation and improvement of the environment and maintenance of local diversity and culture. (Some of these are set out in Section B of this chapter and a fuller illustration of the range of industry action can be found on the World Travel & Tourism Council's. Of course, there are also examples where development has not been sustainable.

Providing Infrastructure

To a greater degree than most activities, Travel & Tourism depends on a wide range of infrastructure services - airports, air navigation, roads, railheads and ports, as well as basic infrastructure services required by hotels, restaurants, shops, and recreation facilities (e.g. telecommunications and utilities).

It is the combination of tourism and good infrastructure that underpins the economic, environmental and social benefits. It is important to balance any decision to develop an area for tourism against the need to preserve fragile or threatened environments and cultures. However, once a decision has been taken where an area is appropriate for new tourism development, or that an existing tourist site should be developed further, then good infrastructure will be essential to sustain the quality, economic viability and growth of Travel &

Tourism. Good infrastructure will also be a key factor in the industry's ability to manage visitor flows in ways that do not affect the natural or built heritage, nor counteract against local interests.

Challenge for the Future

Travel & Tourism creates jobs and wealth and has tremendous potential to contribute to economically, environmentally and socially sustainable development in both developed countries and emerging nations. It has a comparative advantage in that its start up and running costs can be low compared to many other forms of industry development. It is also often one of the few realistic options for development in many areas. Therefore, there is a strong likelihood that the Travel & Tourism industry will continue to grow globally over the short to medium term.

Of course, if Travel & Tourism is managed badly, it can have a detrimental effect - it can damage fragile environments and destroy local cultures. The challenge is to manage the future growth of the industry so as to minimise its negative impacts on the environment and host communities whilst maximising the benefits it brings in terms of jobs, wealth and support for local culture and industry, and protection of the built and natural environment.

Industry Initiatives

Travel & Tourism takes many different forms - from a trip only a few hours away from home to long distance travel overseas. A common belief is that most Travel & Tourism involves large numbers of visitors from developed countries travelling by air to destinations in emerging countries. In fact, in most countries, the domestic tourism market is larger than the inbound market. Of course, the social and cultural impact of inbound visitors is often greater than that of domestic tourists. Whether tourism is domestic or international, it involves visiting a destination away from the area in which one lives and using the services available in that destination. Therefore, tourists' requirements are for travel services to reach their destinations and once there, for services such as shelter, water, food, sanitation and entertainment.

What makes tourism special is that, many of these different products and services are often supplied by different operators: usually small or medium sized businesses in local ownership. This makes tourism a highly fragmented and diverse industry and so co-ordinated, industry-wide action is difficult to achieve. The influence of Travel & Tourism's demand also extends far beyond traditional tourism companies, into upstream suppliers like aircraft manufacturers or food producers and into the downstream service providers for travellers, like retail shops.

Despite the difficulties caused by fragmentation and lengthy supply chains, there has been a steady growth in environmental good practice across the industry in recent years. There are examples of airlines and airports reducing pollution and noise impacts; cruise liners practising marine conservation; hotels implementing energy consumption and waste disposal programmes; car rental companies investing in increasingly fuel efficient fleets and railways sound proofing to dampen noise. The result is that there are a number of excellent initiatives in place designed to improve the environmental management of Travel & Tourism businesses. Of course, more needs to be done.

WTTC with 105 members is the global business leaders' forum for the Travel & Tourism industry. The WTTC have set in place an extensive strategy to promote a culture of sustainable development and have put in place a three tiered structure for its achievement. This involves:

In 1996 the WTTC, the World Tourism Organization and the Earth Council, joined together to launch an action plan entitled "Agenda 21 for the Travel & Tourism Industry: Towards Environmentally Sustainable Development" - a sectional sustainable development programme based on the results of the Rio Earth Summit in 1992. Since the launch of the document, the three organisations have begun a series of regional seminars to increase awareness of the conclusions, and to adapt the programme for local implementation. The programme has held regional seminars in London and Jakarta in 1997 and Victoria Falls and Dominica in 1998.

WTTC has recently introduced a major addition to the programme - the "Alliance for Sustainable Tourism", which invites public and private sector Travel & Tourism organisations to record their Agenda 21 based activities on a central web site and commit to co-operation with all other partners. In order to develop the programme from global principles to community based action, WTTC is also discussing with the International Council for Local Environment Initiatives (ICLEI) on how the principles of "Agenda 21 for Travel & Tourism" can be built into Local Agenda 21 programmes. Furthermore, WTTC is considering pilot projects in 5 cities around the world to serve as models for other destinations.

In 1994, WTTC initiated the "GREEN GLOBE", an Agenda 21 based industry improvement programme, which provides guidance material and a certification process linked to both ISO standards and Agenda 21 principles. There are now 500 "GREEN GLOBE "members in 100 countries dedicated to improving environmental practice. The first certification has commenced with hotels groups in Jamaica and Manchester (UK). "GREEN GLOBE" has also developed a specific Destination Programme, which provides a methodology for Travel & Tourism destinations to implement sustainable development.

The ultimate aim is that "GREEN GLOBE" will become the primary global standard of environmental commitment by the global Travel & Tourism industry and will be recognised by the public as such. Currently, "GREEN GLOBE" has the support of over 20 international industry organisations representing thousands of businesses world-wide and the support of the

World Tourism Organization, the United Nations Environment Programme and the Earth Council. WTTC have also developed "ECoNETT", a web-site containing advice and data on good practice and sources of help and advice. "ECoNETT" is increasingly recognised as a focal point for environmental information, good practice, new techniques and technologies.

The International Hotel & Restaurant Association (IH&RA), based in Paris, represents over 700,000 establishments in more than 150 countries. Its membership comprises some 50 national and international hotel and restaurant chains, over 110 national hotel and restaurant associations, independent hotel operators and restaurateurs, industry suppliers and 130 hotel schools.

The IH&RA has offices in Asia-Pacific and Latin America. It is also the voice of the world's hotels and restaurants and plays a global role in representing, protecting, promoting and informing the industry to enable its members to achieve their business objectives.

The IH&RA has:

- Raised environmental awareness and developed programmes through joint workshops with national hotel associations and regularly encourages them to develop their own environmental awareness programmes;
- Established an annual Environmental Award sponsored by American Express and judged by the United Nations Environment Programme (UNEP) that recognises efforts by independent and chain hotels to "green" the industry;
- Published advice including practical publications such as the "Environmental Action Pack for Hotels" with the International Hotel Environment Initiative and UNEP and "Environmental Good Practice in Hotels" with UNEP;
- Supported regional initiatives such as the Caribbean Action for Sustainable Tourism; and
- Joined forces with UNEP and the International Hotel School Directors' Association to develop an "Environmental Teaching Resource Package for Hospitality Educational Institutes".

Corporate Initiatives

The International Hotel Environment Initiative (IHEI), based in London, England, is a programme of The Prince of Wales Business Leaders Forum. Founded in 1992 by a consortium of chief executives from 10 multinational hotel groups, IHEI is an educational charity designed to encourage continuous improvement in the environmental performance of the global hotel industry. It does this through:

- Raising environmental awareness in the hotel industry by promoting good practiceinternationally;

- Developing hotel-specific guidance, enabling hotels of all sizes to implement environmentalprogrammes; and
- Multiplying the reach and impact of IHEI by working with partners, including hotelassociations, governments, NGOs, tourism bodies and businesses.

IHEI is a catalyst and conduit for hotels to pool their resources and to share experience via a non- competitive platform. In 5 years it has evolved into an organisation with global impact. IHEI has worked in 111 countries, stimulating and assisting with the establishment of local initiatives such as New Zealand's "Environmental Hotels of Auckland, the Asia Pacific Hotel Environment Initiative" and the Caribbean Action for Sustainable Tourism.

Member hotels now represent over 1 million guest rooms and more than 8,000 hotels on 5 continents. The Co-operative Research Centre for Sustainable Tourism, based in Australia, was established in 1997 to enhance the strategic knowledge available to the Travel & Tourism industry through:

- Long-term high-quality scientific and technological research which contributes to the development of an internationally competitive tourism industry;
- Strengthening the links between research and its commercial and other applications;
- Promoting co-operative research; and
- Stimulating education and training, particularly in graduate programmes, through active involvement of researchers from outside the higher education system in educational activities, and of graduate students in major research programmes.

Company Initiatives

The number of initiatives undertaken by individual companies is large. Just two examples from this are as follows:

The Kandalama hotel in Sri Lanka has been a recipient of the "GREEN GLOBE" award, 3 years in a row, for its commitment to environmental excellence.

The hotel has undertaken measures in the following areas to ensure that its operations are more sustainable:

- *Cultural and social*: Hotel employment, providing community infrastructure and development;
- *Natural environment*: Soil erosion measures and planting forests;
- *Pollution*: Sewage, solid waste and noise pollution reduction programmes; and
- *Environmental communication*: Construction of an Eco Park where all waste is treated within the park, a dry debris sorting centre, a lecture room to promote environmental awareness and a sustainable development library.

Canadian Pacific Hotels, the largest hotel conglomerate in Canada, has developed an environmental programme, which is recognised as the most comprehensive in the North American hotel industry. Based on the results of a survey, employee suggestions and the recommendations of a professional environmental consultant, Canadian Pacific Hotels developed a list of 16 goals to be attained by all hotels.

In addition to individual projects implemented at each of the 26 hotels, the goals set for the chain as a whole were ambitious:

- To reduce the amount of waste sent to landfill by 50% across the chain, by launching an extensive recycling programme;
- To redesign purchasing policies to ensure that waste is reduced at source, and supplies used in the hotels are nature friendly.

Inter-regional Level

The Caribbean Action for Sustainable Tourism (CAST) is an alliance for sustainable growth developed by the Caribbean Hoteliers Association with the support of the WTTC, the IHEI and the Caribbean Tourism Organisation. CAST has developed workshops, training courses and guidance material for its members on a wide range of environmental issues, including:

- Setting up environmental management systems;
- Energy efficiency;
- Renewable energy; and
- Waste water management.

Agents and Partnerships for Change

The public sectors, particularly national and local government, have an important role to play by setting the agenda and providing the framework in which action should take place.

The regulatory environment also plays an important role in creating the conditions suitable for sustainable tourism. Self-regulation involving the agreement and co-operation of industry is always likely to be the most effective solution. Therefore, the role of trade associations and industry organisations in distributing information among their members and encouraging participation is essential.

The major partnerships to be formed are between:

- Industry and the public sector - to ensure consistency with the framework;
- Industry and the voluntary sector - to tap into the enormous resources of expertise and goodwill that this sector is able to generate; and
- Industry and the public - both travellers themselves and the people who live in the places they visit to develop more sustainable forms of tourism.

Areas for further Action

The industry is already doing much to improve its performance in terms of sustainable development. The challenge for the new millennium is to move from the existing ad hoc approach to a more systematic one.

To do this will involve a partnership between industry and national governments to deliver the following:

(i) Governments:
- Integration of travel and tourism policy into broader government policies, especially the environment;
- Incentives for the Travel & Tourism industry, backed up where necessary by effective regulation.

(ii) Public/Private partnership:
- Infrastructure planned and developed with a long-term view and within a reference framework based on Agenda 21;
- Indicators and environmental impact assessment tools to enable effective local management and appropriate development.

(iii) International bodies:
- Co-ordination at an international level of environmental action undertaken by all sectors of the Travel & Tourism industry;
- Review of existing voluntary initiatives to improve the quality of reporting, their transparency and credibility, and the assessment of their contribution to sustainability.

(iv) Companies:
- Commitment to place sustainable development issues at the core of the management structure;
- Innovation of process and application through new technology;
- Commitment to education and environmental training of staff.

Influencing Consumer Behaviour to Promote Sustainable Tourism

Problems

At the 1998 World Travel Market, WTTC hosted, as a part of its Environmental Awareness Day, a seminar entitled "Does the Consumer Care?" At this event, MORI presented the latest findings from their Business and the Environment survey - an annual UK survey devoted to public attitudes to the environment. The survey is now in its tenth year and illustrates the challenge facing the Travel & Tourism industry in influencing consumer behaviour to promote sustainable tourism. According to this survey, Travel & Tourism is now more associated with environmental damage than it has been in the past.

Despite this decline in perception, the industry's economic success is not dependent on its green record - public sensitivity to environmental problems on holiday/business trips has not increased and is no more of a deterrent to repeat travel than it was previously. There is a downward trend in the public's willingness to pay extra for environmental protection and environmentally friendly products, including "green" Travel & Tourism. Awareness of companies making environmental commitments is only marginally up.

Therefore, the challenge is to persuade the consumer that it is in their interests to adopt and promote a sustainable approach in their activities and purchasing decisions. Education programmes and the development and widespread acceptance of codes of conduct are useful tools in achieving this step. Once this message has been conveyed, it is then important to back this up with the necessary information to enable consumers to make informed choices. It is here that "ecolabels" and award programmes have value.

Education Programmes

The Foundation for Environmental Education in Europe (FEEE) seeks to promote environmental education by carrying out campaigns and improving awareness of the importance of environmental education. It is composed of a network of international organisations.

The FEEE (headquarters in Denmark) runs three major campaigns in Europe for providing safe and clean beaches and marinas. The award itself is given annually to beaches and marinas that satisfy a number of essential criteria in three separate areas: water quality; beach management and safety; and environmental information and education.

"GREEN GLOBE"'s Dodo Campaign, is based on a cartoon character, who features in 65 Travel & Tourism videos. Dodo explains and promotes the actions that visitors can take to reduce the impacts of their travels. The videos are aimed at children and are designed to be fun, whilst conveying important messages about sustainable Travel & Tourism. The aim is to have these videos shown on in flight and in-room television channels to raise awareness and influence consumer behaviour.

Codes of conduct

Codes of conduct are also used to try and influence consumer behaviour. For example, "Guidelines for Responsible Environmental Tourism" are prepared and distributed by the American Society of Travel Agents to all customers who book holidays through their members' branches. The Guidelines aim to "encourage the growth of peaceful tourism and environmentally responsible travel" and include 10 recommendations to encourage tourists to act responsibly and show respect for their hosts and the environment of their destinations.

The Pacific Asia Tourism Association (PATA) is an industrial association, which promotes the Pacific Asia area's Travel & Tourism destinations, products and services. PATA also serves as a central resource of information and research, travel industry education and training, as well as quality product development with sensitivity for culture, heritage and environment. In 1992, PATA introduced its "Code for Environmentally Responsible Tourism" to strengthen the principles of preservation in the region.

Businesses, organisations and individuals wishing to affirm their support for the PATA Code are encouraged to participate in the PATA Green Leaf programme. The Africa Travel Association has produced "Responsible Traveller Guidelines"; the Japanese Association of Travel Agents has produced the "Declaration of Earth Friendly Travellers" and there are many more examples of industry codes aimed at educating and influencing their customers.

Eco Labelling

There are numerous examples of industry sponsored labelling schemes, whose aim is to recognise good industry practice and influence consumer behaviour into purchasing the labelled products. For example, the "Green Key, Denmark" certificate operated by the Hotel, Restaurant and Leisure Industry Association (HORESTA) has 56 criteria that includes environmental information, water & energy consumption and waste management.

Special features also include ecological food products, outdoor areas, non-smoking rooms, and adaptations for access by disabled persons. There are a number of industries that runs and sponsors award programmes to highlight and promote examples of good practice.

For example, British Airways has run the "Tourism for Tomorrow" awards since 1992 to encourage action to protect the environment. The awards are directed at tour operators, hotels, national parks and heritage sites, and other activities associated with tourism. By selecting projects showing best practice in their field as role models, others are encouraged to follow suit and consider the environment in the everyday running of their tourism business.

The awards are run annually, with a winner selected from each of five regions and an overall winner. In addition, two special awards are made for mass tourism destinations. The awards are run in association with the British Tourist Authority, the Association of British Travel Agents, the Pacific Asia Travel Association and the American Society of Travel Agents. Entries to the awards have been increases every year. American Express also sponsors a variety of environmental awards for international tourism organisations.

Agents and Partnerships for Change

- A broad based approach is called for which requires Travel & Tourism to work with: national governments to raise the profile of environmental and social issues within the education system;
- NGOs to raise awareness of tourism issues in their work and activities and provide feedback to the Travel & Tourism industry;
- Development organisations to communicate with host communities to understand their needs and requirements;

- Local authorities to engage local people through the inclusion of tourism issues in Local Agenda21 plans;
- National and international trade associations, labour representative organisations and training providers to increase awareness and training of staff in environmental and social issues;
- Travel & Tourism publications (such as travel guides);
- Travel & Tourism journalists to raise the profile of reporting environmental and social impacts of tourism among consumers and tourism businesses; and
- The Internet as a source of information for potential travellers.

Areas for further Action

The WTTC/MORI data shows the scale of the task still remaining. The industry has developed a number of initiatives to influence consumer behaviour. However, if consumers do not understand or are not aware of the issues involved and do not demand more sustainable products then, in the long term, it will not be in the industry's interests to move in that direction. The priority for future action, therefore, should be to raise awareness among travellers of the issues associated with tourism and the impact their activities can have on local destinations and cultures.

Broad-based Sustainable Development through Tourism

The Travel & Tourism industry has a vested interest in protecting the natural and cultural resources that are the core of its business. Travel & Tourism has less impacts on natural resources and the environment than other sectors and it has already done much to address the issues arising from its activities.

There are examples, however, from around the world where the impact of Travel & Tourism has been damaging to the local environment and people. Some of the factors which contributes to the harmful impact of tourism are:

- A lack of awareness on the part of those making decisions about tourism development of the social, economic and environmental balance to be pursued in achieving sustainable development;
- A lack of commitment by tourism operators and travellers to contribute to the maintenance of the local environment and culture of the host destination;
- A weak institutional framework with inadequate controls can lead to tourism development which is both inappropriate and intrusive;
- Unfairly traded tourism, whereby local communities are unable to share in its benefits;
- Large flows of visitors in remote or sensitive locations can place considerable strains on local resources (particularly water) and supply systems. Travellers' expectations of the goods and services,

which should be available, can lead to these items or services, being imported from outside or local supply chains, being distorted to meet demands; and

- Tourism can change a destination's cultural make-up and, if poorly developed, can increase crime, prostitution and other social problems.

In order for tourism to realise its potential to achieve broad-based sustainable development, an effective partnership between Government and all sectors of the industry will be required. The following illustrates what is being done:

International Co-operation

IH&RA and the United Nations Organisation for Education, Science and Culture (UNESCO) have signed a co-operation agreement to encourage world-wide hotel chains to sponsor UNESCO cultural heritage sites and attract tourism to them via their marketing campaigns.

National Governments

In India, the government is pump priming local "eco-tourism" activities, which are primarily driven by local women. In Mexico, the government is kick starting village development for "eco-tourism" lodges in the Chiapas region involving the whole community. In England, the government has recently held a national consultation on sustainable tourism and, as a result, is developing a new strategy for tourism, which incorporates the principles of sustainable development as a core component. The Caribbean Tourism Organisation has developed a comprehensive strategy to develop "eco-tourism" in the Caribbean region. This strategy is closely integrated with the goals of the Association for Caribbean States (ACE) for a green Caribbean.

"GREEN GLOBE" has developed a specific "Destinations" programme to recognise those tourist destinations where there is a concerted effort by all those involved in the local tourism industry to improve the quality of the environment. The Destinations process provides a framework to guide tourist locations towards achieving sustainable development based on the principles of Agenda 21. The Destinations programmes are tailor made to reflect local circumstances, such as the level of environmental awareness, action taken to date and available resources. Each programme is based on achieving progressive environmental improvements.

Targets are set within a realistic timetable and are developed by a steering group made up of key partners. The island of Jersey has become the first "GREEN GLOBE" Destination. Vilamoura in Portugal, Dominica in the Caribbean and 3 destinations in the Philippines have also entered the Destination programme.

For example, in 1996 Luso tour SA, a tourism development company, enacted a management plan for Vilamoura whereby employees are given responsibility for individual environmental tasks. The company has invested money into rehabilitating the surrounding natural environment, which includes pine forests and a lake that has significance to local wetland areas. Guests are provided with a copy of the environmental policy and are encouraged to participate in the scheme through specialised brochures.

The campaign includes recycling; treating diseased pine areas; regular cleaning of the beaches and marinas; development of a sewage treatment plant and new buildings in the resort are designed to minimise visual and environmental impacts. For its work in Vilamoura, Lusotour SA is also a winner of the British Airways Tourism for Tomorrow Awards.

The "Africa tourism" brand has been developed by the Open Africa Foundation to encourage products, which embraces sustainable ecological, economic and social development based on Africa's unique cultural, natural and wildlife heritage.

"Open Africa" is also developing a continuous network of "Africa tourism" routes from the Cape to Cairo, known as the "African Dream". The Dream helps to create awareness of the many rural and environmental projects, which exist throughout Africa. "Team Africa", a transcontinental alliance of governments, corporations, institutions, professionals and individuals, provides leadership and motivation in the development of the "African Dream".

Host Communities

"Whale Watch Kaikoura" is an initiative of local Maori people from a small town on the East Coast of New Zealand's South Island. Within a kilometre of the Kaikoura shore is an area ideal for whales, where visitors are guaranteed to see them all year round. The Whale Watch began 11 years ago and is now a booming tourist destination, run by indigenous people with a strong sense of heritage and a view of the future based on strong principles of sustainability.

Jordan Tourism Investments, has revitalised the traditional village of Taybeh, in Jordan, into a cultural tourist resort, with the help and agreement of villagers. With many of the younger generation moving to the cities, the village was losing its character. By restoring its 19th century buildings and reviving old crafts, the village is now thriving again. The village lies 9km south east of the historic city of Petra. Opened in July 1994, the village now accommodates around 60,000 guests each year.

Uluru and Kakadu National Parks are both owned by indigenous Australians, the local Aboriginal communities, and jointly run with the National Parks and Wildlife Service. They are both major tourism destinations and involve indigenous participation in planning, management, and ownership of tourism infrastructure, as well as interpretation for visitors. They bring significant economic, social and cultural benefits to the local indigenous communities. The Conservation Corporation in Africa has established a series of high quality game parks in which local communities are major stakeholders and beneficiaries of tourism. This initiative is also helping to re-invigorate local crafts.

Agents and Partnerships

The challenge facing the tourism industry in moving towards a more sustainable future is set out in "Agenda 21 for the Travel & Tourism Industry". To achieve the goals set out in this document will require a partnership between government departments, national tourism authorities, international and national trade organisations and Travel & Tourism companies.

Working together in close co-operation such partnerships should aim to deliver the following:

- Close co-operation between the public and private sectors to deliver a regulatory regime, which encourages voluntary action but supplement, where necessary, with regulation in areas such as land-use and waste management.
- Agreed common standards and tools to enable the measurement of progress towards achieving sustainable development.
- Certification criteria developed and more widely applied to industry initiatives.
- A commitment to the controlled expansion, where appropriate, of infrastructure.
- Environmental taxes, where applied, should be fair and non-discriminatory. They should be carefully thought out to minimise their impact on economic development, and revenues should be allocated to Travel & Tourism associated environment improvement programmes.
- International, national and local funding bodies should include sustainable development as apart of their criteria, so that in time, all funding would be dependent on sound environmental practice.
- Contemporary research into sustainable tourism needs to be funded and developed. Issues requiring attention include design, carrying capacity, tour operator activities, environmental reporting, auditing and environmental impact assessments.
- Environmental education and training should be increased, particularly in schools, for future hotel and tourism staff.
- Greater investment and commitment to the use of new technology.

Coastal Impact of Tourism

Tourism provides an essential lifeline for many coastal communities. Faced with the prospect of increasing financial hardship, more and more coastal communities have turned to tourism as a means of generating income and survival. Tourism's impact on the coastal zone has, therefore, been largely positive. Of course, as in any area, if Tourism is not properly managed and developed, it can be harmful. Impacts arise from the construction of infrastructure (hotels, marinas, transport, waste treatment facilities, groynes etc.) and from recreation (golf courses, water sports, theme parks etc). Coastal communities are now faced with tourism on a considerable scale, and the host to guest ratio can be very high in such areas. At the same time, coastal communities must try to maintain the resort's attraction as tourist demands change, sometimes quite rapidly.

With coastal regions being primary tourist destinations, sensitive marine and coastal environments can suffer dramatically. For example, as a result of large-scale sea-front tourist development, considerable beach and dune erosion can occur.

Tourism also impacts on environmental quality in the following ways:

- Ribbon development, infrastructure requirements, particularly transport links;
- The treatment and disposal of solid and/or liquid wastes, particularly during peak tourist seasons, may be inadequate or at worst non-existent; and
- Water is often consumed excessively, not only for drinking but for showers, laundry, swimming pools, maintenance of golf courses etc. This can affect the quantity and quality of fresh water available to indigenous coastal populations.

Recreational activities can also have a significant impact on the coastal zone:

- Golf course's impact can be considerable, with those situated directly on coastal habitats(especially sand dunes) in particular;
- Erosion of reefs and coral from divers and swimmers;
- Pollution from boats and jets skis; and
- Noise from motor boats and jet skis, cars and buses, nightlife and other activities.

The development of a sustainable tourism industry in the coastal zone offers numerous opportunities. Opportunities includes, those for nature conservation - which, given the increasing interest in high quality natural and cultural experiences, can help to reverse the decline in market share of many coastal destinations.

Tourism also provides important opportunities for strengthening local industries. Where industries are in decline, tourism ventures can help supplement declining income.

The following examples illustrate what can be done to make the most of the opportunities offered by tourism in the coastal zone:

Calvia is a Municipality on the Mediterranean coast that has undertaken an Agenda 21 project to assist the sustainable development of its tourism sector, in order to counter the negative impact of short-term tourism development since the 1960s. The local council has now implemented a transferable policy aimed at modernising, improving and diversifying the local tourist industry, involving all stakeholders, including the local population.

A Project Plan was enacted, and achievements so far include:

- Indigenous development, based on the sustainable use of available resources;
- High quality services and an appropriate bed night capacity;
- A ban on new development on 1,700 acres;
- Active participation of the residents in community life; and
- Environmental management of municipality buildings, waste recycling, reduction in spending on electricity, and use of environmentally friendly materials for office use.

Quicksilver Tours, Queensland, Australia, is owned by one of the largest tourism operators to the Great Barrier Reef. Quicksilver have five large catamarans, which take about 1,000 tourists a day to dive on the reef. They have their own reef site with fixed diving platforms. They employ a team of biologists, both for environmental management and assessment as well as widespread environmental interpretation. Recent assessment of the reef, in the vicinity of the operation, shows that it is being maintained in pristine condition.

Kingfisher Bay Resort is found at Fraser Island, Queensland. It is a large five star "ecotourism" resort built in a beautiful, but fragile environment off the Queensland coast. Its concept, design, construction and management were conceived using the latest ecologically sustainable principles. It is a state-of-the-art "ecotourism" resort, which has won Australia's top tourism awards, and its economic and environmental success has influenced new coastal tourism developments.

Maho Bay's camps and studios in the US Virgin Islands have based their product on a commitment to minimise impact on the environment, conserve natural resources, engage in active and passive environmental education of their guests, and contribute to the local economy. Specific initiatives introduced at Maho Bay include the following: use of new technology; purchasing policies; waste management; environmental education; energy and water conservation; and support for local communities and culture.

These initiatives show an appreciation of the need for alternative solutions to issues such as packaging and waste disposal through landfill. These are issues, which as the industry grows, will be increasingly important for the Travel & Tourism industry as a whole to address.

The agents, partnerships for change and areas for further action in relation to tourism in the coastal zone are similar to the development of broad based sustainable tourism in general. A number of issues do, of course, have particular importance for the coastal zone.

Above all, the key to success is better participation at destination level among all the stakeholders concerned. In the case of the coastal zone, there are a number of additional organisations with an interest in coastal policy, marine conservation, shipping etc., which needs to be identified and included in partnerships for the coastal zone.

Successful planning for tourism is very important for the future of the industry in coastal regions, because a significant percentage of tourism occurs within the geographical parameters of the definition of a coastal zone. Concerted support from all countries involved (and the industries within them) is vital to protect the shared natural resources that coastal zones represent.

Historically, the influence most hoteliers have on the environmental impact of their business is limited to working within existing buildings, or after a new site has been completed. In April 1998, the IHEI convened a group of hoteliers, tour operators, architectural firms and sustainable development specialists with the goal of creating a partnership to be called the "Sitting and Design Programme".

The new initiative's mission will be to define responsible planning and design specifications that will cause minimal environmental damage at new sites. Particular attention will be paid to sites located within ecologically sensitive areas and upon waterfronts.

The "Siting and Design Programme" will strive to reach hotel owners, investors and developers to bring these issues to the attention of the entire industry. Linkages with government authorities that uphold responsible development standards would complete the partnership.

Travel & Tourism has a number of advantages over other industry sectors:

- It creates jobs and wealth whilst;
- At the same time, it can contribute to sustainable development;
- It tends to have low start-up costs;
- Is a viable option in a wide range of areas and regions;
- Is likely to continue to grow for the foreseeable future; and
- The industry is, in a large part, aware of the need to protect the resource on which it is based - local culture and built and natural environment - and it is committed to these resources' preservation and enhancement.

The industry is, therefore, making a concerted effort to build up programmes for sustainable development. However, it cannot do this alone. If Travel & Tourism is to continue to flourish and to contribute to sustainable development, it needs help from national Governments.

This assistance is needed in two forms: - both positive encouragement for sustainable tourism initiatives and an understanding that policy decisions in other areas can effect Travel & Tourism. In practical terms, what this means is the following:

The first point of action needed from Governments is to incorporate Agenda 21 principles into tourism policies at international and national level, and to promote their inclusion in regional and local tourism strategies. By providing such a lead and establishing a coherent global framework based on Agenda 21, national governments will make a vital contribution to developing a more sustainable tourism industry.

Governments should also recognise that Travel & Tourism is a core service sector which should always be considered when looking at policies to expand trade, increase employment, modernise infrastructure and encourage investment - at both domestic and international level. It should also be included in national statistics with its economic impact calculated by means of a national tourism satellite account.

Governments should also consider helping Travel & Tourism by seeking to minimise regulatory impediments and by offering appropriate investment incentives. By supporting tourism and allowing it to compete in open and fair markets, tourism's benefits can be more easily secured. Finally, governments can address some of the fundamental barriers to tourism growth by looking at how to expand and modernise infrastructure, to apply taxes fairly and to invest in human resource development. If the programme of action outlined above can be undertaken by national governments in co-operation with continued industry commitments and initiatives for sustainable tourism then we can look to a brighter future.

7

The Future of Tourism and Hotel Organisation

ORGANIZATION OF A LODGING ESTABLISHMENT

As their facilities grow in size, lodging managers are faced with the need to group certain jobs in order to ensure efficient coordination and control of activities. These job groupings are usually called departments. In general, departments might be grouped as front of the house (those departments in which employees have guest contact, such as front desk), and back of the house (where employees have little guest contact, such as accounting).

However, separating departments by function is the most common method of organizing a hotel or a lodging business. The limited-service hotel, a full-service hotel with under 500 rooms, and a full-service hotel with over 500 rooms. There may be as few as 2 or as many as 50 employees in a particular department. In a very small lodging business, such as a bed-and-breakfast, the owner can supervise each department. However, as the lodging business increases in size (i.e., above 20 rooms), it is most effective to create managerial positions within departments.

Typically, the rooms department (called the front desk department in a limited-service facility) includes reservations, the front office, housekeeping, and telephone or PBX. In smaller full-service hotels, security and engineering might also be included in the rooms department. Responsibilities of the rooms department include reservations, guest reception, room assignment, tracking the status of rooms (available or occupied), prompt forwarding of mail and phone messages, security, housekeeping of guest rooms and public spaces such as lobbies, and answering guests' questions.

To perform these many duties effectively, the rooms department may be divided into a number of specialized subunits. To complicate matters, in many instances these subunits are also referred to as departments. For example, the laundry department. Because of its specialized function, little of the knowledge and skills required to manage a laundry operation is transferable to other areas of hotel operations. The front office is one of the most important departments in a hotel, as it often offers the only contact between guests and staff. A hotel's front office is where guests are greeted when they arrive, where they are registered and assigned to a room, and where they check out. Usually, the telephone operator, other guest communications functions, and the bell staff or those employees responsible for delivering luggage and messages and attending to special guest requests also fall under the front office umbrella.

The reservations department takes and tracks the hotel's future bookings. The housekeeping department is responsible for cleaning guest rooms and public spaces. Because of their specialized nature, the security and engineering departments are discussed in separate sections. A great deal of interdependence exists among the subunits of the rooms department.

For example, reservations must inform the front office of the number of presold rooms each day to ensure that a current inventory of salable rooms is always available. On the other hand, the front office must let reservations know whenever walk-in guests (those who do not have reservations) register. A similar level of cooperation is required between the front office and housekeeping. When a guest checks out, the front office must inform housekeeping so that the room may be cleaned.

Once a room is cleaned, housekeeping must inform the front office so that the room may be sold. Certain tasks within the rooms department must occur in a specific order. For example, housekeeping cannot properly provision a guest room if the laundry does not supply enough clean towels or bed sheets. Engineering cannot replace a defective light switch in a guest room if housekeeping does not report the problem. Effective management of this busy department calls for standardized plans, procedures, schedules, and deadlines, as well as frequent direct communication between the executives who manage the key operating units of the rooms department.

Security

The hotel and lodging business is vulnerable to security and safety problems. Problems can be created by guests, employees, or intruders. Security breaches can result in embezzlement, theft, arson, robbery, and even terrorism. Depending on the size of a hotel or a lodging establishment, the security function may be handled by a fully staffed department on site, contracted to an outside security company, or assigned to designated staff members or on-premises supervisory personnel in the rooms department. In a larger, full-service hotel, the director of security may report directly to the general manager. In smaller hotels, the security function might become a task of the rooms department.

Engineering.

Typically, the engineering department's responsibilities include preventive maintenance; repair; replacement; improvement and modification to furniture, fixtures, and equipment (FFE); and ensuring uninterrupted provision of utilities (gas, electricity, water). Preventive maintenance involves routine checks and inspection of the key components of all equipment.

Maintenance of recreational facilities may be part of the engineering department's responsibilities. In particular, swimming pools require extensive maintenance to ensure proper filtration and to prevent the accumulation of algae and other conditions unsuitable for swimming.

Prompt repair minimizes loss of productivity in other hotel operating departments and inconvenience to hotel guests. When a particular FFE has reached the end of its useful life and repair is no longer cost-effective, replacement is indicated. Improvement projects enhance the existing operation or reduce operating costs of the facility. Modification projects alter the existing operation to accommodate one or more new functions.

One hotel might have a large engineering staff that includes plumbers, carpenters, painters, electricians, and other technicians. Another might have maintenance personnel who have general knowledge and understanding of the hotel's operations but rely on outside contractors for specialized jobs. In larger, full-service hotels, engineering may be a separate department, with a director who reports directly to the resident manager.

The primary function of the food and beverage department is to provide food and drink to a hotel's guests. In earlier times, when an inn had a single dining room that could hold a limited number of guests, this was a fairly simple task. Today, however, providing food and drink is much more complicated.

A large hotel might well have a coffee shop, a gourmet restaurant, a poolside snack bar, room service, two banquet halls, and ten function rooms where food and beverages are served. It might also have a lounge, a nightclub, and a lobby bar. On a busy day (or night), it's quite likely that functions will be booked in many outlets at the same time. In addition, some outlets may have multiple events scheduled for a single day. As you can see, there is great diversity in the types of activities performed by a food and beverage department, requiring a significant variety of skills on the part of its workers.

Food Department

Because of the diversity of services provided, the food and beverage department is typically split into subunits. The executive chef, a person of considerable importance and authority in any full-service hotel, runs the food production, or kitchen, department. A variety of culinary specialists who are responsible for different aspects of food preparation report to the executive chef.

The actual serving of food in a large hotel's restaurants is usually the responsibility of a separate department, headed by the assistant food and beverage director. The food service department is composed of the individual restaurant and outlet managers, maitre d's, waiters, waitresses, and bus help. Because of their special duties and concerns, many large hotels have a separate subunit that is responsible only for room service. Because of the high value and profit margins associated with the sale of alcoholic beverages, some hotels have a separate department that assumes responsibility for all outlets where alcoholic beverages are sold. The person responsible for this department is the beverage manager.

Most full-service hotels also do a considerable convention and catering business. The typical convention uses small function rooms for meetings and larger rooms for general sessions, trade shows, exhibits, and banquets. As a hotel or lodging business increases the use of its facilities for conventions and meetings, it may form a separate convention services department.

The convention services department and its personnel are introduced to the client, a meeting planner, or an association executive by the marketing and sales department. The convention services department then handles all of the client's meeting and catering requirements. Individually catered events include parties, wedding receptions, business meetings, and other functions held by groups. To provide for the unique needs of these types of customers, hotels often organize separate catering and convention departments. Depending on the size of the hotel, the job of cleaning the food and beverage outlets themselves as well as of washing pots and pans, dishes, glasses, and utensils is often delegated to a subunit known as the stewarding department.

It is only through continuous cooperation and coordination that a hotel's food service function can be carried out effectively. A guest who is dining in a hotel restaurant requires the joint efforts of the kitchen, food service, beverage, and stewarding departments. A convention banquet cannot be held without the efforts of the convention and catering department along with the food production, beverage, and stewarding departments. The sequence of events and cooperation required among the food and beverage staff is even more important than in the rooms department, thus increasing the importance of communication between managers and employees alike.

Another challenge faced by management is the diversity of the employees in the food and beverage department; the dishwasher in the stewarding department is at a dramatically different level than the sous chef in the kitchen. Coordination is not as important an issue in the marketing and sales department, which is generally much smaller than the food and beverage department. The primary responsibility of the sales managers who make up the marketing and sales department is sales, or the selling of the hotel facilities and services to individuals and groups. Sales managers sell rooms, food, and beverages to potential clients through advertising, attendance at association and conference meetings, and direct contacts.

The marketing and sales department is also removed from most of the day-to-day operational problems faced by other departments. The division of work among the sales managers is based on the type of customers a hotel is attempting to attract. Individual sales managers often specialize in corporate accounts, conventions, or tour and travel markets. Sales managers' accounts are sometimes subdivided along geographical lines into regional or national accounts. The sales staff of the largest full-service hotels usually does not exceed a dozen or so. These sales managers work more or less independently in their particular market segments.

The human resources department serves no customers, books no business, and prepares no meals, yet it plays a vital role in a hotel's efficient operation. The three functions of the human resources department are employee recruitment, benefits administration, and training. The director of human resources is also expected to be an expert on federal and state labour laws and to advise managers in other departments on these topics.

The human resources department's major challenge is in its interactions with other hotel departments. Although the human resources department recruits, interviews, and screens prospective employees, the final hiring decision rests within the department in which the potential employee will be working. The same is true of promotion and disciplinary decisions; the human resources department's input is, in most cases, limited to advice and interpretation of legal questions.

The human resources department's effectiveness depends on its manager's ability to form effective working relationships with managers of other departments. In many hotels, the accounting department combines staff functions and line functions, or those functions directly responsible for servicing guests.

The accounting department's traditional role is recording financial transactions, preparing and interpreting financial statements, and providing the managers of other departments with timely reports of operating results (line functions). Other responsibilities, carried out by the assistant controller for finance, include payroll preparation, accounts receivable, and accounts payable (staff functions). Another dimension of the accounting department's responsibilities deals with various aspects of hotel operations, cost accounting, and cost control throughout the hotel.

The two areas of central concern to the accounting department are rooms and food and beverage. The accounting department's front office cashier is responsible for tracking all charges to guest accounts. At the close of each business day, which varies by hotel but typically occurs at midnight or after the bulk of guests' transactions have been completed (i.e., check-in, restaurant charges, retail charges, etc.), the night auditor is responsible for reconciling all guest bills with the charges from the various hotel departments.

Although the front office cashier and the night auditor physically work at the front desk and, in the case of the cashier, have direct contact with guests, they are members of the accounting department and report to the assistant controller of operations.

The food and beverage department may be responsible for food preparation and service, but the accounting department is responsible for collecting revenues. The food and beverage controller and the food and beverage cashiers keep track of both the revenues and expenses of the food and beverage department. The food and beverage controller's job is to verify the accuracy and reasonableness of all food and beverage revenues. In addition to tracking and preparing daily reports on the costs of the food and beverages used in the hotel, in many cases the accounting department is also responsible for purchasing and storeroom operations.

Finally, the director of systems is responsible for designing the accounting and control systems used throughout the hotel. As you can see, the accounting department is anything but a passive staff unit contending with routine recordkeeping. The accounting department is also responsible for collecting and reporting most of a hotel's operational and financial statistics, which provide important data for decision making and budget preparation purposes.

The head of the accounting department may report not only to the hotel's general manager but also to the hotel chain's financial vice president or to the hotel's owner. The reason for this dual responsibility and reporting relationship is to afford the hotel corporation an independent verification of the financial and operating results of the hotel. In addition to being in charge of overseeing all of the departments that we have discussed, the hotel's general manager (GM) is responsible for defining and interpreting the policies established by top management.

The general manager serves as a liaison to the hotel's owner or corporate parent, sets (or communicates) the overall strategic course of the hotel, sets hotel-wide goals, coordinates activities between departments, and arbitrates interdepart-mental disputes. It is common practice in a large, full-service hotel for a director of public relations to report directly to the GM. The GM also has corporate-level responsibilities, participates on civic boards and committees, and engages in industry-related activities such as serving on the local tourism commission or hotel-motel association.

In addition to possessing a high level of technical skill (i.e., a thorough understanding of each operating department in the hotel), the general manager must also be decisive, analytical, and skilled with both computers and people. He or she must be able to see the big picture and how all of the parts of the hotel fit into the overall organization. An executive may be promoted to relieve the general manager of some operational duties. This is often accomplished by elevating the duties and responsibilities of one particular department head without relieving that person of regular departmental duties.

The title of this position is usually resident manager. It is quite common (and logical) for the general manager to select the manager of the rooms department to be resident manager. Responsibilities of the resident manager include serving as acting GM in the GM's absence, representing the GM on interdepartmental hotel committees, and taking responsibility for important special projects such as major hotel renovations, VIP guests, and operating reports that require in-depth analysis for the regional or corporate offices.

Patterns of Authority

The delegation of authority creates a chain of command, the formal channel that defines the lines of authority from the top to the bottom of an organization. The chain of command consists of a series of relationships from the highest position in the organization to the lowest. The chain of command specifies a clear reporting relationship for each person in the organization and should be followed in both downward and upward communication. Following the chain of command enables each new employee, no matter what his or her position, to know exactly for whom and to whom he or she is responsible.

When designing an organizational structure, managers must consider the distribution of authority. Defined simply, authority is the organizationally sanctioned right to make a decision. Authority can be distributed throughout an organization or held in the hands of a few select employees. Decentralization is the process of distributing authority throughout an organization. In a decentralized organization, an organization member has the right to make a decision without obtaining approval from a higher-level manager.

Centralization is the retention of decision-making authority by a high-level manager. Traditionally, hotel and lodging management has been very centralized, probably due to its roots in small, owner-operated lodging. In recent years, as the hotel and lodging industry has expanded, decentralization has become a more frequent style of operation.

Decentralization has several advantages. Managers are encouraged to develop decision-making skills, which help them advance in their careers. The autonomy afforded by this style of operation also increases job satisfaction and motivation. When employees are encouraged to perform well, the profitability of the organization increases. Many hotel and lodging organizations have begun to empower employees and supervisors to make decisions that typically have been made by managers.

One example that we have already discussed is the use of the quality circle. For example, if a front desk agent determines that a guest's bill is incorrect, in a decentralized organization the agent has the power to make the correction immediately. If that same front desk agent determines that a guest's stay has been unsatisfactory, he or she has the power to reduce the guest's bill by an amount previously specified by management. Additional challenges, control of the process, and quality assessment become part of everyone's job, and each employee is given the authority to take positive actions that will lead to high quality and improved performance.

Span of Control

Span of control refers to the number of people who report to one manager or supervisor. A wide span of control results in a flat organization— that is, a large number of employees reporting to one supervisor. A narrow span of control results in a tall organization, in which a small number of employees report to a supervisor, necessitating a larger number of supervisors. No formula exists for determining the ideal span of control. The following factors determine the most appropriate span of control: task similarity, training and professionalism, task certainty, frequency of interaction, task integration, and physical dispersion.

When a large number of employees perform similar tasks, the span of control can be increased. When the employees perform very different tasks, the supervisor must give each subordinate more individual attention in order to keep in touch with the different types of tasks; this requires a narrower span of control.

For example, the rooms department manager might easily manage the front desk agents and housekeepers until the brand standards for check-in or checkout of a guest increase in complexity and the standards for the various types of rooms and their cleaning procedure increase in detail. At this time, the rooms department manager's span of control must be narrowed. The better trained and more skilled a subordinate is, the less supervision is required. For example, a front desk agent might require a higher level of training and skill than a room service waiter. Thus, a front desk supervisor can supervise more employees (wider span of control) than the room service supervisor (narrower span of control).

Task certainty refers to the predictability of a task. Routine tasks allow management to devise standard procedures for subordinates to follow, minimizing questions about the job and widening the span of control. On the other hand, close supervision is called for when tasks are ambiguous and uncertainty is great. For example, the task of checking a guest in or out of the hotel can be documented and standard procedures can be created, so the front desk manager can have a relatively wide span of control over the front desk agents.

However, because of the diversity of customers the sales manager encounters, the tasks of a hotel sales manager are less certain. The director of sales is responsible for coaching the sales managers, observing sales calls, and ensuring deal closings; these tasks require a hands-on approach that limits the number of employees the director of sales can handle, narrowing the span of control. If the supervisor-subordinate relationship requires frequent interaction, the span of control must be narrow. If interaction is infrequent, the span of control can be wide. For example, the hotel controller must review regularly the status of collections and payments with staff.

In contrast, the frequency of interaction between the chief engineer and his or her subordinates is directed by written work orders in most circumstances and thus requires less direct communication, enabling a wider span of control.

If the supervisor must integrate and coordinate the tasks of subordinates, the span of control narrows. For example, in the production of a meal for one table of four guests with different appetizers, salads, and entrées, the chef must have a narrow span of control to ensure that each component of the meal is assembled correctly and delivered to service personnel on a timely basis. The span of control of the executive housekeeper can be much wider because the procedure for cleaning and preparing each guest room is similar, if not exactly the same, for every room.

Physical dispersion refers to the distribution of employees within the lodging establishment. For example, if the executive housekeeper has guest room attendants on 20 floors in two buildings and the front desk manager has all front desk agents located in one place, the span of control would narrow for the executive housekeeper and widen for the front desk manager.

The ideal number of people that one person can supervise depends on a variety of factors. Consistent with trends in organizational structure such as teams, quality circles, and employee empowerment, many hotel and lodging organizations are widening their span of control. The objective behind these trends is to develop a flatter, more responsive organizational structure in which employees can make decisions without going through several levels of management.

Functional Organisation Design

The most important strength of a functional organizational design is efficiency. The performance of common tasks allows for work specialization, which increases overall productivity. Workers develop specialized skills and knowledge more rapidly. Training is easier because of the similarity of tasks and the resulting opportunities for inexperienced workers to learn from experienced workers. This helps new employees quickly learn the kinds of behaviour that lead to success and promotion. Coordination of activities within functional departments is easier than in more broadly based organizations.

A functional organization fosters efficiency, teamwork, and coordination of activities within individual units. However, the functional organization's most important strength is also the source of its greatest shortcoming. The success of a hotel as a business is measured by its overall performance and not by the performance of any one department. A hotel with spotless guest rooms will not be successful if guests' front desk experiences are not up to par. Even if guests' dining experiences are superb, the hotel will fall flat on its face if its rooms are dismal.

It is sometimes difficult for each department to fully appreciate its role in the overall success of the organization. It is vital that each department keep in mind the hotel-wide goals of customer service and profitability rather than focus narrowly on its own concerns. Some means must be found to coordinate the activities of functional departments and to set hotel-wide strategies and goals. A hotel's functional organization demands strong leadership.

New initiatives in hotels often require cooperation and coordination between functional departments. New ideas tend to be stillborn if department heads lack a hotel-wide perspective or have difficulty coordinating their activities. The tendency to concentrate on doing things right often overshadows the organization's ability to do the right thing. The GM, as the chief executive of the hotel, emerges as the single person capable of providing the overall organizational direction, decision making, coordination, and arbitration needed to make a hotel's functional departments work together effectively. A hotel simply cannot run itself from the departmental level. Thus, the GM must be a strong leader to be effective.

Meetings and Committees

An organizational chart is useful in identifying the formal reporting and authority relationships of a hotel or a lodging enterprise. However, it is not of much help in coordinating administrative units at the department and subdepartment level. Consider this scenario. If the director of sales increases group bookings without consulting other hotel departments, a disaster is in the making. If the reservations department is not consulted, the sales department might guarantee more rooms to a group than are actually available at a price lower than the reservations department's quarterly goal. If the convention services manager is not consulted, necessary meeting rooms might not be available.

If the food and beverage department is not consulted, the group might be sold a banquet that exceeds the hotel's capabilities. If the accounting department is not consulted, credit terms might be extended that violate the credit manager's policies. If the front office is not consulted, the group might experience lengthy delays at check-in (groups are usually preassigned rooms and keys).

The executive operating committee (EOC) of a hotel, made up of the general manager and senior executives from each department, is designed to increase the level of coordination between departments. There is no standard membership for this committee, but it usually comprises those executives who report directly to the general manager. The EOC is also responsible for a hotel's major budgetary units, such as the food and beverage and housekeeping units. EOC functions depend on how the hotel GM chooses to use the group, the GM's style, and the structure of other management meetings in the hotel.

Typically, the EOC meets weekly, focusing on matters ranging from day-today operational issues (daily function schedules and labour and food cost control) to comparing budgets with actual operating results. Many hotels increase communications through an elaborate structure of additional committees and meetings, including some or all of the following: operations, staff, sales forecast and marketing, departmental, subdepartmental, credit, safety, energy conservation, and employee meetings. The operations committee comprises the general manager, department heads, front office manager, manager on duty, and representatives from housekeeping, security, engineering, and food and beverage. This committee might meet four or five times per week for 15 to 20 minutes to review upcoming activities and assess the results of previous activities.

The staff committee might include the GM, department heads, and all subdepartment heads who report to the department heads. This committee, which might meet weekly for one or two hours, reviews the prior week's performance, the current week's activities, the next week's plans, and special projects. The staff committee also presents performance awards to employees.

The sales forecast and marketing committee might meet one to four times per month for several hours so the GM and department heads can review room demand for the coming 90 days and devise strategies to increase room nights (and thus bring in more revenue) and to increase average daily rates by up-selling potential guests to higher-rated rooms with perhaps more amenities or services.

The departmental committee consists of the department head and his or her subdepartment heads, managers, and supervisors. Meeting once or twice per month for an hour or so, the group reviews departmental issues. Similarly, subdepartment committees meet monthly for about an hour so the subdepartment head, managers, and supervisors can address issues unique to their subdepartment, such as the selection of a new type of floor cleaner by the housekeeping department or a more energy-efficient light bulb by the engineering department.

The credit committee includes the general manager, the controller, sales, the front office, reservations, catering, and the credit manager. Meeting monthly for an hour, the committee reviews those guests and clients of the hotel who were granted credit but have not settled their account. The safety committee typically comprises representatives from human resources, food and beverage, housekeeping, and engineering. Meeting monthly for an hour or so, the committee reviews safety programmes and safety records, addresses problems, and discusses the implementation of new safety regulations.

In some full-service hotels, an energy conservation committee includes the chief engineer, resident manager, food and beverage staff, human resource representatives, rooms staff, and housekeeping representatives. The committee typically meets monthly for an hour to discuss strategies and programmes for controlling energy costs. Most full-service hotels convene a monthly meeting or at least an annual meeting of all hotel management and employees to review performance and to distribute awards. This event ranges from an hourlong meeting to a company-wide celebration lasting several hours.

The Future Organization of Hotels

As new business practices are evolving as fast as our technologies, resistance to change has become a primary cause of business failure. The future success of a hotel will be driven in large part by the ability to foresee and capitalize on change. As we go through global transitions, the successful hotel will examine the key factors that will not only define success but also the ability to survive in coming years. These key organizational trends must be acknowledged by the successful hotel organization: visionary leadership, globalization, diversity, flexibility, flat structure, customer focus, zero defects, network orientation, and being in the information fast lane.

The organization must be able to respond to increasingly globalized sales, the movement to maintaining sales offices in many countries and hotel properties across the globe, and an increasingly globalized labour market. Intercontinental Hotels Group recently introduced a new organization structure to more efficiently use regional and global resources to drive higher levels of innovation, customer focus, and revenues.

Diversity means the organization must respond to a workforce that is heterogeneous sexually, racially, and chronologically; innovation and conflict/ communication issues; and different styles of interaction, dress, presentation, and physical appearance. Flexibility in the modern hotel organization means assuring that systems, processes, and people can respond differently to different situations; fewer detailed rules and procedures; greater autonomy and encouragement of initiative; customizing employment relationships to include telecommuting and job-sharing; and lifetime employability rather than lifetime employment.

The trend toward flatness in hotel organizations means fewer levels of management, workers empowered to make decisions, and fewer differences in responsibility. The organization's employees need to believe in a sense of entrepreneurship that reacts proactively to market diversity. Traditional organizations that follow well-documented rules must give way to leaders who can balance a sense of discipline with one of flexibility.

If the customer is king or queen in the 21st century, hotel organizaions will be best served by focusing less on their hotel assets as measures of success and more on their customers. This involves a fundamental shift from viewing the real estate asset as the wealth creator to seeing the customer as the key to building shareholder wealth. A customer focus must reflect business decisions at all levels of developing and operating a hotel organization. Pursuing such a course will inevitably impact shareholder wealth.

The Japanese concept of zero defects in products and services can yield tremendous benefits for a hotel business organization. In practical terms, the hotel industry finds it extremely difficult to meet the standard of zero defects in service. Hotel services are based primarily on people, not on computers or other equipment. Twenty years ago, a business executive did not expect a consistent and predictable level of service wherever he or she traveled.

Today that is the standard, not the exception, as is the expectation of sophisticated technology in hotel rooms to support business needs. With customer discrimination so acute, it is not surprising that brand loyalty is a diminishing commodity in the hotel industry. Today's hotel organization must recognize the need for visionary leadership. The old command-and-control model of leadership is giving way to a focus on leadership in ideas, information, inspiration, vision, and teamwork. A failing hotel organization is overmanaged and underled.

The networked hotel organization can facilitate direct communication across unit and property boundaries, ignoring the chain of command; cross-unit team structures; outsourcing and downsizing; strategic alliances with competitors and others; customization; and decentralization. Being in the information fast lane is critical. The traditional role of information technology as a back office support for accounting and bookkeeping has clearly moved to front and centre stage. Information technology today influences all aspects of business from corporate strategies to organizational structure.

Technology was once viewed as a way to reduce costs by replacing people. That attitude has been firmly supplanted by the idea of seeking information technology support for the creative work all organizations must pursue. Information technology must enable organizations to react more speedily to market needs and, of course, produce the fulfillment of customer demands both quickly and accurately. To do this it must operate on a decentralized basis. Information technology delivers, but it has to deliver the right information to the right people at the right time.

The Hotel Staffing System

Staffing, which is one of a hotel's most important management functions, is an ongoing challenge because of the high rate of employee and manager turnover. Full-service hotels can experience annual turnover rates in excess of 100 per cent in certain employee classifications. Some managers consider an annual employee turnover rate of 33 per cent low. (In other words, in a single year, one-third of a hotel's employees must be replaced.) At this rate, the entire hotel must be completely restaffed every three years. The higher the turnover rate, the larger the number of employees who must be replaced. For example, if a hotel with 450 employees has a 75 per cent annual turnover rate, it will be completely restaffed every 16 months.

In an attempt to reduce employee turnover, hotel and lodging businesses are giving increasing attention to job design, seeking to enhance those job characteristics that give the employee the greatest satisfaction and motivation. Good job design must take into account the needs of employees as well as the demands of the job. Well-thought-out job design begins when management conducts a job analysis—that is, a thorough evaluation of the specific tasks performed for a particular job and the time required to perform them. Job analysis is an ongoing process, as many jobs change with improvements in technology and pressure to improve product quality.

The job analysis is the basis for the job description and job specification. A job description includes the job title, pay, a brief statement of duties and procedures, working conditions, and hours. The job specification is an outline of the qualifications necessary for a particular job. In response to the limits of specialization, organizations can redesign jobs to improve coordination, productivity, and product quality while responding to an employee's needs for learning, challenge, variety, increased responsibility, and achievement.

Such job redesign often involves job rotation, the systematic movement of employees from one job to another; job enlargement, an increase in the number of tasks an employee will do in the job; job enrichment, the attempt to give the employee more control over job-related activities; and flextime, a flexible work schedule that permits employee input in establishing work schedules. In team-driven job redesign, a concept similar to job rotation, employees can transfer back and forth among teams that provide different services or products.

Hotels recruit employees from a variety of sources. Newspapers and employee referrals are used to recruit nonskilled hourly employees. Supervisory and management employees generally are recruited through colleges and universities, promotions from within, professional associations, and management recruiters. Hotels that take more time in making their selections are more successful in retaining employees.

Discussions of employee training and development often concentrate on training techniques without giving a full explanation of what a hotel is trying to accomplish. As training and development impart job skills and educate employees, supervisors, and managers, they also improve current and future employee performance, which affects the bottom line. Effective training includes problem solving, problem analysis, quality measurement and feedback, and team building.

Performance evaluation, also called performance appraisal, is the systematic review of the strengths and weaknesses of an employee's performance. The major difficulty in a performance appraisal is quantifying those strengths and weaknesses. The performance of some jobs is easy to quantify, while for others it is more difficult. An important part of the appraisal process is a well-established job description, so that the employee and the supervisor have similar expectations.

Compensation includes the monetary and nonmonetary rewards that managers, supervisors, and employees receive for performing their jobs. In order to set compensation levels, the human resources department must periodically conduct job evaluations, which determine the value of the job to the hotel. Knowledge of the value of the job to the organization and of wage rates for each job classification allows the hotel to establish a fair compensation policy.

If you complete your course of study and graduate with a bachelor of science degree in hotel management, most likely you will enter the business at the managerial level. Along the way you will have learned that a successful manager provides clear direction, encourages open communication, coaches and supports people, provides objective recognition, establishes ongoing controls, follows up and gives subordinates feedback, selects the right people to staff the organization, understands the financial implications of decisions, encourages innovation and new ideas, gives subordinates clear-cut decisions when needed, and consistently demonstrates a high level of integrity.

There are three levels of management careers in the hotel or lodging business: first-line, middle, and top. First-line refers to those who have day-to-day contact with the guests and clients of a lodging business. The first-line manager oversees the work of the supervisors and line employees. In a hotel or lodging business, first-line positions may include assistant manager of housekeeping, assistant front office manager, and assistant restaurant manager.

First-line managers are responsible for a hotel's basic work, such as checking guests in and out, making up the guests' rooms, and preparing and serving the meals. First-line managers are in daily or near-daily contact with line employees. Middle management of most hotel or lodging businesses includes the department manager, general manager, and any position between those levels.

Depending on the size of the hotel, the regional manager (who supervises the general managers of the hotels in his or her region) can also fall into this category. Unlike first-line managers, those in middle management plan, organize, lead, and control other managers' activities and are responsible for the performance of their departments. Top management comprises a small group of managers such as the chief executive officer, president, or vice president.

Top management is responsible for the performance of the entire hotel business as well as for supervision of the middle managers. The top manager is accountable to the owners of the financial resources used by the organization, such as the stockholders or executive board. As you have already seen, there are numerous attractive careers in the hotel and lodging business.

The following is one of the many paths your career might follow:

1. Assistant manager of the reservations department
2. Reservations department manager
3. Rooms department manager
4. Resident manager
5. General manager
6. Regional manager

In a full-service hotel or lodging business, the movement from entry-level position to general manager might encompass 15 years. Career advancement in a limited-service hotel or lodging business can occur more rapidly. A career in a limited-service hotel or lodging establishment might commence at the assistant general manager level, with movement to general manager within three years and to district or regional manager within five to eight years. This accelerated pace is due in large part to the more restricted range of services the manager must master before advancing.

The four basic components of organizational structure include job specialization, departmentalization, patterns of authority, and span of control. Job specialization includes increased worker productivity and efficiency, but it increases the need for managerial control and coordination. Work teams can be used to alleviate the routine caused by job specialization. A similar concept, the quality circle, can also enhance employee productivity. The departments of a full-service hotel and lodging establishment include rooms, food and beverage, marketing and sales, human resources, and accounting. These departments report directly to the general manager or to a resident manager who is responsible to the general manager. In smaller hotel or lodging businesses, the audit, front desk, housekeeping, maintenance, and sales departments all might report directly to the general manager.

While patterns of authority remain centralized in many hotel or lodging businesses, increasingly employees have become empowered to make decisions that typically have been made by managers. Decentralization is the distribution of authority throughout an organization. Centralization is the retention of decision-making authority by a high-level manager. Span of control refers to the number of people who report to one manager or supervisor. In a narrow span of control, fewer subordinates report to each supervisor, resulting in a tall organization. In a wide span of control, a larger number of subordinates report to each supervisor, resulting in a flat organization.

The level of coordination and communication between departments can be increased by the activities of committees. The executive operating committee includes the general manager and designated department heads. Other committees include operations, staff, sales forecasting and marketing, departmental, subdepartmental, credit, safety, and energy conservation. Larger organizations conduct an annual meeting for all employees of the organization, to discuss company performance and to distribute awards. Staffing is an ongoing challenge in the hotel and lodging industry because of the high percentage of employee turnover. Successful staffing depends on providing adequate job descriptions, including job specifications, as well as realizing that job descriptions must be flexible. In some cases, it becomes necessary to redesign jobs; this can involve job rotation, job enlargement, job enrichment, and flextime.

Employees must be properly trained; effective training includes problem solving, problem analysis, quality measurement, feedback, and team building. Successful managers enjoy certain common characteristics including providing clear direction, feedback, and recognition; encouraging open communication and innovation; and establishing ongoing controls. The management of a hotel or a lodging business falls into one of three categories: first-line, middle, or top.

8

Tourism Marketing: As a Important Tool of Careers

A market is a social arrangement that allows buyers and sellers to discover information and carry out a voluntary exchange of goods or services. It is one of the two key institutions that organize trade, along with the right to own property. Allowing markets to arrive at a pareto efficient outcome is one of the key components of capitalism. In everyday usage, the word "market" may refer to the location where goods are traded, sometimes known as a marketplace, or to a street market.

The function of a market requires, at a minimum, that both parties expect to become better off as a result of the transaction. Markets generally rely on price adjustments to provide information to parties engaging in a transaction, so that each may accurately gauge the subsequent change of their welfare. In less sophisticated markets, such as those involving barter, individual buyers and sellers must engage in a more lengthy process of haggling in order to gain the same information. Markets are efficient when the price of a good or service attracts exactly as much demand as the market can currently supply.

The chief function of a market, then, is to adjust prices to accommodate fluctuations in supply and demand in order to achieve allocative efficiency. An economic system in which goods and services are exchanged by market functions is called a market economy. An alternative economic system in which non-market forces determine prices are called planned economies or command economies. The attempt to combine socialist ideals with the incentive system of a market is known as market socialism. Although many markets exist in the traditional sense—such as a flea market—there are various other types of them and various organizational structures to assist their functions. A market can be organized as an auction, as a shopping centre, as a complex institution such as a stock market, and as an informal discussion between two individuals.

In economics, a market that runs under laissez-faire policies is a free market. It is "free" in the sense that the government makes no attempt to intervene through taxes, subsidies, minimum wages, price ceilings, etc.

Markets may be distorted by a seller or sellers with monopoly power, or a buyer with monopsony power. Also, the level of organization or negotiation power of buyers, markedly affects the functioning of the market. Markets where price negotiations do not arrive at efficient outcomes for both sides are said to experience market failure.

Most markets are regulated by state wide laws and regulations. While barter markets exist, most markets use currency or some other form of money. Markets of varying types can spontaneously arise whenever a party has interest in a good or service that some other party can provide. Hence there can be a market for cigarettes in correctional facilities, another for chewing gum in a playground, and yet another for contracts for the future delivery of a commodity.

Market failure

If advertising is poor, definitely there will be market failure. Market failure is a term used to describe a situation in which markets do not efficiently allocate goods and services. To economists, the term would normally be applied to situations where the inefficiency is particularly dramatic, or when it is suggested that non-market institutions would be more efficient and wealth-producing than their private alternatives.

On the other hand, the term "market failure" is also often used to describe situations where market forces do not serve the perceived public interest. However, the focus is on market failure as defined by mainstream economics. Economists use model-like theorems to explain or understand such cases.

The two main reasons that markets fail are:

- The inadequate expression of costs or benefits in prices and thus into microeconomic decision-making in markets.
- Sub-optimal market structures.

The existence of a market failure in a certain economic activity is often used as an argument that the activity in question should not be directed by market forces. This generally leads to a debate on the question of what - if anything - should be used to replace markets. The most common response to a market failure in the present day is to use the government to produce certain goods and services. However, government intervention may cause nonmarket failure by the intevention itself causing externalitites.

Types of Market Failures

Imperfect Competition

In economic theory, imperfect competition, is the competitive situation in any market where the conditions necessary for perfect competition are not satisfied.

Forms of imperfect competition include:

- Monopoly, in which there is only one seller of a good.

- Oligopoly, in which there is a small number of sellers.
- Monopolistic competition, in which there are many sellers producing highly differentiated goods.
- Monopsony, in which there is only one buyer of a good.
- Oligopsony, in which there is a small number of buyers.

There may also be imperfect competition in markets due to buyers or sellers lacking information about prices and the goods being traded. There may also be imperfect competition due to a time lag in a market. For example, in the 1990s, there was a shortage of computer programmers, but becoming a skilled programmer requires several years of experience.

This drove up salaries. Another example is the "jobless recovery". There are many growth opportunities available after a recession, but it takes time for employers to react, leading to high unemployment. High unemployment decreases wages, which makes hiring more attractive, but it takes time for new jobs to be created.

Market Power

In economics, market power is the ability of a firm to alter the market price of a good or service. A firm with market power can raise price without losing all customers to competitors. When a firm has market power it faces a downward-sloping demand curve. In perfectly competitive markets, market participants have no market power. A firm with market power has the ability to individually affect either the total quantity or the prevailing price in the market.

If the demand curve is downward sloping then the decrease in supply as a result of the exercise of market power creates an economic deadweight loss in comparison with a situation of perfect competition. This is often viewed as socially undesirable, and as a result, many countries have anti-trust or other legislation with the aim of limiting the ability of firms to accrue market power. Such legislation often regulates mergers and sometimes introduces a judicial power to compel divestiture.

A firm usually has market power by virtue of it controlling a large portion of the market. In extreme cases - monopoly and monopsony - the firm controls the entire market. However, market size alone is not a good indicator of market power. Highly concentrated markets may be contestable if there are no barriers to entry or exit, limiting the incumbent firm's ability to raise its price above competitive levels.

Market power gives firms the ability to engage in unilateral anti-competitive behaviour. Some of the behaviours that firms with market power are accused of engaging in include predatory pricing, product tying, and creation of overcapacity or other barriers to entry. If no individual participant in the market has significant market power, then anti-competitive behaviour can take place only through collusion, or the exercise of a group of participants' collective market power. When several firms control a significant share of market sales, the resulting market structure is called an oligopoly or oligopsony. An oligopoly may engage in collusion, either tacit or overt, and thereby exercise market power. An explicit agreement in an oligopoly to affect market price or output is called a cartel.

The behaviour of firms in perfect competition or monopoly can be treated as a simple optimization, but an oligopoly requires game theoretic analysis. Monopoly power is an example of market failure which occurs when one or more of the participants has the ability to influence the price or other outcomes in some general or specialized market. The most commonly discussed form of market power is that of a monopoly, but other forms such as monopsony, and more moderate versions of these two extremes, exist. Market participants that have market power are sometimes referred to as "price makers", while those without are sometimes called "price takers".

A well known example of monopolistic market power is Microsoft's market share in PC operating systems. The United States v. Microsoft case concerned the allegation that Microsoft illegally exercised its market power by bundling its web browser with its operating system. Some have suggested that Wal Mart exercises monopsonistic market power; its size allows it to extract extremely low prices from its suppliers.

Monopoly

In economics, is defined as a persistent market situation where there is only one provider of a product or service. Monopolies are characterized by a lack of economic competition for the good or service that they provide and a lack of viable substitute goods. Monopoly should be distinguished from monopsony, in which there is only one buyer of the product or service; it should also, strictly, be distinguished from the phenomenon of a cartel. In a monopoly a single firm is the sole provider of a product or service; in a cartel a centralized institution is set up to partially coordinate the actions of several independent providers.

Strategies in Marketing

Marketing strategy is a powerful process that gives an organization a competitive advantage in the marketplace. While just defining a marketing strategy will not automatically create a competitive advantage, it will allow the organization to concentrate its resources on the greatest opportunities to increase sales and achieve a sustainable competitive advantage. The word strategy comes from the Greek word strategies meaning general. Strategy is what generals use to win battles.

Thus properly understood, marketing strategy is a high-level exercise involving the "generals" of the organization in determining how to build on the firm's strengths while taking advantage of competitors' weaknesses. Marketing strategy is most effective when it is a vital component of corporate strategy, defining how the organization will engage customers, prospects and the competition in the market arena for consistent success. A marketing strategy also serves as the foundation of a marketing plan. A marketing plan contains a set of specific actions required to successfully implement a specific marketing strategy. For example: "Use a low cost product to attract consumers. Once our organization, via our low cost product, has established a relationship with consumers, our organization will sell additional, higher-margin products and services that enhance the consumer's interaction with the low-cost product or service."

A strategy is different from a tactic. While it is possible to write a tactical marketing plan without a sound, well-considered strategy, it is not recommended. Without a sound marketing strategy, a marketing plan has no foundation. Marketing strategies serve as the fundamental underpinning of marketing plans designed to reach marketing objectives. It is important that these objectives have measurable results.

A good marketing strategy should integrate an organization's marketing goals, policies, and action sequences into a cohesive whole. The objective of a marketing strategy is to provide a foundation from which a tactical plan is developed. This allows the organization to carry out its mission effectively and efficiently. Marketing strategies are partially derived from broader corporate strategies, corporate missions, and corporate goals. They should flow from the firm's mission statement. They are also influenced by a range of microenvironmental factors. Marketing strategies are dynamic and interactive. They are partially planned and partially unplanned.

Commercial Planning

In the modern world of business, it is useless to be a creative original thinker unless you can also sell what you create. Management cannot be expected to recognize a good idea unless it is presented to them by a good salesman. The success of a new product depends not only on the idea behind the product, but also on the marketing of the new product before, during and after the product launch. Commercializing a product is commonly known as Commercial Planning. No concrete methods are currently available for New Product Launching. However, to launch a new product. This describes a set of activities and products, that are essential for launching a new product. New Product Launching is part of the New Product Development method.

Strategic Management

An organization's strategy must be appropriate for its resources, environmental circumstances, and core objectives. The process involves matching the company's internal resources and capabilities to the external business environment the organization faces.

Strategy formulation involves:

- Doing a situation analysis: Both internal and external; both micro-environmental and macro-environmental.

- Concurrent with this assessment, objectives are set. This involves crafting vision statements, mission statements, overall corporate objectives, strategic business unit objectives, and tactical objectives.
- These objectives should, in the light of the situation analysis, suggest a strategic plan. The plan provides the details of how to achieve these objectives.

This three-step strategy formulation process is sometimes referred to as determining where you are now, determining where you want to go, and then determining how to get there. These three questions are the essence of strategic planning. SWOT Analysis: I/O Economics for the external factors and RBV for the internal factors.

Strategy implementation involves:

- Allocation of sufficient resources
- Establishing a chain of command or some alternative structure
- Assigning responsibility of specific tasks or processes to specific individuals or groups
- It also involves managing the process. This includes monitoring results, comparing to benchmarks and best practices, evaluating the efficacy and efficiency of the process, controlling for variances, and making adjustments to the process as necessary.
- When implementing specific programmes, this involves acquiring the requisite resources, developing the process, training, process testing, documentation, and integration with legacy processes.

Strategy formulation and implementation is an on-going, never-ending, integrated process requiring continuous reassessment and reformation. Strategic management is dynamic. It involves a complex pattern of actions and reactions.

It is partially planned and partially unplanned. Strategy is both planned and emergent, dynamic, and interactive. Some people feel that there are critical points at which a strategy must take a new direction in order to be in step with a changing business environment. These critical points of change are called strategic inflection points.

Strategic management operates on several time scales. Short term strategies involve planning and managing for the present. Long term strategies involve preparing for and preempting the future. Marketing strategist Derek Abell has suggested that understanding this dual nature of strategic management is the least understood part of the process. He claims that balancing the temporal aspects of strategic planning requires the use of dual strategies simultaneously. Strategic Management is actually a solid foundation or a framework within which all the functioning managerial operations are bundled together. This is the highest level corporate activity that sets the terms and goals for a company that it should follow for prosperity.

Strategic management techniques can be viewed as bottom-up, top-down, or collaborative processes. In the bottom-up approach, employees submit proposals to their managers who, in turn, funnel the best ideas further up the organization. This is often accomplished by a capital budgeting process. Proposals are assessed using financial criteria such as return on investment or cost-benefit analysis.

The proposals that are approved form the substance of a new strategy, all of which is done without a grand strategic design or a strategic architect. The top-down approach is the most common by far. In it, the CEO, possibly with the assistance of a strategic planning team, decides on the overall direction the company should take. Some organizations are starting to experiment with collaborative strategic planning techniques that recognize the emergent nature of strategic decisions.

In most corporations there are several levels of strategy. Strategic management is the highest in the sense that it is the broadest, applying to all parts of the firm. It gives direction to corporate values, corporate culture, corporate goals, and corporate missions. Under this broad corporate strategy there are often functional or business unit strategies. Functional strategies include marketing strategies, new product development strategies, human resource strategies, financial strategies, legal strategies, and information technology management strategies.

The emphasis is on short and medium term plans and is limited to the domain of each department's functional responsibility. Each functional department attempts to do its part in meeting overall corporate objectives, and hence to some extent their strategies are derived from broader corporate strategies. Many companies feel that a functional organizational structure is not an efficient way to organize activities so they have re-engineered according to processes or strategic business units . A strategic business unit is a semi-autonomous unit within an organization. It is usually responsible for its own budgeting, new product decisions, hiring decisions, and price setting. An SBU is treated as an internal profit centre by corporate headquarters. Each SBU is responsible for developing its business strategies, strategies that must be in tune with broader corporate strategies.

The "lowest" level of strategy is operational strategy. It is very narrow in focus and deals with day-to-day operational activities such as scheduling criteria. It must operate within a budget but is not at liberty to adjust or create that budget. Operational level strategy was encouraged by Peter Drucker in his theory of management by objectives . Operational level strategies are informed by business level strategies which, in turn, are informed by corporate level strategies. Business strategy, which refers to the aggregated operational strategies of single business firm or that of an SBU in a diversified corporation refers to the way in which a firm competes in its chosen arenas.

Corporate strategy, then, refers to the overarching strategy of the diversified firm. Such corporate strategy answers the questions of "in which businesses should we compete?" and "how does being in one business add to the competitive advantage of another portfolio firm, as well as the competitive advantage of the corporation as a whole?" Since the turn of the millennium, there has been a tendency in some firms to revert to a simpler strategic structure. This is being driven by information technology.

It is felt that knowledge management systems should be used to share information and create common goals. Strategic divisions are thought to hamper this process. Most recently, this notion of strategy has been captured under the rubric of dynamic strategy, popularized by the strategic management textbook authored by Carpenter and Sanders. This work builds on that of Brown and Eisenhart as well as Christensen and portrays firm strategy, both business and corporate, as necessarily embracing ongoing strategic change, and the seamless integration of strategy formulation and implementation.

Such change and implementation are usually built into the strategy through the staging and pacing facets. Management by Objectives is a process of agreeing upon objectives within an organization so that management and employees buy in to the objectives and understand what they are. Management By Objectives term was first popularized by Peter Drucker in 1954 in his book 'The Practice of Management'.

It is all too easy for managers to fail to outline, and agree with their employees, what it is that everyone is trying to achieve. MBO substitutes for good intentions a process that requires rather precise written description of objectives and timelines for their monitoring and achievement. The process requires that the manager and the employee agree to what the employee will attempt to achieve in the period ahead, and that the employee accept and buy into the objectives .

For example, whatever else a manager and employee may discuss and agree in their regular discussions, let us suppose that they feel that it will be sensible to introduce a key performance indicator to show the development of sales revenue in a part of the firm. Then the manager and the employee need to discuss what is being planned, what the time-schedule is and what the indicator might or might not be. Thereafter the two of them should liaise to ensure that the objective is being attended to and will be delivered on time.

Organizations have scarce resources and so it is incumbent on the managers to consider the level of resourcing but also to consider whether the objectives that are jointly agreed within the firm are the right ones and represent the best allocation of effort. Also, reliable Management information systems are needed to establish relevant objectives and monitor their "reach ratio" in an objective way.

MBO is often achieved using set targets. MBO introduced the SMART criteria: Objectives for MBO must be SMART . However, it has been reported in recent years that this style of management receives criticism in that it triggers employees' unethical behaviour of distorting the system or financial figures to achieve the targets set by their short-term, narrow bottom-line, and completely self-centered thinking.

Marketing Strategy Tools and Models

Ansoffs Matrix

A common tool used within marketing was developed by Igor Ansoff in 1957.

His model gives organisation five strategic business options:

1. *Market Penetration:* This involves increasing sales of an existing product and penetrating the market further by either promoting the product heavily or reducing prices to increase sales.
2. *Product Development:* The organisation develops new products to aim within their existing market, in the hope that they will gain more custom and market share. For Example Sony launching the Playstation 2 to replace their existing model.
3. *Market Development:* The organisation here adopts a strategy of selling existing products to new markets. This can be done either by a better understanding of segmentation, *i.e* who else can possibly purchase the product or selling the product to new markets overseas.
4. *Diversification:* Moving away from what you are selling to providing something new *e.g*. Moving over from selling foods to selling cars.
5. *Consolidation:* Where the organisation adopts a strategy of withdrawing from particular markets, scaling back on operations and concentrating on its existing products in existing markets.

Product Life Cycle

The product life cycle concept suggests that a product passes through four stages of evolution. Introduction, growth, maturity and decline. As a product evolves and passes through theses four stages profit is affected, and different strategies have to be employed to ensure that the product is a success within its market. As a new product much time will be spent by the organisation to create awareness of it presence amongst its target market. Profits are negative or low because of this reason. Growth: If consumer clearly feels that this product will benefit them in some ways and they accept it, the organisation will see a period of rapid sales growth. Maturity: Rapid sales growth cannot last forever. Sales slow down as the product sales reach peak as it has been accepted by most buyers. Decline: Sales and profits start to decline, the organisation may try to change their pricing strategy to stimulate growth, however the product will either have to be re-modified, or replaced within the market.

Value Chain Analysis

Michael Porter in 1985 introduced in his book ' The competitive advantage' the concept of the Value Chain. He suggested that activities within the organisation add value to the service and products that the organisation produces, and all these activities should be run at optimum level if the organisation is to gain any real competitive advantage. If they are run efficiently the value obtained should exceed the costs of running them *i.e.* customers should return to the organisation and transact freely and willingly. Michael Porter suggested that the organisation is split into 'primary activities' and 'support activities'.

Primary Activities

- *Inbound logistics*: Refers to goods being obtained from the organisations suppliers ready to be used for producing the end product.
- *Operations*: The raw materials and goods obtained are manufactured into the final product. Value is added to the product at this stage as it moves through the production line.
- *Outbound logistics*: Once the products have been manufactured they are ready to be distributed to distribution centres, wholesalers, retailers or customers.
- *Marketing and Sales*: Marketing must make sure that the product is targeted towards the correct customer group. The marketing mix is used to establish an effective strategy, any competitive advantage is clearly communicated to the target group by the use of the promotional mix.
- *Services:* After the product/service has been sold what support services does the organisation have to offer. This may come in the form of after sales training, guarantees and warranties.

With the above activities, any or a combination of them, maybe essential for the firm to develop the competitive advantage which Porter talks about in his book.

Support Activities

The support activities assist the primary activities in helping the organisation achieve its competitive advantage.

They include:

- *Procurement:* This department must source raw materials for the organisation and obtain the best price for doing so. For the price they must obtain the best possible quality
- *Technology development:* The use of technology to obtain a competitive advantage within the organisation. This is very important in today's technological driven environment. Technology can be used in production to reduce cost thus add value, or in research and development to develop new products, or via the use of the internet so customers have access to online facilities.
- *Human resource management*: The organisation will have to recruit, train and develop the correct people for the organisation if they are to succeed in their objectives. Staff will have to be motivated and

paid the 'market rate' if they are to stay with the organisation and add value to it over their duration of employment. Within the service sector *e.g.* airlines it is the 'staff' who may offer the competitive advantage that is needed within the field.

- *Firm infrastructure:* Every organisations needs to ensure that their finances, legal structure and management structure works efficiently and helps drive the organisation forward.

As you can see the value chain encompasses the whole organisation and looks at how primary and support activities can work together effectively and efficiently to help gain the organisation a superior competitive advantage.

SWOT Analysis

A tool used by organisations to help the firm establish its Strengths, Weaknesses, Opportunities and Threats . A SWOT analysis is used as a framework to help the firm develop its overall corporate, marketing, or product strategies.

Note: Strengths and Weaknesses are internal factors which are controllable by the organisation. Opportunities and threats are external factors which are uncontrollable by the organisation.

Strength examples could include:

- A strong brand name.
- Market share.
- Good reputation.
- Expertise and skill.
- Weaknesses could include:
- Low or no market share.
- No brand loyalty.
- Lack of experience.
- Opportunities could include:
- A growing market.
- Increased consumer spending.
- Selling internationally.
- Changes in society beneficial to your company.

Threats could include:

- Competitors
- Government policy *e.g.* taxation, laws
- Changes in society not beneficial to your company

A SWOT analysis is an excellent tool to use if the organisation wants to take a step back and assess the situation they are in. Issues raised from the analysis are then used to assist the organisation in developing their marketing mix strategy. A SWOT analysis must form the part of any prudent marketing strategy.

Generic Strategies

For an organisation to obtain a sustainable competitive advantage Michael Porter suggested that they should follow either one of three generic strategies.

Strategy 1: Cost Leadership

This strategy involves the organisation aiming to be the lowest cost producer within their industry. The orgainisation aims to drive cost down through all the elements of the production of the product from sourcing, to labour costs. The cost leader usually aims at a broad market, so sufficient sales can cover costs. Low cost producers include Easyjet airline, Ryan air, Asda and Walmart. Some organisation may aim to drive costs down but will not pass on these cost savings to their customers aiming for increased profits clearly because their brand can command a premium rate.

Strategy 2: Differentiation

To be different, is what organisations strive for. Having a competitive advantage which allows the company and its products ranges to stand out is crucial for their success. With a differentiation strategy the organisation aims to focus its effort on particular segments and charge for the added differentiated value. If we look at Brompton folding cycles their compact design differentiates them from other folding bike companies. New concepts which allow for differentiation can be patented, however patents have a certain life span and organisation always face the danger that their idea that gives the competitive advantage will be copied in one form or another.

Strategy 3: Niche Strategies

Here the organisation focuses its effort on one particular segment and becomes well known for providing products/services within the segment. They form a competitive advantage for this niche market and either succeed by being a low cost producer or different within that particular segment. Examples include Roll Royce and Bentley.

Are you 'Stuck in the Middle'

The danger some organisation face is that they try to do all three and become what is known as stuck in the middle. The have no clear business strategy, be all to all consumers, which adds to their running costs causing a fall in sales and market share. 'Stuck in the middle' companies are usually subject to a takeover or merger.

Industry Analysis Model

Porters fives forces model is an excellent model to use to analyse a particular environment of an industry. So for example, if we were entering the PC industry, we would use porters model to help us find out about:

- Competitive Rivalry
- Power of suppliers
- Power of buyers
- Threats of substitutes
- Threat of new entrants.

The five main factors are key factors that influence industry performance, hence it is common sense and practical to find out about these factors before you enter the industry.

Competitive Rivalry

A starting point to analysing the industry is to look at competitive rivalry. If entry to an industry is easy then competitive rivalry will likely to be high. If it is easy for customers to move to substitute products for example from coke to water then again rivalry will be high.

Generally competitive rivalry will be high if:

- There is little differentiation between the products sold between customers.
- Competitors are approximately the same size of each other.
- If the competitors all have similar strategies.
- It is costly to leave the industry hence they fight to just stay in

Power of Suppliers

Suppliers are also essential for the success of an organisation. Raw materials are needed to complete the finish product of the organisation. Suppliers do have power.

This power comes from:

- If they are the only supplier or one of few suppliers who supply that particular raw material.
- If it costly for the organisation to move from one supplier to another
- If there is no other substitute for their product.

Power of Buyers

Buyers or customers can exert influence and control over an industry in certain circumstances.

This happens when:

- There is little differentiation over the product and substitutes can be found easily.
- Customers are sensitive to price.
- Switching to another product is not costly.

Threat of Substitutes

Are there alternative products that customers can purchase over your product that offer the same benefit for the same or less price?

The threat of substitute is high when:

- Price of that substitute product falls.
- It is easy for consumers to switch from one substitute product to another.
- Buyers are willing to substitute.

Threat of New Entrant

The threat of a new organisation entering the industry is high when it is easy for an organisation to enter the industry *i.e.* entry barriers are low. An organisation will look at how loyal customers are to existing products, how quickly they can achieve economy of scales, would they have access to suppliers, would government legislation prevent them or encourage them to enter the industry.

So to summaries porters five forces model is essential to carry to help you understand your industry in depth before you enter it.

Diffusion of Innovation

This extension of the product life cycle was developed by Everett M. Rogers in 1962 and simply looks who adopts products at the different stages of the life cycle. Rogers identified five types of purchasers as the product moves through its life cycle stage.

He suggested:

1. Innovator who make up 2.5% of all purchases of the product, purchase the product at the beginning of the life cycle. They are not afraid of trying new products that suit their lifestyle and will also pay a premium for that benefit.
2. Early Adopters make up 13.5% of purchases, they are usually opinion leaders and naturally adopt products after the innovators. This group of purchasers are crucial because adoption by them means the product becomes acceptable, spurring on later purchasers.
3. Early Majority make up 34% of purchases and have been spurred on by the early adopters. They wait to see if the product will be adopted by society and will purchase only when this has happened. They early majority usually have some status in society.
4. Late Majority make up another 34% of sales and usually purchase the product at the late stages of majority within the life cycle.
5. Laggards make up 16% of total sales and usually purchase the product near the end of its life. They are the 'wait and see' group. They wait to see if the product will get cheaper. Usually when they purchase the product a new version is already on the market. Some may call Laggards, bargain hunters!

Boston Consultancy Group

This product portfolio matrix classifies product lines into four categories.

The BCG models suggests that organisations should have a healthy balance of products within their range. The Boston Consultancy Group classified these products as following:

Question Mark/Problem Child

These are products with low market share but operate in high market growth rates. The company puts a lot of resources in this product in the hope that it will eventually increase market share and generate cash returns in the future.

Star

Stars have high market shares that operate in growing markets. The product at this stage should be generating positive returns for the company.

Cash Cow

Cash Cow are products at the mature stage of the lifecycle, they generate high amounts of cash for the company, but growth rate is slowing. There are chances that the product may slip into decline, appropriate marketing mix strategies should be employed to try to prevent this from happening.

Managing income

Accounting is the measurement, disclosure or provision of assurance about financial information that helps managers, investors, tax authorities and other decision makers make resource allocation decisions. The names come from the use of financial accounts. Financial accounting is one branch of accounting and historically has involved processes by which financial information about a business is recorded, classified, summarized, interpreted, and communicated. Accounting is also widely referred to as the "language of business".

Auditing, a related but separate discipline, has two sub-disciplines: Internal and External auditing. External auditing is the process whereby an independent auditor examines an organization's financial statements and accounting records in order to express an opinion — that conveys reasonable but not absolute assurance — as to the truth and fairness of the statements and the accountant's adherence to Generally Accepted Accounting Principles in all material respects.

Internal auditing is an examination in which management, and not the external public, is the main beneficiary. It is carried out usually by auditors employed by the company, but sometimes by external service providers. The internal auditor's role is broader, and basically depends on what kind of assurance management wants.

It usually certifies the efficiency and effectiveness of processes, departments, projects or internal controls. The Institute of Internal Auditors is generally accepted as the custodian of Internal Auditing best practice. At the heart of accounting is the measurement of financial transactions which are transfers of legal property rights made under contractual relationships. Non-financial transactions are specifically excluded due to conservatism and materiality principles. Practitioners of accountancy are known as accountants.

There are many professional bodies for accountants throughout the world. Many allow their members to use titles indicating their membership. Examples are Chartered Certified Accountant, Chartered Accountant and Certified Public Accountant. Accountancy attempts to create accurate financial reports that are useful to managers, regulators, and other stakeholders such as shareholders, creditors, or owners. The day-to-day record-keeping involved in this process is known as bookkeeping.

At the heart of modern financial accounting is the double-entry bookkeeping system. This system involves making at least two entries for every transaction: a debit in one account, and a corresponding credit in another account. The sum of all debits should always equal the sum of all credits. This provides an easy way to check for errors. This system was first used in medieval Europe, although claims have been made that the system dates back to Ancient Greece. According to critics of standard accounting practices, it has changed little since. Accounting reform measures of some kind have been taken in each generation to attempt to keep bookkeeping relevant to capital assets or production capacity. However, these have not changed the basic principles, which are supposed to be independent of economics as such. In recent times, the divergence of accounting from economic principles has resulted in controversial reforms to make financial reports more indicative of economic reality.

Accountancy's infancy dates back to the earliest days of human agriculture and civilization, when the need to maintain accurate records of the quantities and relative values of agricultural products first arose. Simple accounting is mentioned in the Christian Bible in the book of Matthew, in the Parable of the Talents. Twelfth century writer Ibn Taymiyyah mentioned in his book Hisba, detailed accounting systems used by the Muslims as early as in the mid-seventh century.

The accounting practices were influenced by the Roman and the Persian civilizations that Muslims interacted with. The most detailed example of a complex governmental accounting system is the Divan of Umar, the second Caliph of Islam in which all revenues and disbursements were recorded. The Divan of Umar has been described in detail by various Islamic historians and was used by Muslim rulers with mofidications and enhancements until the fall of the Ottoman Empire.

Applied Modern Accountancy in Hotel

The first book on accounting was written by a Croatian merchant Benedetto Cotrugli, who is also known as Benedikt Kotruljeviæ, from the city of Dubrovnik. During his life in Italy he met many merchants and decided to write, Della Mercatvra et del Mercante Perfetto in which he elaborated on the principles of modern, double-entry book-keeping. He finished his lifework in 1458. However, his work was not published until 1573, as a result of which his contributions to the field have been overlooked by the general public.

For this reason, Luca Pacioli, also known as Friar Luca dal Borgo, is credited for the "birth" of accounting. His Summa de arithmetica, geometrica, proportioni et proportionalita, a synthesis of the mathematical knowledge of his time, includes the first published description of the method of keeping accounts that Venetian merchants used at that time, known as the double-entry accounting system. Although Pacioli codified rather than invented this system, he is widely regarded as the "Father of Accounting".

The system he published included most of the accounting cycle as we know it today. He described the use of journals and ledgers, and warned that a person should not go to sleep at night until the debits equalled the credits! His ledger had accounts for assets, liabilities, capital, income, and expenses — the account categories that are reported on an organization's balance sheet and income statement, respectively. He demonstrated year-end closing entries and proposed that a trial balance be used to prove a balanced ledger. His treatise also touches on a wide range of related topics from accounting ethics to cost accounting.

The first known book in the English language on accounting was published in London by John Gouge in 1543. It is described as A Profitable Treatyce called the Instrument or Boke to learn to know the good order of the keeping of the famous reconynge, called in Latin, Dare and Habere, and, in English, Debitor and Creditor.

A short book of instructions was also published in 1588 by John Mellis of Southwark, in which he says, "I am but the renuer and reviver of an ancient old copy printed here in London the 14 of August 1543: collected, published, made, and set forth by one Hugh Oldcastle, Scholemaster, who, as appeareth by his treatise, then taught Arithmetics, and this booke in Saint Ollaves parish in Marko Lane." John Mellis refers to the fact that the principle of accounts he explains is "after the forme of Venice".

A book described as The Merchants Mirrour, or directions for the perfect ordering and keeping of his accounts formed by way of Debitor and Creditor, after the Italian manner, by Richard Dafforne, accountant, published in 1635, contains many references to early books on the science of accountancy. In this book, headed "Opinion of Book-keeping's Antiquity," the author states, on the authority of another writer, that the form of book-keeping referred to had then been in use in Italy about two hundred years, "but that the same, or one in many parts very like this, was used in the time of Julius Caesar, and in Rome long before."

An early Dutch writer appears to have suggested that double-entry book-keeping was even in existence among the Greeks, pointing to scientific accountancy having been invented in remote times. There were several editions of Richard Dafforne's book - the second edition in 1636, the third in 1656, and another in 1684. The book is a very complete treatise on scientific accountancy, beautifully prepared and containing elaborate explanations.

The numerous editions tend to prove that the science was highly appreciated in the 17th century. From this time on, there has been a continuous supply of literature on the subject, many of the authors styling themselves accountants and teachers of the art, and thus proving that the professional accountant was then known and employed.

The requirements for entry in the profession of accounting vary from country to country. Accountants may be licensed by a variety of organisations, such as the British qualified accountancy bodies including Association of Chartered Certified Accountants and Institute of Chartered Accountants, and are recognized by titles such as Chartered Certified Accountant and Chartered Accountant, Certified Public Accountant, Certified Management Accountant, Certified General Accountant, or Certified Practising Accountant .

Some Commonwealth countries often recognise both the certified and chartered accounting bodies. The majority of "public" accountants in New Zealand and Canada are Chartered Accountants; however, Certified General Accountants are also authorized by legislation to practise public accounting and auditing in all Canadian provinces, except Ontario and Quebec, as of 2005. There is, however, no legal requirement for an accountant to be a paid-up member of one of the many Institutes and other bodies which are effectively a form of professional trade union. Unlike the Law Society, which can legally stop a solicitor from practising, accountancy institutes do not have such authority. However, auditors are regulated.

Before the Enron and other accounting scandals, there were five large firms and were called the Big Five. Since Arthur Andersen's assurance practice split with a plurality joining KPMG in the US and Deloitte and Touche outside of the US, Arthur Andersen left from the group. Previous to this there were also groupings referred to as the "Big Six" and the "Big Eight". Enron turned out to be only the first of a series of accounting scandals that enveloped the accounting industry in 2002.

This is likely to have far-reaching consequences for the U.S. accounting industry. Application of International Accounting Standards originating in International Accounting Standards Board headquartered in London and bearing more resemblance to UK than current US practices is often advocated by those who note the relative stability of the UK accounting system. Accounting reform of a far more comprehensive sort is advocated by those who see issues with capitalism or economics, and seek ecological or social accountability.

According to Accountancy Age's 2005 league table, fee income amongst the Top 50 accounting firms in the UK rose from £6.3bn to £7.0bn. This followed two successive years in which fee income had declined, largely a result of the sale by some of the larger firms of their consultancy arms. Fee income in most business areas - audit, tax, corporate finance and consultancy - rose in the 2005 survey, with insolvency and wealth management being the only segments where revenue fell. Price water house Coopers remains the largest firm with fee income totalling £1,780m followed by Deloitte, KPMG and Ernst and Young .

The combined revenue of the Big Four accounted for £5.0bn, 72% of the fee income of the Top 50, down from 78-79% in the years up to the 2002 survey and the third year in succession a decline in their share has occurred . Ernst and Young's fee income is the smallest of the largest four firms, but still over three times that of the next largest firm, Grant Thornton. The amount of fee income tapers off amongst the mid-tier firms so that in total there were only 25 firms that each generated more than £15m of revenue in the 2005 survey. For more details regarding British qualified accountancy professionals, please refer to the page of British qualified accountants.

Management Accounting

Management accounting is concerned with the provisions and use of accounting information to managers within organizations, to provide them with the basis in making informed business decisions that would allow them to be better equipped in their management and control functions.

Unlike financial accountancy information, management accounting information is used within an organization and is usually confidential and access to which is only available to a select few.

According to CIMA, The Chartered Institute of Management Accountants, Management Accounting is "the process of identification, measurement, accumulation, analysis, preparation, interpretation and communication of information used by management to plan, evaluate and control within an entity and to assure appropriate use of and accountability for its resources. Management accounting also comprises the preparation of financial reports for non management groups such as shareholders, creditors, regulatory agencies and tax authorities".

Aims:

- Formulating strategies;
- Planning and constructing business activities;
- Making decisions;
- Well use of resources;
- Supporting financial reports preparation; and
- Safeguarding assets.

In the late 1980s, accounting practitioners and educators were heavily criticized on the grounds that management accounting practices had changed little over the preceding 60 years, despite radical changes in the business environment. Professional accounting institutes, perhaps fearing that management accountants would increasingly be seen as superfluous in business organizations, subsequently devoted considerable resources to the development of a more innovative skills set for management accountants. The distinction between 'traditional' and 'innovative' management accounting practices can be illustrated by reference to cost control techniques. Traditionally, management accountants' principal technique was variance analysis, which is a systematic approach to the comparison of the actual and budgeted costs of the raw materials and labour used during a production period.

While some form of variance analysis is still used by most manufacturing firms, it nowadays tends to be used in conjunction with innovative techniques such as life cycle cost analysis and activity-based costing, which are designed with specific aspects of the modern business environment in mind. Lifecycle costing recognizes that managers' ability to influence the cost of manufacturing a product is at its greatest when the product is still at the design stage of its product lifecycle, since small changes to the product design may lead to significant savings in the cost of manufacturing the product. Activity-based costing recognizes that, in modern factories, most manufacturing costs are determined by the amount of 'activities' and that the key to effective cost control is therefore optimizing the efficiency of these activities. Activity-based accounting is also known as Cause and Effect accounting.

Both lifecycle costing and activity-based costing recognize that, in the typical modern factory, the avoidance of disruptive events is of far greater importance than reducing the costs of raw materials. Activity-based costing also de-emphasizes direct labour as a cost driver and concentrates instead on activities that drive costs, such as the provision of a service or the production of a product component.

The most significant recent direction in managerial accounting is throughput accounting, which recognizes the interdependencies of modern production processes and provide managers with a tool that will allow them to measure the contribution per unit of constrained resource for any given product, customer or supplier. A seldom expressed alternative view of management accounting is that it is neither a neutral or benign influence in organizations, rather a mechanism for management control through surveillance. This view locates management accounting specifically in the context of management control theory.

There are several related professional qualifications in the field of accountancy including:

- Management Accountancy Qualifications
  - CIMA
  - MA
  - Institute of Cost and Works Accountants of India
  - AAFM
- Other Professional Accountancy Qualifications
  - Chartered Certified Accountant,
  - Chartered Accountant,
  - Certified Public Accountant,

Accounting Management is the practical application of management techniques to control and report on the financial health of the organization. It involves the analysis, planning, implementation, and control of programmes designed to provide financial data reporting for managerial decision making.

This includes the maintenance of bank accounts, developing financial statements, cash flow and financial performance analysis. Accounting management is a mandatory knowledge module of any MBA programme. Accounting is often referred to as billing management. The goal is to gather usage statistics for users. Using the statistics the users can be billed and usage quota can be enforced.

Examples:

- Disk usage
- Link utilisation
- CPU time

For non-billed networks, 'Administration' replaces 'Accounting'. The goals of Administration is to administer the set of authorized users, by establishing users, passwords and permissions; and to administer the operations of the equipment such as by performing software backup and synchronization.

Activity-based Costing

Activity-based costing is a method of allocating costs to products and services. It is generally used as a tool for planning and control. This is a necessary tool for doing value chain analysis. The concepts of ABC were developed in the manufacturing sector of the U.S. during the 1970s and 80s.

During this time, the Consortium for Advanced Manufacturing-International, now known simply as CAM-I, provided a formative role for studying and formalizing the principles that have become more formally known as Activity-Based Costing. Robin Cooper and Robert Kaplan, proponent of the Balanced Scorecard, brought notice to these concepts in a number of articles published in Harvard Business Review beginning in 1988.

Cooper and Kaplan described ABC as an approach to solve the problems of traditional cost management systems. These traditional costing systems are often unable to determine accurately the actual costs of production and of the costs of related services. Consequently managers were making decisions based on inaccurate data especially where there are multiple products.

Instead of using broad arbitrary percentages to allocate costs, ABC seeks to identify cause and effect relationships to objectively assign costs. Once costs of the activities have been identified, the cost of each activity is attributed to each product to the extent that the product uses the activity. In this way ABC often identifies areas of high overhead costs per unit and so directs attention to finding ways to reduce the costs or to charge more for costly products. Activity-based costing was first clearly defined in 1987 by Robert S. Kaplan and W. Bruns as a stage in their book Accounting and Management. They initially focused on manufacturing industry where increasing technology and productivity improvements have reduced the relative proportion of the direct costs of labour and materials, but have increased relative proportion of indirect costs. For example increased automation has reduced labour, which is a direct cost, but has increased depreciation, which is an indirect cost.

Traditionally cost accountants had arbitrarily added a broad percentage onto the direct costs to allow for the indirect costs. However as the percentages of overhead costs had risen, this technique became increasingly inaccurate because the indirect costs were not caused equally by all the products. For example one product might take more time in one expensive machine than another product, but since the amount of direct labour and materials might be the same, the additional cost for the use of the machine would not be recognised when the same broad 'on-cost' percentage is added to all products. Consequently, when multiple products share common costs, there is a danger of one product subsidising another.

Like manufacturing industries, financial institutions also have diverse products which can cause cross-product subsidies. Since personnel expenses represent the largest single component of non-interest expense in financial institutions, these costs must also be attributed more accurately to products and customers. Activity based costing, even though developed for manufacturing, can therefore be a useful tool for doing this. This extended use of ABC to financial institutions was presented in 1990 in an article appearing in the Journal of Bank Cost and Management Accounting by Richard Sapp, David Crawford and Steven Rebishcke.

Direct labour and materials are relatively easy to trace directly to products, but it is more difficult to directly allocate indirect costs to products. Where products use common resources differently, some sort of weighting is needed in the cost allocation process. The measure of the use of a shared activity by each of the products is known as the cost driver. For example, the cost of the activity of bank tellers can be ascribed to each product by measuring how long each product's transactions takes at the counter and then by measuring the number of each type of transaction.

Even in activity-based costing, some overhead costs are difficult to assign to products and customers, for example the chief executive's salary. These costs are termed 'business sustaining' and are not assigned to products and customers because there is no meaningful method. This lump of unallocated overhead costs must nevertheless be met by contributions from each of the products, but it is not as large as the overhead costs before ABC is employed.

Although some may argue that costs untraceable to activities should be "arbitrarily allocated" to products, it is important to realise that the only purpose of ABC is to provide information to management. Therefore, there is no reason to assign any cost in an arbitrary manner. Management accountants can be creative in finding other ways to represent these costs on internal reporting statements.

managing budget

Budget generally refers to a list of all planned expenses and revenues. A budget is an important concept in microeconomics, which uses a budget line to illustrate the trade-offs between two or more goods. A personal budget is among the most important concepts of personal finance. In a personal or family budget all sources of income are identified and expenses are planned with the intent of matching outflows to inflows .

There are a wide variety of personal budgeting methods and tools that can be employed to help individuals and families with the budgeting process. Also the level of planned finance available to a person, corporation or government, as set by a certain person.

The budget of a government is a summary or plan of the intended revenues and expenditures of that government. In the United States, the federal budget is prepared by the Office of Management and Budget, and submitted to Congress for consideration. Invariably, Congress makes many and substantial changes.

Nearly all American states are required to have balanced budgets, but the federal government is allowed to run deficits. In the UK the budget is prepared by the Chancellor of the Exchequer, the second most important member of the government, and must be passed by Parliament. The Parliament seldom makes changes to the budget. The budget of a company is compiled annually. A finished budget usually requires considerable effort and can be seen as a financial plan for the new financial year.

While traditionally the Finance department compiles the company's budget, modern software allows hundreds or even thousands of people in the various departments to contribute their expected revenues and expenses to the final budget. If the actual numbers delivered through the financial year turn out to be close to the budget, this will demonstrate that the company understands their business and has been successfully driving it in the direction they had planned.

On the other hand, if the actuals diverge wildly from the budget, this sends out an 'out of control' signal and the share Cost-plus pricing is a pricing method commonly used by firms. It is used primarily because it is easy to calculate and requires little information. There are several varieties, but the common thread in all of them is that you first calculate the cost of the product, then include an additional amount to represent profit. Cost-plus pricing is often used on government contracts, and has been criticized as promoting wasteful expenditures.

Calculating Price Using the Cost-plus Method

There are several ways of determining cost, and the profit can be added as either a percentage markup or an absolute amount. One example is:

$$P = (AVC + FC\%) \times (1 + MK\%)$$

where:

- P = price
- AVC = average variable cost
- FC% = percentage allocation of fixed costs
- MK% = percentage markup

For example: If variable costs are 30 yen, the allocation to cover fixed costs is 10 yen, and you feel you need a 50% markup then you would charge a price of 60 yen:

P = (30 + 10) × (1 + 0.50)

P = 40 × 1.5

P = 60

An alternative way of doing a similar calculation is:

$$P = (AVC + FC\%)/(1 \text{ “ } MK\%)$$

To make things simpler, some firms, particularly retailers, ignore fixed costs and just use the purchase price paid to their suppliers as the cost term. They indirectly incorporate the fixed cost allocation into the markup percentage. To simplify things even further, sometimes a fixed amount is applied rather than a percentage. This fixed amount is usually determined by head-office to make it easy for franchisees and store managers. This is sometimes referred to as turnkey pricing. Another variant of cost plus pricing is activity based pricing.

This involves being more careful in determining costs. Instead of using arbitrary expense categories when allocating overhead, every activity is linked to the resources it uses. Cost will need to be recalculated and the percentage markup will likely need to be adjusted as the product goes through its life cycle. This is sometimes referred to as product life cycle pricing, although it is seldom done deliberately or in a planned and organized manner. Price skimming and penetration pricing are also types of product life cycle pricing but they are demand based pricing methods rather cost based.

Advantages of Cost-plus Pricing:

- Easy to calculate
- Minimal information requirements
- Easy to administer
- Tends to stabilize markets - insulated from demand variations and competitive factors
- Insures seller against unpredictable, or unexpected later costs
- Ethical advantages

Disadvantages:

- Tends to ignore the role of consumers
- Tends to ignore the role of competitors
- Use of historical accounting costs rather than replacement value
- Use of "normal" or "standard" output level to allocate fixed costs
- Inclusion of sunk costs rather than just using incremental costs

- Ignores opportunity costs
- Contractors may not focus on performance because the cost is always covered by the client

In microeconomics, Production is simply the conversion of inputs into outputs. It is an economic process that uses resources to create a commodity that is suitable for exchange. This can include manufacturing, storing, shipping, and packaging. Some economists define production broadly as all economic activity other than consumption.

They see every commercial activity other than the final purchase as some form of production. Production is a process, and as such it occurs through time and space. Because it is a flow concept, production is measured as a "rate of output per period of time".

There are three aspects to production processes:

1. The quantity of the commodity produced,
2. The form of the good produced,
3. The temporal and spatial distribution of the commodity produced.

A production process can be defined as any activity that increases the similarity between the pattern of demand for goods, and the quantity, form, and distribution of these goods available to the market place. A production process is efficient if a given quantity of outputs cannot be produced with any less inputs. It is said to be inefficient when there exists another feasible process that, for any given output, uses less inputs. Some economists use the term X-efficiency to indicate that production processes tend to be inherently inefficient due to satisfying behaviour.

The "rate of efficiency" is simply the amount of outputs divided by the amount of inputs. If a production process uses 50 units of input to produce one unit of output it is more efficient than a process that uses 55 units of input to produce the same level of output. It is said to be 10% more efficient .

The inputs or resources used in the production process are called factors by economists. The myriad of possible inputs are usually grouped into four or five categories.

These factors are:

- Raw materials
- Labour services
- Capital goods
- Land

Sometimes a fifth category is added, entrepreneurial and management skills, a subcategory of labour services. Capital goods are those goods that have previously undergone a production process. They are previously produced means of production. Some textbooks use "technology" as a factor of production.

In the "long run" all of these factors of production can be adjusted by management. The "short run" however, is defined as a period in which at least one of the factors of production is fixed. A fixed factor of production is one whose quantity cannot readily be changed. Examples include major pieces of equipment, suitable factory space, and key managerial personnel. A variable factor of production is one whose usage rate can be changed easily. Examples include electrical power consumption, transportation services, and most raw material inputs. In the short run, a firm's "scale of operations" determines the maximum number of outputs that can be produced. In the long run, there are no scale limitations.

The total product of a variable factor of production identifies what outputs are possible using various levels of the variable input. This can be displayed in either a chart that lists the output level corresponding to various levels of input, or a graph that summarizes the data into a "total product curve". The diagram shows a typical total product curve. In this example, output increases as more inputs are employed up until point A. The maximum output possible with this production process is Qm.

If there are other inputs used in the process, they are assumed to be fixed. The average physical product is the total product divided by the number of units of variable input employed. It is the output of each unit of input. If there are 10 employees working on a production process that manufactures 50 units per day, then the average product of variable labour input is 5 units per day.

The average product typically varies as more of the input is employed, so this relationship can also be expresses as a chart or as a graph. A typical average physical product curve is shown. It can be obtained by drawing a vector from the origin to various points on the total product curve and plotting the slopes of these vectors.

The marginal physical product of a variable input is the change in total output due to a one unit change in the variable input or alternatively the rate of change in total output due to an infinitesimally small change in the variable input. The discrete marginal product of capital is the additional output resulting from the use of an additional unit of capital. The continuous marginal product of a variable input can be calculated as the derivative of quantity produced with respect to variable input employed. The marginal physical product curve is shown. It can be obtained from the slope of the total product curve.

Because the marginal product drives changes in the average product, we know that when the average physical product is falling, the marginal physical product must be less than the average. Likewise, when the average physical product is rising, it must be due to a marginal physical product greater than the average. For this reason, the marginal physical product curve must intersect the maximum point on the average physical product curve.

MPP keeps increasing till it reaches its maximum. Up until this point every additional unit has been adding more value to the total product than the previous one. From this point onwards, every additional unit adds less to the total product compared to the previous one. But the average product is still increasing till MPP touches APP. At this point, an additional unit is adding the same value as the average product. From this point onwards, MPP starts to reduce and so does APP because every additional unit is adding less to APP than the average product. But the total product is still increasing because every additional unit is still contributing positively. Therefore, during this period, both, the average as well as marginal products, are decreasing, but the total product is still increasing. Finally we reach a point when MPP crosses the x-axis.

At this point every additional unit starts to diminish the product of previous units, possibly by getting into their way. Therefore the total product starts to decrease at this point. This is point A on the total product curve.

Diminishing returns can be divided into three categories:

1. Diminishing Total returns, which implies reduction in total product with every additional unit of input. This occurs after point A in the graph.
2. Diminishing Average returns, which refers to the portion of the APP curve after its intersection with MPP curve.
3. Diminishing Marginal returns, refers to the point where the MPP curve starts to slope down and travels all the way down to the x-axis and beyond. Putting it in a chronological order, at first the marginal returns start to diminish, then the average returns, followed finally by the total returns.

These curves illustrate the principle of diminishing marginal returns to a variable input. This states that as you add more and more of a variable input, you will reach a point beyond which the resulting increase in output starts to diminish. This point is illustrated as the maximum point on the marginal physical product curve. It assumes that other factor inputs are held constant.

An example is the employment of labour in the use of trucks to transport goods. Assuming the number of available trucks is fixed, then the amount of the variable input labour could be varied and the resultant efficiency determined. At least one labourer is necessary. Additional workers per vehicle could be productive in loading, unloading, navigation, or around the clock continuous driving.

But at some point the returns to investment in labour will start to diminish and efficiency will decrease. The most efficient distribution of labour per piece of equipment will likely be one driver plus an additional worker for other tasks. Resource allocations and distributive efficiencies in the mix of capital and labour investment will vary per industry and according to available technology. Trains are able to transport much more in the way of goods with fewer "drivers" but at the cost of greater investment in infrastructure.

With the advent of mass production of motorized vehicles, the economic niche occupied by trains has become more specialized and limited to long haul delivery. There is an argument that if the theory is holding everything constant, the production method should not be changed, *i.e.*, division of labour should not be practiced. However, the rise in marginal product means that the workers use other means of production method, such as in loading, unloading, navigation, or around the clock continuous driving. For this reason, some economists think that the "keeping other things constant" should not be used in this theory.

The total, average, and marginal physical product curves mentioned are just one way of showing production relationships. They express the quantity of output relative to the amount of variable input employed while holding fixed inputs constant. Because they depict a short run relationship, they are sometimes called short run production functions. If all inputs are allowed to be varied, then the diagram would express outputs relative to total inputs, and the function would be a long run production function. If the mix of inputs is held constant, then output would be expressed relative to inputs of a fixed composition, and the function would indicate long run economies of scale.

Rather than comparing inputs to outputs, it is also possible to assess the mix of inputs employed in production. An isoquant relates the quantities of one input to the quantities of another input. It indicates all possible combinations of inputs that are capable of producing a given level of output. Rather than looking at the inputs used in production, it is possible to look at the mix of outputs that are possible for any given production process. This is done with a production possibilities frontier. It indicates what combinations of outputs are possible given the available factor endowment and the prevailing production technology. You can use a lot of labour with a minimal amount of capital, or you could invest heavily in capital equipment that requires a minimal amount of labour to operate, or any combination in between. For most goods, there are more than just two inputs.

For example in agriculture, the amount of land, water, and fertilizer can all be varied to produce different amounts of a crop. An isoquant, in the two input case, is a curve that shows all the ways of combining two inputs so as to produce a given level of output. In the three input case it will be a surface. Iso is Latin for equal and quant is short for quantity. Movement along an isoquant depicts a constant rate of output, but a changing input ratio.

A unique isoquant can be constructed for every level of output, and a family of isoquants can be created to represent various output levels. Isoquants further from the origin represent greater amounts of output. Isoquants are usually considered to be everywhere dense, meaning an infinite number of them could be plotted in any two input space. A typical isoquant is illustrated in the diagram to the right. At point A in the diagram Ka units of capital are combined with La units of labour to produce 100 units of output.

It is downward sloping, convex to the origin, and non-intersecting . A complete isoquant is actually a closed curve, but only the "down sloping to the right" portion makes economic sense. The upward sloping parts of isoquants, for example, indicate that level of output could be produced by less of both inputs so this section is of little interest to decision makers. The economic section of the isoquants is defined by a pair of lines called ridge lines. The "downward to the right" slope of the economic region of an isoquant is due to the possibility of substituting one input for another in the production process while keeping the level of output constant. Isoquants are typically convex to the origin reflecting the fact that the two factors are substitutable for each other at varying rates.

This rate of substitutability is called the "marginal rate of technical substitution" or occasionally the "marginal rate of substitution in production". It measures the reduction in one input per unit increase in the other input that is just sufficient to maintain a constant level of production. For example, the marginal rate of substitution of labour for capital gives the amount of capital that can be replaced by one unit of labour while keeping output unchanged.

To move from point A to point B in the diagram, the amount of capital is reduced from Ka to Kb while the amount of labour is increased only from La to Lb. To move from point C to point D, the amount of capital is reduced from Kc to Kd while the amount of labour is increased from La to Lb. The marginal rate of technical substitution of labour for capital is equivalent to the absolute slope of the isoquant at that point. It is equal to 0 where the isoquant becomes horizontal, and equal to infinity where it becomes vertical.

The opposite is true when going in the other direction. In this case we are looking at the marginal rate of technical substitution capital for labour. It can also be shown that the marginal rate of substitution labour for capital, is equal to the marginal physical product of labour divided by the marginal physical product of capital.

In the unusual case of two inputs that are perfect substitutes for each other in production, the isoquant would be linear. If, on the other hand, there is only one production process available, factor proportions would be fixed, and these zero-substitutability isoquants would be shown as horizontal or vertical lines.

Fixed Assets Management

Fixed assets management is an accounting process that seeks to track fixed assets for the purposes of financial accounting, preventive maintenance, and theft deterrence. Many organizations face a significant challenge to track the location, quantity, condition, maintenance and depreciation status of their fixed assets.

A popular approach to tracking fixed assets utilizes serial numbered Asset Tags, often with bar codes for easy and accurate reading. Periodically, the owner of the assets can take inventory with a mobile barcode reader and then produce a report. Off-the-shelf software packages for fixed asset management are marketed to businesses small and large. Some Enterprise Resource Planning systems are available with fixed assets modules.

Free Cash Flow

Free cash flow measures a firm's net increase in:

- Cash from operations,
- Less the dividends paid to preferred shareholders, and
- Less expenditures necessary to maintain assets.

Increases in non-cash current assets may, or may not be deducted, depending on whether they are considered to be maintaining the status quo, or to be investments for growth.

Problems with Capx

- The expenditures for maintenance of assets is only part of the capx reported on the Statement of Cash Flows. It must be separated from the expenditures for growth purposes. This split is not a requirement under GAAP, and is not audited. Management is free to disclose maintenance capx or not. Therefore this input to the calculation of free cash flow is easy to manipulate. Since it is a very large number, maintenance capx's questionable validity is the basis for some people's dismissal of 'free cash flow'.
- A second problem with the maintenance capx measurement is its intrinsic 'lumpyness'. By their nature, expenditures for capital assets that will last decades are infrequent, but costly when they occur. 'Free cash flow', in turn, will be very different from year to year. No particular year will be a 'norm' that can be expected to be repeated.

Uses of the Metric

- Free cash flow measures the ease with which businesses can grow and pay dividends to shareholders. Even profitable businesses may have negative cash flows. Their requirement for increased financing will result in increased financing costs reducing future income. It is easier to grow with organic cash flows than with additional financing.
- According to the discounted cash flow valuation model, the intrinsic value of a company is the present value of all future free cash flows, plus the cash proceeds from its eventual sale. The presumption is that the cash flows are used to pay dividends to the shareholders. Bear in mind the lumpyness discussed.
- Some investors prefer using free cash flow instead of net income to measure a company's financial performance, because free cash flow is more difficult to manipulate than net income. The problems with this presumption are itemized at cash flow and return of capital.
- The payout ratio is a metric used to evaluate the sustainability of distributions from REITs, Oil and Gas Royalty Trusts, and Income

Trust. The distributions are divided by the free cash flow. Distributions may include any of income, flowed-through capital gains or return of capital.

This metric is used only by shareholders. Debt holders are not concerned with maintaining the operating capital assets, or with growing the business. Nor are they concerned with taxes paid since their payments come first. The appropriate metric for debt holders is EBITDA.

Change Management

There are several phrases regarding organizational change and development that look and sound a lot alike, but have different meanings. As a result of the prominence of the topic, there seems to be increasingly different interpretations of some of these phrases, while others are used interchangeably. Without at least some sense of the differences between these phrases, communications about organizational change and development can be increasingly vague, confusing and frustrating.

There are different overall types of organizational change, including planned versus unplanned, organization-wide versus change primarily to one part of the organization, incremental versus transformational, etc.. Knowing which types of change you are doing helps all participants to retain scope and perspective during the many complexities and frequent frustrations during change.

Successful change efforts often include several key roles, including the initiator, champion, change agent, sponsor and leaders. Organization-wide change in corporations should involve the Board of Directors. Whether their members are closely involved in the change or not, they should at least be aware of the change project and monitor if the results are being achieved or not. As the change agent, you might be performing different roles during the project.

Appreciative Inquiry is a recent and powerful breakthrough in organizational change and development. It's based on the philosophy that "problems" are often caused as much by our perception of them as problems as by other influencing factors. The philosophy has spawned a strong movement that, in turn, has generated an increasing number of models, tools and tips, most of which seem to build from the positive perceptions of those involved in the change effort.

There are numerous well-organized approaches from which to manage a change effort. Some of the approaches have been around for many years — we just haven't thought of them as such. For example, many organizations undertake strategic planning. The implementation of strategic planning, when done in a systematic, cyclical and explicit approach, is strategic management. Strategic management is also one model for ensuring the success of a change effort. There are numerous, major methods and movements to regularly increase the performance of organizations. Each includes regular recurring activities to establish organizational goals, monitor progress towards the goals, and make adjustments to achieve those goals more effectively and efficiently. Any or all of the following approaches will improve organizational performance depending on if they are implemented comprehensively and remain focused on organizational results. Some of the following, *e.g.*, organizational learning and knowledge management, might be interpreted more as movements than organization performance strategies because there are wide interpretations of the concepts, not all of which include focusing on achieving top-level organizational results.

However, if these two concepts are instilled across the organization and focus on organizational results, they contribute strongly to organizational performance. On the other hand, the Balanced Scorecard, which is deliberately designed to be comprehensive and focused on organizational results, will not improve performance if not implemented from a strong design.

Index